Navigating the Digital Landscape: File Systems in Operating Systems Unveiled

Table of Content

Chapter 1: The Foundation: Understanding File Systems

- Definition and significance of file systems in operating environments.
- The role of file systems in organizing and storing data.
- Overview of fundamental components such as directories, files, and metadata.
- Understanding the hierarchical structure of file systems.
- Explanation of common file operations like create, read, update, and delete (CRUD).
- The interaction between applications and file systems during these operations.
- Techniques for navigating through file systems using command-line interfaces and graphical interfaces.
- Understanding path structures and file addressing.
- Introduction to different file system types, including FAT, NTFS, ext4, and more.
- Comparative analysis of file system characteristics and use cases.

Chapter 2: Evolution of File Systems in Operating Systems

- Tracing the evolution of file systems from early computing to modern operating systems.
- Key milestones and innovations in file system development.
- Examining early file systems like FAT16 and FAT32.
- Understanding the limitations and advantages of legacy file systems.
- Exploring the shift towards 64-bit file systems for improved scalability.
- The impact of 64-bit architecture on file system design.
- The emergence of networked file systems like NFS and SMB.
- Enabling file sharing and collaboration across distributed environments.
- The integration of file systems with cloud computing.
- How cloud-based file systems enhance storage and accessibility.

Chapter 3: Critical Components: Anatomy of File Systems

- Breaking down the architecture of file systems into layers.
- Understanding the interaction between the kernel, file system drivers, and user space.
- The role of inodes and file allocation tables in file system structures.
- How these components manage and track file information and storage allocation.
- Explaining the concept of journaling for file system integrity.
- How logging mechanisms facilitate error recovery and system stability.
- Various directory structures, such as tree-structured and hash-based.
- How directory structures impact file retrieval and organization.
- Understanding the importance of metadata in file systems.
- How metadata stores information about files, permissions, and attributes.

Chapter 4: Efficiency and Performance Tuning in File Systems

- Defining key performance metrics, including throughput, latency, and IOPS.
- Evaluating the impact of file system design on overall system performance.
- Strategies for optimizing file access speed and reducing latency.
- Cache management and prefetching techniques for enhanced efficiency.
- The importance of proper disk partitioning for optimal file system performance.
- Techniques for aligning partitions to improve data access speed.
- Exploring the use of compression and deduplication in file systems.
- Balancing storage savings with processing overhead.
- Addressing challenges related to concurrent file access.
- Scalability considerations for file systems in growing environments.

Chapter 5: Security Measures: Safeguarding File Systems

- Overview of access control lists (ACLs) and permissions in file systems.
- How file systems regulate user and group access to files and directories.
- Implementing encryption to secure data at rest.
- File-level and disk-level encryption techniques.
- The role of audit trails in tracking file access and modifications.
- Logging mechanisms for detecting unauthorized activities and security breaches.
- Techniques for ensuring data integrity through hash functions.
- Periodic integrity checks to identify and rectify file corruption.
- Establishing best practices for securing file systems.
- User education and awareness to mitigate security risks.

Chapter 6: Emerging Trends in File Systems Technology

- Exploring the integration of machine learning for predictive file system behavior.
- AI-driven algorithms for automated file system optimization.
- The shift towards object storage as an alternative to traditional file systems.
- Advantages and challenges of object-based storage.
- The concept of immutable file systems for enhanced security.
- Use cases and implications of immutability in file storage.
- Evolving trends in distributed file systems for cloud and edge computing.
- Challenges and innovations in managing files across distributed nodes.
- Strategies for integrating and managing file systems across hybrid and multi-cloud environments.
- Ensuring data consistency and accessibility in diverse cloud infrastructures.

Chapter 7: Challenges and Solutions in File Systems Management

- Addressing challenges related to file fragmentation.
- Strategies for defragmentation and optimizing file allocation.
- Identifying challenges associated with managing large-scale file systems.
- Scalability solutions, including sharding and distributed file storage.
- Common challenges in implementing reliable backup and recovery strategies.
- Techniques for ensuring data resilience and rapid recovery.
- The importance of routine maintenance for file systems.
- Automating maintenance tasks to minimize downtime and disruptions.
- Challenges arising from file system compatibility issues.
- Strategies for achieving interoperability between different file system types.

Chapter 8: Future Horizons: Innovations in Operating System File Systems

- Exploring the integration of non-volatile memory technologies in file systems.
- The impact on data access speed and system responsiveness.
- Leveraging machine-generated metadata for enhanced file categorization.
- Automating metadata management for improved efficiency.
- The potential for blockchain technology in creating secure and transparent file systems.
- The concept of self-healing file systems capable of automatic error correction.
- Exploring the integration of augmented reality in file system interactions.
- User interfaces and file management through augmented reality applications.
- Implementing dynamic policies for file system management based on real-time conditions.
- Speculating on the potential impact of quantum computing on file systems.

Introduction

In the dynamic realm of technology, where data reigns supreme, a profound understanding of the intricacies of file systems within operating systems is indispensable. The very fabric of the digital landscape is intricately woven with the efficiency, security, and adaptability of these file systems, dictating the fundamental mechanisms governing how data is stored, retrieved, and managed.

The comprehensive guide, aptly titled "Navigating the Digital Landscape: File Systems in Operating Systems Unveiled," endeavors to serve as an illuminating beacon, guiding readers through the labyrinth of complexities that enshroud file systems. It embarks on a journey that transcends mere theoretical constructs, aiming to provide readers with a visceral and comprehensive insight into the profound significance and intricate functionality of file systems.

From the foundational concepts that form the bedrock of file system architecture to the cutting-edge innovations that propel these systems into the future, this book is designed as a holistic exploration. It is a journey that traverses through the very heart of operating systems, unraveling the intricate threads that bind and structure the digital world. In essence, it is an odyssey through the backbone of technology, where the nuances of file systems come to life, influencing every facet of digital interactions.

The digital landscape, ever-shifting and dynamic, demands a guide that not only dissects the core principles but also adapts to the evolving nature of technology. "Navigating the Digital Landscape" seeks to fulfill this need, offering readers a roadmap that spans from the rudimentary understanding of file systems to the nuanced grasp of their pivotal role in the broader operating system framework.

As we delve into the chapters of this guide, we explore the very foundations that lay the groundwork for file systems, understanding their architecture, components, and the intricacies of file operations. We trace the evolutionary path of file systems, acknowledging their historical significance while navigating through the transformative journey that has brought us to the sophisticated landscape of contemporary operating systems.

Critical components of file systems, from inodes and file allocation tables to journaling and logging mechanisms, come under scrutiny, revealing the inner workings that ensure the integrity and efficiency of these systems. It's not merely a theoretical exploration; rather, it's a practical guide that equips readers with the knowledge to optimize file systems for enhanced efficiency and performance.

The guide extends its reach to address the paramount importance of security measures in safeguarding file systems. Access control mechanisms, encryption strategies, and integrity checks take center stage as we unravel the layers of protection required to secure the digital assets encapsulated within file systems.

In acknowledging the perpetual evolution of technology, the guide turns its gaze towards the horizon of emerging trends in file systems. Machine learning integration, object storage paradigms, and the integration of blockchain technology are dissected, offering readers a glimpse into the potential future trajectories of file system development.

Challenges and solutions in file systems management are not overlooked. From the perennial issue of data fragmentation to scalability challenges and the imperative nature of backup and recovery, the guide provides practical insights and strategies to navigate these hurdles effectively.

The concluding chapters peer into the future horizons, where innovations in non-volatile memory integration, machine-generated metadata, and augmented reality applications converge to shape the next frontier of file system technology. It is a forward-looking exploration that encourages readers to anticipate and adapt to the transformative landscape that lies ahead.

In essence, "Navigating the Digital Landscape" is more than a guide; it is a companion for those seeking mastery in the art and science of file systems within operating systems. It demystifies the complexities, unravels the intricacies, and empowers readers to not only understand but actively navigate the digital landscape with confidence and expertise. As technology continues its relentless evolution, this guide stands as a testament to the perpetual quest for knowledge and proficiency in the ever-expanding universe of file systems.

Chapter 1: The Foundation: Understanding File Systems

Definition and significance of file systems in operating environments.

A file system is a crucial component in the architecture of operating environments, serving as a structured method for organizing and storing data on computer storage devices. It encompasses a set of rules and protocols that govern how data is stored, retrieved, and managed on storage media such as hard drives, solid-state drives, and external storage devices. The significance of file systems lies in their role as a bridge between the high-level software applications and the low-level physical storage hardware, providing an abstraction layer that facilitates efficient and organized data access.

In essence, a file system enables users and applications to interact with stored information in a logical and coherent manner. It establishes a hierarchical structure of directories and files, allowing users to navigate and locate specific pieces of data with ease. This hierarchical organization contributes to the efficiency of data management by categorizing information into a tree-like structure, which aids in maintaining order and facilitating quick retrieval. Furthermore, file systems define the rules for naming files and directories, ensuring consistency and clarity in identifying and accessing stored data.

The management of file attributes is another fundamental aspect of file systems. These attributes include metadata such as file size, creation date, modification date, and permissions, providing essential information about each file. Permissions, in particular, dictate the level of access that users or applications have to a file, thereby ensuring data security and integrity. The enforcement of access control through permissions helps prevent unauthorized modifications or deletions, contributing to the overall reliability of the file system.

One key role of file systems is to abstract the complexities of storage devices and their physical characteristics. This abstraction allows users and applications to interact with data in a uniform manner, regardless of the underlying storage technology. Different types of storage media, such as hard disk drives and solid-state drives, may have distinct characteristics and mechanisms for data storage. The file system acts as a mediator, providing a standardized interface that shields users and applications from the intricacies of various storage devices.

The concept of file systems becomes even more significant in multi-user and networked operating environments. In such scenarios, the file system facilitates concurrent access to data by multiple users or applications while maintaining data integrity. File locking mechanisms and transactional operations ensure that conflicting modifications do not compromise the consistency of the stored information. Additionally, networked file systems enable seamless sharing and collaboration, allowing users to access and modify data stored on remote servers or other networked devices.

Fault tolerance and data recovery are critical aspects addressed by advanced file systems. In the event of unexpected system failures or hardware malfunctions, file systems implement mechanisms such as journaling and versioning to recover data and maintain system stability. Journaling, for instance, logs changes before they are committed, enabling the file system to recover to a consistent state in case of an abrupt interruption. Versioning allows users to revert to previous versions of files, providing a safety net against accidental data loss or unwanted modifications.

As technology evolves, so do the requirements for file systems. Modern file systems are designed to accommodate the increasing volumes of data generated in today's digital age. They incorporate features such as support for large file sizes, efficient data compression, and optimized storage allocation algorithms to make the most efficient use of available storage space. Additionally, advancements in file system design aim to enhance performance, with features like caching and indexing to expedite data retrieval and improve overall system responsiveness.

The choice of a file system is often influenced by the specific needs and characteristics of the intended use case. Different operating systems may employ distinct file systems tailored to their design philosophies and requirements. For instance, systems like Microsoft Windows commonly use the NTFS (New Technology File System), while Linux distributions may opt for ext4 (Fourth Extended Filesystem) or other variants. The compatibility and interoperability of file systems across platforms play a crucial role in facilitating data exchange and collaboration in heterogeneous computing environments.

In conclusion, file systems are a foundational element in the architecture of operating environments, serving as a vital link between software applications and storage hardware. Their hierarchical organization, attribute management, access control mechanisms, and fault tolerance features contribute to the efficient and reliable management of data. As computing environments become increasingly complex and data-centric, the evolution of file systems continues to address emerging challenges and optimize performance. The significance of file systems in maintaining order, enabling collaboration, and ensuring data integrity underscores their essential role in the seamless functioning of modern operating environments.

The role of file systems in organizing and storing data.

File systems play a pivotal role in the organization and storage of data within the realm of computing, serving as a fundamental framework that dictates how information is structured, accessed, and managed on storage devices. At its core, a file system provides the necessary infrastructure to arrange data in a logical and hierarchical manner, introducing a systematic approach to storing files and directories. This hierarchical structure forms the backbone of efficient data organization, facilitating ease of navigation and retrieval for users and applications alike. By categorizing data into directories and sub-directories, file systems establish a coherent framework that mirrors the real-world organization of information, offering users an intuitive means of locating and interacting with their stored data.

The significance of file systems is particularly evident in their role as intermediaries between high-level software applications and the low-level physical storage hardware. This abstraction layer shields users and applications from the complexities of interacting directly with storage devices, providing a standardized interface for data manipulation. It allows users to create, modify, delete, and retrieve files without having to grapple with the intricate details of how data is stored on a specific storage medium. In essence, the file system creates a virtual environment that translates user-friendly commands into the intricate operations required to manage data at the hardware level.

In addition to establishing a structured organization for data, file systems define and manage a plethora of attributes associated with each file. Metadata, such as file size, creation date, modification date, and permissions, adds a layer of information that is crucial for effective data management. These attributes not only provide valuable insights into the nature and history of a file but also contribute to security and access control. Permissions, for instance, regulate who can access, modify, or delete a particular file, ensuring that sensitive data remains secure and that inadvertent alterations are prevented.

The concept of abstraction that file systems introduce extends beyond the organization of data; it also encapsulates the diversity of storage technologies. Different types of storage media, ranging from traditional hard disk drives to modern solid-state drives, exhibit distinct characteristics and mechanisms for data storage. File systems bridge the gap between these varied technologies, offering a unified interface that remains consistent irrespective of the underlying storage hardware. This adaptability allows users and applications to interact with data seamlessly, regardless of the specific storage medium in use, thereby enhancing the overall flexibility and compatibility of computing environments.

In multi-user and networked operating environments, the role of file systems becomes even more pronounced. File systems must facilitate concurrent access to data by multiple users or applications while ensuring data integrity and consistency. This is achieved through mechanisms such as file locking, which prevents conflicting modifications, and transactional operations, which enable a series of changes to be treated as a single, atomic unit. Networked file systems, on the other hand, extend the scope of data accessibility beyond local devices, enabling users to share and collaborate on files stored on remote servers or other networked storage devices.

An essential aspect of file systems lies in their ability to ensure fault tolerance and data recovery. Unforeseen events such as system failures or hardware malfunctions can potentially lead to data loss or corruption. To mitigate these risks, file systems implement features like journaling and versioning. Journaling involves logging changes before they are committed, allowing the file system to recover to a consistent state in case of abrupt interruptions. Versioning, on the other hand, provides users with the capability to revert to previous versions of files, acting as a safeguard against accidental data loss or unwanted modifications.

As technology advances, modern file systems evolve to meet the increasing demands of a data-centric world. They incorporate features such as support for large file sizes, efficient data compression, and optimized storage allocation algorithms to make the most effective use of available storage space. Performance enhancements, including caching and indexing, are also integrated to expedite data retrieval and improve overall system responsiveness. The evolution of file systems reflects the ongoing efforts to address emerging challenges and optimize their functionality in the context of evolving computing environments.

The choice of a file system is often influenced by the specific needs and characteristics of the intended use case. Various operating systems may employ different file systems, each tailored to its design philosophies and requirements. For example, Microsoft Windows commonly utilizes the NTFS (New Technology File System), while Linux distributions may opt for ext4 (Fourth Extended Filesystem) or other variants. The compatibility and interoperability of file systems across platforms are vital considerations, ensuring seamless data exchange and collaboration in heterogeneous computing environments.

In conclusion, the role of file systems in organizing and storing data is multifaceted and indispensable in the landscape of computing. They provide a structured framework for data organization, offering users and applications a systematic and intuitive means of managing information. Beyond organization, file systems act as crucial intermediaries, abstracting the complexities of storage hardware and presenting a unified interface for data manipulation. Their ability to manage attributes, enforce access control, and ensure fault tolerance further solidifies their significance in the efficient and reliable management of data. As computing environments continue to evolve, the ongoing development of file systems remains integral to meeting the challenges and demands of an increasingly data-driven world.

Overview of fundamental components such as directories, files, and metadata.

A comprehensive understanding of the fundamental components of file systems necessitates an exploration of directories, files, and metadata—integral elements that collectively shape the organization and structure of stored data. At the core of any file system lies the concept of directories, providing a hierarchical framework for the systematic arrangement of data. These directories, often referred to as folders in graphical user interfaces, enable users to categorize and group related files, fostering an organized and intuitive approach to data management. The hierarchical structure establishes a clear relationship between parent and child directories, creating a navigable tree-like arrangement that mirrors the logical organization of information.

Files, as the primary units of data storage, represent the tangible entities within the file system. A file encapsulates information, whether it be textual documents, images, executable programs, or other forms of data. Each file is assigned a unique name within its respective directory, facilitating identification and access. The diverse nature of files, ranging from simple text documents to complex multimedia files, underscores the versatility of file systems in accommodating various data types. The file system's role in defining and managing the attributes of files, including size, creation date, modification date, and permissions, contributes to the comprehensive characterization of stored data.

Metadata, a critical aspect of file systems, extends beyond the content of files to encompass additional information that enhances the understanding and management of data. This supplementary layer of information includes details such as file size, providing insights into the volume of data a file occupies on storage media. Creation and modification dates offer a historical perspective, outlining when a file was initially created and when it was last altered. Permissions, a crucial subset of metadata, regulate access control, determining which users or processes have the rights to read, write, or execute a particular file. Metadata thus enriches the contextual understanding of files, playing a pivotal role in effective data management and security.

Directories, files, and metadata collectively form the triad that defines the structure and functionality of file systems. Directories establish the organizational framework, providing a structured hierarchy that facilitates intuitive navigation and data retrieval. Files, as the bearers of data, represent the tangible entities stored within the file system, showcasing the diversity of information that can be accommodated. Metadata, on the other hand, augments the basic attributes of files, offering a more comprehensive understanding of data by incorporating details about size, dates, and access permissions. This symbiotic relationship among directories, files, and metadata ensures that file systems provide not only a coherent organization of data but also the necessary contextual information for efficient and secure data management.

The hierarchical arrangement of directories is a defining feature of file systems, contributing significantly to the organization and accessibility of data. Directories serve as containers for files and subdirectories, creating a structured and navigable hierarchy that simplifies the task of locating specific pieces of information. The parent-child relationships between directories establish a logical order, with each directory encapsulating a specific category or theme. Users can traverse this hierarchy, moving from higher-level directories to lower-level ones, enabling an intuitive exploration of stored data. This hierarchical organization, coupled with the ability to create, rename, and delete directories, empowers users to tailor the structure of the file system to their specific needs and preferences.

Files, as the elemental units of data storage, are central to the functionality of file systems. A file represents a distinct collection of information, whether it be a document, image, audio clip, or program executable. The file system provides a mechanism for naming and identifying each file within its respective directory. The file name serves as a human-readable label, allowing users to distinguish and recognize files based on their content or purpose. Beyond nomenclature, files are characterized by their content and format, determining how the data within them is interpreted and processed by associated applications. The diversity of files accommodated by file systems underscores their adaptability to the wide array of data types encountered in computing environments.

Metadata, often described as data about data, elevates the understanding and management of files within a file system. This additional layer of information augments the basic attributes associated with files, offering a more nuanced view of stored data. File size, a fundamental metadata attribute, provides insights into the space occupied by a file on the storage medium, influencing considerations of storage capacity and efficiency. Creation and modification dates furnish a temporal context, documenting when a file was originally generated and when it was last altered. Permissions, another critical subset of metadata, dictate the level of access granted to users or processes, safeguarding data security and integrity. Metadata, therefore, serves as a bridge between the tangible content of files and the broader context in which they exist, enriching the understanding and utility of stored data.

The interplay between directories, files, and metadata encapsulates the essence of file systems, offering a holistic framework for the organization and storage of data. Directories establish a hierarchical structure that fosters intuitive navigation, creating a logical order that mirrors the conceptual organization of information. Files, as the carriers of diverse data types, populate this structure, showcasing the versatility of file systems in accommodating a broad spectrum of information. Metadata, with its detailed attributes, enhances the contextual understanding of files, providing essential information about size, dates, and access permissions. Together, these fundamental components synergize to create a robust and flexible environment for data management, contributing to the seamless functioning of file systems in diverse computing scenarios.

Understanding the hierarchical structure of file systems.

The hierarchical structure of file systems is a foundational organizational framework that plays a pivotal role in the systematic arrangement and efficient management of stored data. At its essence, this structure establishes a clear and logical order, resembling a tree-like hierarchy composed of directories and files. Directories, often referred to as folders in graphical user interfaces, serve as containers that house files and subdirectories. This parent-child relationship between directories creates a nested structure, with higher-level directories encapsulating lower-level ones. This hierarchical arrangement fosters an intuitive and navigable environment, allowing users to traverse the structure, locate specific files, and organize data according to their preferences and requirements.

The hierarchical nature of file systems mirrors the real-world organization of information, facilitating an approach to data management that aligns with human cognition. Users encounter familiar concepts such as parent and child directories, akin to navigating through physical folders and subfolders in a filing cabinet. This intuitive structure enhances user experience, enabling individuals to conceptualize and navigate their stored data in a manner that aligns with their mental models. The hierarchical arrangement also allows for the creation of a logical taxonomy, where directories can represent categories, themes, or projects, contributing to a more systematic and comprehensible organization of information.

Each level in the hierarchy contributes to the overall organization of data in a manner that reflects a user's workflow or the nature of the stored information. For instance, a user might create a top-level directory for work-related documents, with subdirectories for specific projects or departments. Within these subdirectories, individual files or additional subdirectories may be organized, creating a hierarchical structure that mirrors the organizational hierarchy of the user's work environment. This hierarchical approach fosters a sense of order and facilitates quick and intuitive access to relevant data, streamlining the user's workflow.

Moreover, the hierarchical structure inherently supports the concept of relative paths, which are crucial for referencing and accessing files. A relative path indicates the location of a file or directory relative to the current working directory. The hierarchical arrangement simplifies the specification of these paths, as users can navigate through the structure using easily comprehensible representations such as ".." to refer to the parent directory. This simplifies file referencing and allows for the creation of portable and adaptable scripts and programs that can be independent of the absolute file system paths.

Directories in a hierarchical file system are dynamic entities, affording users the flexibility to create, rename, move, and delete them as needed. This adaptability empowers users to tailor the hierarchy to evolving requirements, accommodating changes in projects, priorities, or organizational structures. The ability to create subdirectories within directories adds an additional layer of granularity, allowing users to organize information at multiple levels, each serving a specific purpose. As a result, the hierarchical structure becomes a dynamic and responsive framework, capable of adapting to the evolving needs and complexities of data management.

The hierarchical structure of file systems is not confined to a single user's environment; it extends seamlessly to multi-user and networked operating environments. In such scenarios, directories can represent shared spaces accessible to multiple users. The hierarchical structure then becomes a collaborative tool, enabling users to collectively organize and access shared data. Networked file systems, where data is stored on remote servers accessible over a network, leverage the hierarchical structure to facilitate access to shared resources while maintaining a logical and orderly arrangement. This adaptability to both individual and collaborative use cases underscores the versatility and universality of the hierarchical structure.

Furthermore, the hierarchical structure enhances the scalability of file systems. As data volumes grow, users can scale their organizational framework by creating additional directories and subdirectories without sacrificing the navigability and coherence of the overall structure. This scalability ensures that the hierarchical structure remains an effective tool for data management, regardless of the size or complexity of the stored data. Users can maintain a structured and organized environment even as the volume and diversity of their data increase over time.

In conclusion, the hierarchical structure of file systems represents a fundamental and versatile organizational framework that underpins the effective management of stored data. It establishes a logical order through parent-child relationships between directories, creating an intuitive and navigable environment for users. This hierarchical approach mirrors human cognitive processes, aligning with real-world concepts of organization and facilitating an intuitive understanding of data. The adaptability of the hierarchical structure, allowing users to create, modify, and organize directories dynamically, ensures that it remains a responsive tool that can evolve with changing needs. Whether in individual, collaborative, or networked environments, the hierarchical structure remains a cornerstone of efficient data management, offering a scalable and versatile solution for organizing and accessing diverse sets of information.

Explanation of common file operations like create, read, up-date, and delete (CRUD).

Commonly referred to as CRUD operations, create, read, up-date, and delete represent the fundamental set of actions that users and applications perform on data within a file system, encapsulating the core processes of data management. The first operation, create, involves the generation of new files or directories within the file system. Users initiate this process by providing a name for the file or directory, specifying its location within the hierarchical structure, and potentially assigning initial content. This operation is fundamental to the expansion of the data repository, enabling the incorporation of new information into the file system. Create operations are versatile, allowing users to establish folders for organizational purposes or generate files to store diverse types of data, ranging from textual documents to multimedia content.

Read operations are the cornerstone of data retrieval within a file system. Once files or directories are created, users and applications can initiate read operations to access and retrieve the stored information. The read operation allows for the examination of file content, providing users with visibility into the data contained within a specific file or the listing of files within a directory. This operation is crucial for extracting information for viewing, processing, or transferring purposes. Read operations enable users to interact with the content they have stored, facilitating the seamless integration of data into their workflows and the execution of various applications that require access to specific files or directories.

Update operations involve the modification of existing files or directories within the file system. Users can initiate updates to alter the content of files, change file names, or reorganize the hierarchical structure by moving files to different directories. These modifications may also include changes to metadata attributes such as file size, modification date, or access permissions. Update operations are pivotal for keeping data relevant and accurate over time. They allow users to refine and enhance existing information, reflecting changes in the real-world context or the evolving requirements of data management. The update operation is a dynamic process that accommodates the fluid nature of information within the file system.

Delete operations involve the removal of files or directories from the file system. Users may initiate delete operations to eliminate outdated or unnecessary information, freeing up storage space and decluttering the file system. The delete operation requires users to specify the target file or directory, and upon confirmation, the selected data is permanently removed. Care must be taken during delete operations to prevent accidental loss of valuable information. Additionally, some file systems implement safeguards such as recycle bins or confirmation prompts to mitigate the risk of unintentional deletions. Delete operations play a crucial role in the lifecycle management of data, allowing users to maintain an organized and efficient file system by eliminating redundant or obsolete information.

Collectively, these CRUD operations form the backbone of data manipulation within file systems, empowering users and applications to interact with stored information in a dynamic and purposeful manner. The synergy between these operations enables a holistic approach to data management, from the creation of new content to its retrieval, modification, and eventual removal. The CRUD paradigm is not limited to local file systems but extends to networked and distributed environments, where users can perform these operations on files and directories located on remote servers or shared storage devices.

Moreover, the CRUD operations are integral to the development of applications and software systems that rely on data storage and retrieval. Application developers incorporate these operations to enable users to interact with the application's data, whether it involves creating new records, reading existing information, updating details, or deleting obsolete entries. The CRUD paradigm provides a standardized and intuitive framework for developers to implement data manipulation functionalities, fostering consistency and ease of use across various software applications.

In the context of database systems, CRUD operations are often associated with the manipulation of records within database tables. Create operations involve the insertion of new records, read operations retrieve existing records, update operations modify record attributes, and delete operations remove records from the database. This extension of the CRUD paradigm to databases exemplifies its universality and adaptability across diverse data management scenarios.

As technology advances, the implementation of CRUD operations continues to evolve, incorporating features and optimizations to enhance efficiency, security, and user experience. The advent of version control systems, for example, introduces nuanced variations of CRUD operations that enable users to track changes to files over time, facilitating collaboration and code management in software development. Additionally, the integration of metadata and access control mechanisms refines the granularity of CRUD operations, allowing for more sophisticated control over data attributes and permissions.

In conclusion, the CRUD operations—create, read, update, and delete—form the bedrock of data manipulation within file systems, providing users and applications with a comprehensive set of actions to interact with stored information. These operations encapsulate the core processes of data management, from the creation of new content to its retrieval, modification, and eventual removal. The universality of the CRUD paradigm extends its applicability to various data management scenarios, encompassing local file systems, networked environments, and database systems. As technology progresses, the nuanced implementation of CRUD operations reflects ongoing efforts to refine and optimize data manipulation functionalities, ensuring their relevance and effectiveness in the dynamic landscape of computing and information management.

The interaction between applications and file systems during these operations.

The interaction between applications and file systems during the fundamental CRUD operations—create, read, update, and delete—is a dynamic and intricate process that involves the seamless collaboration between software applications and the underlying file system infrastructure. During the create operation, applications initiate the creation of new files or directories by interfacing with the file system through system calls or application programming interfaces (APIs). The application provides essential information such as the desired file or directory name, location within the hierarchical structure, and, in some cases, initial content. This information is then translated by the file system into the necessary low-level operations to allocate storage space, update directory structures, and set metadata attributes. The successful completion of the create operation establishes the newly generated file or directory within the file system, making it available for subsequent interactions.

In the context of read operations, applications interact with the file system to access and retrieve specific files or directories. Through system calls or APIs, applications specify the target file or directory, and the file system, in turn, retrieves the relevant data and provides it to the requesting application. This interaction is characterized by the translation of high-level commands from the application into low-level file system operations, such as locating the file within the storage medium and retrieving its content. The read operation facilitates the seamless integration of data into applications, enabling users to view, process, or manipulate the retrieved information according to their needs.

Update operations involve the modification of existing files or directories, requiring coordinated interactions between applications and the file system. Applications initiate update operations by providing the necessary instructions to alter file content, metadata attributes, or hierarchical structure. The file system processes these instructions, ensuring the appropriate modifications while managing potential concurrency issues to maintain data consistency. The interaction during update operations is bidirectional, with the application informing the file system of desired changes, and the file system, in turn, executing these changes and updating the relevant data structures. This collaborative process ensures that data remains accurate and up-to-date as applications dynamically interact with the file system.

Similarly, delete operations involve a coordinated effort between applications and the file system to remove files or directories from the storage medium. Applications trigger delete operations by specifying the target data for removal, and the file system executes the necessary low-level operations to deallocate storage space, update directory structures, and eliminate metadata entries. The interaction during delete operations requires careful handling to prevent accidental data loss, and some file systems implement safeguards such as confirmation prompts or recycle bins to mitigate risks. Successful collaboration between applications and the file system during delete operations ensures the efficient removal of obsolete or redundant data, contributing to the maintenance of an organized and streamlined file system.

The interaction between applications and file systems extends beyond individual CRUD operations, encompassing broader considerations such as access control, metadata management, and transactional consistency. Access control mechanisms, facilitated by the file system, regulate the permissions associated with files and directories, ensuring that applications adhere to specified security protocols.

Applications interface with the file system to request access permissions, and the file system enforces these permissions to safeguard data integrity and prevent unauthorized operations. This collaborative effort between applications and the file system is crucial for maintaining the security and confidentiality of stored information.

Metadata management is another aspect of interaction between applications and file systems, involving the handling of additional information about files and directories. Applications can retrieve and update metadata attributes, such as file size, creation date, and modification date, to enrich the contextual understanding of data. The file system, in turn, ensures the accurate maintenance of metadata and facilitates its retrieval for applications. This collaborative exchange of metadata information enhances the comprehensibility and utility of stored data, allowing applications to access valuable details about files and directories.

Transactional consistency becomes paramount in scenarios where multiple applications or processes concurrently interact with the file system. Transactional operations ensure that a series of CRUD operations are treated as a single, atomic unit, preventing data inconsistencies and maintaining the integrity of the file system. Applications coordinate with the file system to initiate transactional operations, providing a set of instructions that should be executed as a cohesive unit. The file system executes these operations in a manner that guarantees either the successful completion of all specified actions or the rollback to a consistent state in case of failures or interruptions. This collaborative effort between applications and the file system during transactional operations is crucial for ensuring data consistency in dynamic and concurrent computing environments.

In distributed or networked file systems, the interaction between applications and the file system becomes more complex. Applications on client machines communicate with the file system on remote servers, introducing considerations such as network latency, data transfer protocols, and distributed file locking mechanisms. Remote file systems allow applications to perform CRUD operations on files located on servers, requiring communication protocols such as NFS (Network File System) or SMB (Server Message Block). The collaboration between applications and distributed file systems involves the negotiation of access permissions, data retrieval over the network, and the orchestration of transactions to maintain consistency across distributed storage locations.

As technology advances, the interaction between applications and file systems evolves to accommodate emerging paradigms and challenges. Cloud-based file systems, for example, introduce new dimensions to this interaction by incorporating features such as seamless data synchronization across devices, scalability in storage capacity, and advanced access control in shared environments. Applications leverage cloud-based APIs to interact with file systems hosted on cloud platforms, and the file system infrastructure ensures the reliable storage, retrieval, and management of data in distributed and virtualized environments.

In conclusion, the interaction between applications and file systems during CRUD operations is a dynamic and collaborative process that involves the translation of high-level commands from applications into low-level file system operations. Whether creating, reading, updating, or deleting data, applications interface with the file system through system calls or APIs, initiating a coordinated exchange that ensures the seamless execution of data management tasks. This interaction extends beyond individual CRUD operations to encompass broader considerations such as access control, metadata management, and transactional consistency. In networked or distributed environments, the collaboration becomes more intricate, involving communication protocols, data transfer mechanisms, and distributed file locking. As technology progresses, this interaction continues to evolve, adapting to new paradigms such as cloud-based file systems and addressing the challenges posed by dynamic computing environments. The symbiotic relationship between applications and file systems remains foundational to the effective and reliable management of data in diverse computing scenarios.

Techniques for navigating through file systems using command-line interfaces and graphical interfaces.

Navigating through file systems is an essential skill for users interacting with computers, and the techniques employed vary between command-line interfaces (CLIs) and graphical interfaces (GUIs). In a command-line environment, users rely on a text-based interface to interact with the file system. The primary tool for navigation is the command prompt, where users input textual commands to perform operations. To navigate through directories, users commonly use the 'cd' (change directory) command followed by the desired directory name. The use of relative or absolute paths helps specify the location of directories or files within the file system. The 'ls' command (or 'dir' on Windows) allows users to list the contents of the current directory, providing a snapshot of available files and subdirectories. Recursive navigation involves chaining directory changes to access deeper levels within the hierarchical structure. Users can employ shortcuts such as ".." to refer to the parent directory or "." to denote the current directory, streamlining navigation.

Contrastingly, graphical interfaces provide users with a visual representation of the file system, making navigation more intuitive. File managers, such as Windows Explorer or macOS Finder, present directories and files as graphical icons, enabling users to interact with the file system using mouse-based actions. Double-clicking on directories or files opens them, akin to navigating through physical folders. Graphical interfaces often feature a hierarchical tree view, allowing users to expand or collapse directory branches for a comprehensive overview. The breadcrumb navigation bar displays the current location within the file system, facilitating quick jumps to parent directories. The presence of back and forward buttons aids in revisiting previously accessed locations. Additionally, GUIs often provide search functionalities and the ability to create shortcuts or bookmarks for rapid access to frequently used directories.

In command-line interfaces, file and directory manipulation involves various commands. The 'mkdir' command creates new directories, 'touch' generates empty files, and 'rm' removes files or directories. To move or rename files, the 'mv' command is employed, while the 'cp' command duplicates files. Wildcards, such as '*' and '?', are utilized for pattern matching during operations, enhancing efficiency. File permissions and ownership can be managed through commands like 'chmod' and 'chown'. To view the contents of files, the 'cat' command displays text files, while 'less' and 'more' offer paged viewing. Pipes ('|') allow users to chain commands, redirecting the output of one command as input for another. For editing text files, CLI users often turn to text editors like 'nano', 'vim', or 'emacs', each with its unique set of functionalities.

Graphical interfaces offer a more visual approach to file and directory manipulation. In file managers, users can create new directories or files through context menus or dedicated buttons. Copying and moving files involves dragging and dropping items between directories. Renaming files or directories can be achieved through right-click options. Deleting files prompts a confirmation dialog to prevent accidental data loss. GUIs provide graphical representations of file properties, including size, type, and modification dates. Advanced file operations such as compression and extraction of archives are often integrated into the file manager, reducing the need for external tools. Text files can be edited using built-in text editors or opened in specialized applications associated with their file types.

Searching for files or directories is an integral part of file system navigation. In command-line interfaces, the 'find' command offers a powerful tool for searching based on various criteria such as name, size, or modification time. Combined with options like '-exec,' users can perform actions on the located files. The 'grep' command allows users to search within the content of files, providing a versatile text-based search tool. Additionally, the 'locate' command relies on a pre-built index to quickly locate files, enhancing search speed. Command-line users often leverage regular expressions for more complex and flexible search patterns.

Graphical interfaces streamline file and directory searches through integrated search functionalities. Users can initiate searches from a dedicated search bar, entering file names or keywords. Search results are displayed in a separate window, presenting a visual list of matching files or directories. Filters and sorting options help refine search results based on various criteria. The graphical search process is more intuitive, especially for users less familiar with complex search syntax. Moreover, GUIs often support indexed search, providing faster results by utilizing pre-built indexes similar to the 'locate' command in CLI.

In both command-line and graphical interfaces, file system navigation involves understanding and managing file permissions. In CLI, the 'chmod' command is used to modify permissions, with symbolic notation or octal values representing permission settings. The 'chown' command changes the ownership of files or directories. Understanding the concepts of read, write, and execute permissions for the owner, group, and others is crucial for effective file system management. ACLs (Access Control Lists) offer a more granular control mechanism for permissions on some systems, extending beyond the traditional Unix permissions model.

Graphical interfaces provide an intuitive approach to managing file permissions. In the properties or information dialogs of files and directories, GUI users can visually set permissions using checkboxes or dropdown menus. The owner and group are often displayed along with their associated permissions, allowing for quick identification and modification. Some file managers provide a graphical representation of permission settings, making it easier for users to comprehend the access control of files and directories. While this visual representation simplifies the process, it is essential for users to understand the underlying permission concepts to navigate efficiently.

Error handling and troubleshooting during file system navigation differ between command-line and graphical interfaces. In CLI, error messages are typically displayed in the terminal, providing detailed information about the nature of the issue. Users can analyze error messages to identify problems, such as permission issues or non-existent files. CLI also offers a range of diagnostic tools, including commands like 'ls' with various options to reveal hidden files or directories, aiding in uncovering potential issues.

Graphical interfaces present errors through dialog boxes or notifications. When an operation encounters a problem, a pop-up window notifies users of the issue. While this visual representation simplifies the process for users less familiar with command-line error messages, it may lack the detailed information available in the CLI. However, GUIs often include user-friendly error messages with suggested actions, making it easier for users to understand and address the encountered problems.

Accessibility is a crucial consideration in file system navigation. In CLI, users with visual impairments or those who prefer keyboard-based navigation can leverage screen readers and keyboard shortcuts. Command-line tools are often compatible with accessibility features provided by terminal emulators. Users can customize font sizes, color schemes, and text-to-speech options to enhance readability and usability.

Graphical interfaces cater to accessibility through features like high-contrast themes, magnification options, and screen reader compatibility. Operating systems with GUIs incorporate accessibility settings that allow users to adjust the interface based on their needs.

Additionally, GUI file managers often support keyboard shortcuts for users who prefer or require keyboard-based interactions. The availability of accessibility features in both CLI and GUI environments ensures that users with diverse needs can navigate the file system effectively.

In conclusion, techniques for navigating through file systems differ between command-line interfaces and graphical interfaces, each offering distinct advantages and considerations. Command-line interfaces rely on text-based commands, providing flexibility, efficiency, and powerful scripting capabilities. Users navigate through directories, manipulate files, and perform CRUD operations using commands like 'cd,' 'ls,' 'cp,' and 'rm.' Graphical interfaces, on the other hand, present a visual representation of the file system, making navigation more intuitive for users who may be less familiar with command-line syntax. File managers such as Windows Explorer or macOS Finder offer point-and-click interactions, drag-and-drop functionality, and integrated search features.

The command-line environment excels in efficiency, scripting capabilities, and the ability to work remotely through SSH. Users benefit from a more direct and granular control over file operations, with detailed error messages aiding in troubleshooting. In contrast, graphical interfaces prioritize ease of use, visual navigation, and accessibility. Graphical file managers provide a user-friendly experience with intuitive icons, context menus, and visual representations of file properties. Error handling is simplified through dialog boxes and notifications, making it more approachable for users who may not be familiar with command-line syntax.

Both interfaces cater to a diverse user base, accommodating various preferences, skill levels, and accessibility needs. Understanding the strengths and limitations of each approach allows users to choose the most suitable technique for their specific tasks and workflow. In many cases, users may find a combination of both command-line and graphical interfaces beneficial, depending on the context and requirements of their file system navigation. The coexistence of these techniques underscores the adaptability of computing environments to diverse user preferences and the ongoing evolution of file system interaction paradigms.

Understanding path structures and file addressing.

Path structures and file addressing are fundamental concepts in the realm of computing, playing a pivotal role in navigating and accessing files within a file system. A path serves as a virtual roadmap, guiding users and applications to the precise location of files or directories within the hierarchical structure of the file system. Understanding path structures is essential for efficient file management and is a cornerstone skill for users and developers alike.

In the context of path structures, there are two primary types: absolute paths and relative paths. Absolute paths provide a complete and unambiguous route from the root directory to the target file or directory. This unambiguous specificity makes absolute paths universally applicable, irrespective of the current working directory. On Unix-based systems, an absolute path might start with the root directory represented by a forward slash ('/'), followed by subsequent directory names in the hierarchy. For instance, '/home/user/documents/file.txt' is an absolute path that unequivocally identifies the location of the 'file.txt' within the 'documents' directory under the 'user' directory in the 'home' directory.

Conversely, relative paths are contingent upon the current working directory and offer a more concise means of file addressing. Instead of specifying the entire path from the root directory, a relative path denotes the route from the current working directory to the target file or directory. For example, if the current working directory is '/home/user/' and the target file is located in the 'documents' directory, a relative path might be 'documents/file.txt.' The reliance on the current working directory makes relative paths context-dependent, offering flexibility but necessitating awareness of the current directory's position within the file system hierarchy.

File addressing encompasses the techniques and conventions used to identify and locate files within a given path structure. In both absolute and relative paths, file addressing relies on conventions like file names, directory names, and separators to specify the target location accurately. File names serve as unique identifiers for individual files within a directory, facilitating their differentiation and retrieval. These names can include alphanumeric characters, underscores, hyphens, and periods, among others. Understanding the conventions for naming files is crucial to avoid naming conflicts and ensure clarity in file addressing.

Directories, often referred to as folders in graphical user interfaces, contribute to the hierarchical organization of the file system. Each directory has a name and can contain both files and subdirectories. In a path structure, directories are separated by a directory separator, such as a forward slash ('/') in Unix-like systems or a backslash ('\') in Windows. For example, in the path '/home/user/documents/file.txt,' the directories are 'home,' 'user,' and 'documents,' forming a hierarchical structure that guides the file addressing process.

The concept of separators extends to the root directory, which is the highest-level directory in a file system hierarchy. In Unix-like systems, the root directory is represented by a single forward slash ('/'), while in Windows, it is denoted by the drive letter followed by a colon ('C:'). Understanding the root directory is crucial for constructing absolute paths, as it serves as the starting point for navigating the entire file system.

Additionally, the notion of parent and child directories is integral to file addressing. The parent directory is one level higher in the hierarchy than the current working directory, while the child directory is one level lower. Relative paths often leverage references to the parent directory using the '..' notation. For example, in the path '/home/user/documents/../images/picture.jpg,' the '..' signifies a move up one level from 'documents' to the 'user' directory. This mechanism aids in constructing flexible and adaptable relative paths.

An important consideration in file addressing is the concept of case sensitivity. In some file systems, particularly those used in Unix-like environments, file names are case-sensitive, meaning 'File.txt' and 'file.txt' would be treated as distinct entities. In contrast, certain file systems, such as those in Windows, are case-insensitive, treating 'File.txt' and 'file.txt' as the same file. Awareness of the case sensitivity of a file system is crucial for accurate file addressing, as mismatches in letter casing can lead to errors in file retrieval and manipulation.

File extensions, typically denoted by a period ('.') followed by a few characters, play a significant role in file addressing. The extension often indicates the file type or format and is utilized by applications to interpret and handle the file content appropriately. For example, a file named 'document.docx' is likely a Word document, while 'image.jpg' is likely a JPEG image file. Understanding file extensions is essential for users and applications to interact effectively with files based on their content and intended use.

In command-line interfaces, users interact with the file system using commands that incorporate path structures for effective file addressing. The 'cd' (change directory) command is utilized to navigate through directories, with users providing either absolute or relative paths as arguments. For example, 'cd /home/user/documents' or 'cd documents' would both change the current working directory to the 'documents' directory. Similarly, commands like 'ls' (list) or 'dir' display the contents of the current directory or a specified directory, aiding users in understanding the structure and contents of their file system.

File addressing in command-line interfaces also involves manipulation commands such as 'cp' (copy), 'mv' (move), and 'rm' (remove). These commands take file paths as arguments, specifying the source and destination locations for the respective operations. For example, 'cp file.txt /backup/' copies the 'file.txt' to the 'backup' directory, while 'mv document.docx /home/user/documents/' moves the document to the 'documents' directory. Understanding these commands and their syntax is crucial for effective file manipulation in the command-line environment.

In graphical interfaces, users navigate the file system using file managers, which provide a visual representation of directories, files, and their hierarchical relationships. File managers offer intuitive means of file addressing through point-and-click interactions. Users can double-click on directories to enter them, click on files to open or manipulate them, and use drag-and-drop actions for file relocation. The graphical representation simplifies file addressing, especially for users who may find command-line syntax challenging or prefer visual interactions.

Graphical file managers also include features such as breadcrumbs, which display the current path in a navigable format. Breadcrumbs allow users to quickly jump to parent directories or any level within the hierarchy. The graphical interface often integrates a search functionality, enabling users to locate files based on names or keywords. Additionally, file managers support context menus that provide various options for file addressing, including copy, move, rename, and delete operations.

In conclusion, a comprehensive understanding of path structures and file addressing is indispensable for effective navigation and manipulation of files within a file system. Path structures, whether absolute or relative, provide the roadmap for users and applications to pinpoint the exact location of files and directories within the hierarchical structure. The conventions of file names, directory names, separators, and case sensitivity contribute to the precision and accuracy of file addressing. Whether in command-line interfaces or graphical interfaces, users leverage these concepts to interact with the file system, executing operations such as navigation, copying, moving, and deleting files. The coexistence of command-line and graphical interfaces ensures that users can choose the most suitable approach based on their preferences, skills, and the requirements of their computing tasks. Ultimately, path structures and file addressing form the foundation for effective file system management in diverse computing environments.

Introduction to different file system types, including FAT, NTFS, ext4, and more.

File systems are integral components of modern computing environments, providing the organizational framework for storing, retrieving, and managing data on storage devices. Different file system types have emerged over the years, each with its unique features, strengths, and use cases. Understanding the characteristics of prominent file systems, such as FAT, NTFS, ext4, and more, is essential for users, system administrators, and developers seeking to make informed decisions about storage solutions and compatibility.

The File Allocation Table (FAT) file system represents one of the earliest and most widely adopted file systems in the history of personal computing. Originally developed for MS-DOS, FAT has undergone several iterations, including FAT12, FAT16, and FAT32, accommodating changes in storage capacities and file size limits. FAT's simplicity and compatibility across various operating systems make it a versatile choice for USB drives, memory cards, and other removable storage media. However, its limitations in supporting large file sizes and lack of advanced features such as file permissions make it less suitable for contemporary computing environments.

New Technology File System (NTFS) stands as a significant evolution beyond FAT, developed by Microsoft to address the shortcomings of its predecessor. Introduced with Windows NT, NTFS offers several advancements, including support for larger file sizes, enhanced security features, and improved fault tolerance. NTFS implements a journaling mechanism, recording changes to the file system in a log, which aids in recovering from unexpected system crashes or power failures. The inclusion of access control lists (ACLs) allows for more granular control over file and directory permissions, making NTFS a robust choice for enterprise-level file management, particularly in Windows environments.

In the realm of Unix and Linux operating systems, the Extended File System (ext) family has played a pivotal role, with ext4 being the most recent iteration. ext4 builds upon the foundations laid by its predecessors—ext, ext2, and ext3—introducing several improvements in terms of performance, scalability, and reliability. Known for its backward compatibility with ext3, ext4 incorporates features such as support for larger file systems and files, delayed allocation for improved performance, and extents, which enhance the storage efficiency of large files. ext4 remains a popular choice for Linux distributions, offering a balance between performance and compatibility.

Another notable file system in the Linux ecosystem is Btrfs (B-tree file system), designed to address the evolving needs of modern computing. Btrfs employs a copy-on-write mechanism, ensuring data consistency and integrity by creating a new copy of data before modifying it. This approach enhances fault tolerance and facilitates features like snapshots, which allow users to create point-in-time copies of the file system. Btrfs also supports features like transparent compression, subvolumes, and online resizing, making it suitable for a wide range of applications, from desktop use to storage systems.

ZFS (Zettabyte File System) is a file system initially developed by Sun Microsystems and later embraced by the open-source community, notably employed in FreeBSD and various Linux distributions. ZFS introduces a revolutionary combination of file system and volume manager, presenting a unified storage solution. Its features include data integrity checks with checksums, snapshots for efficient backup and recovery, and support for massive storage capacities. ZFS's copy-on-write architecture, similar to Btrfs, ensures the preservation of data consistency, while features like deduplication and compression contribute to efficient storage utilization.

The High-Performance File System (HPFS) emerged as IBM's response to the limitations of the FAT file system. Initially introduced with OS/2, HPFS featured advancements such as improved support for large volumes, long file names, and efficient space utilization. HPFS demonstrated enhanced performance in comparison to FAT, particularly in scenarios involving large files and directories. However, as OS/2 gradually faded from prominence, HPFS lost relevance in the broader computing landscape.

Apple's Hierarchical File System (HFS) served as the default file system for Macintosh computers for many years, introducing a hierarchical structure for organizing files and directories. HFS evolved into HFS+ (Mac OS Extended), offering support for larger file sizes and introducing features like journaling for improved reliability. However, with the transition to Apple File System (APFS) starting with macOS High Sierra, HFS+ is gradually being phased out. APFS brings modern features such as native encryption, efficient snapshotting, and enhanced performance, aligning with the demands of Apple's evolving hardware and software ecosystem.

exFAT (Extended File Allocation Table) is a file system introduced by Microsoft to bridge the gap between FAT32 and NTFS, particularly catering to scenarios involving large file sizes and removable storage. exFAT eliminates the file size limitations of FAT32, allowing for seamless compatibility with large video files, high-resolution images, and other data-intensive content. Its design prioritizes simplicity and interoperability across different platforms, making it a popular choice for USB drives and memory cards.

As computing environments continue to diversify, network file systems have become instrumental in facilitating shared storage across networks. The Network File System (NFS), developed by Sun

Microsystems, is a widely adopted standard in Unix and Linux environments. NFS enables file sharing and access between networked systems, allowing users and applications to interact with files as if they were local. NFS has evolved through multiple versions, with NFSv4 introducing enhanced security features, improved performance, and support for complex file operations.

Similarly, the Common Internet File System (CIFS), also known as Server Message Block (SMB), is a network file system widely used in Windows environments. CIFS/SMB enables file and printer sharing across diverse operating systems, allowing seamless collaboration in mixed-platform environments. SMB has undergone several revisions, with SMB3 being the latest version, introducing features like encryption, improved performance, and support for large file transfers.

In conclusion, the landscape of file systems encompasses a diverse array of types, each tailored to specific requirements and preferences. From the historical significance of FAT to the robustness of NTFS in Windows environments, the evolutionary journey from ext to ext4 in the Linux realm, and the emergence of innovative file systems like Btrfs, ZFS, and APFS, each file system type reflects a response to the evolving needs of computing. The efficiency of exFAT for removable storage, the networked capabilities of NFS and SMB, and the forward-looking features of ZFS and Btrfs demonstrate the continual innovation in file system design. As computing technologies advance, the selection of an appropriate file system becomes a crucial consideration for optimizing storage, ensuring data integrity, and aligning with the diverse demands of contemporary computing environments.

Comparative analysis of file system characteristics and use cases.

A comparative analysis of file system characteristics and use cases is instrumental in understanding the diverse landscape of storage solutions, each designed to meet specific requirements and adapt to varying computing environments. Examining file systems such as FAT, NTFS, ext4, Btrfs, ZFS, HFS+, exFAT, NFS, and SMB allows for a comprehensive evaluation of their strengths, weaknesses, and optimal use scenarios.

The File Allocation Table (FAT) file system, with its roots deeply embedded in the history of personal computing, is characterized by simplicity and cross-platform compatibility. FAT's straightforward structure facilitates easy implementation and interoperability across different operating systems, making it a suitable choice for removable storage media like USB drives and memory cards. However, its limitations in supporting large file sizes and lack of advanced features such as file permissions limit its application in contemporary computing environments, where data storage demands have grown exponentially.

In contrast, the New Technology File System (NTFS) represents a significant leap forward in terms of sophistication and functionality. Developed by Microsoft, NTFS is the default file system for Windows operating systems. NTFS addresses the limitations of FAT by supporting larger file sizes, implementing journaling for improved fault tolerance, and incorporating access control lists (ACLs) for enhanced security. These features make NTFS particularly well-suited for enterprise-level file management, where security, reliability, and support for large volumes of data are paramount.

The ext4 file system, a member of the Extended File System family, serves as a staple in the Linux ecosystem. Building upon its predecessors, ext4 introduces improvements in performance, scalability, and reliability. With backward compatibility with ext3, ext4 accommodates larger file sizes, implements delayed allocation for enhanced performance, and incorporates extents to improve storage efficiency for large files. The adaptability of ext4 positions it as a versatile choice for Linux distributions, striking a balance between compatibility and modern storage needs.

Btrfs, or B-tree file system, stands out as a modern file system designed to address the evolving demands of contemporary computing. Employing a copy-on-write mechanism and supporting features such as snapshots, transparent compression, and subvolumes, Btrfs is well-suited for a variety of applications. Its ability to efficiently handle large volumes of data, facilitate easy backups through snapshots, and provide flexibility in storage management makes it suitable for both desktop and server environments, offering a robust solution for data-intensive tasks.

ZFS (Zettabyte File System), initially developed by Sun Microsystems and embraced by the open-source community, represents a holistic approach to storage. Acting as both a file system and a volume manager, ZFS introduces features like data integrity checks with checksums, snapshots, and support for massive storage capacities. The copy-on-write architecture ensures data consistency, while features like deduplication and compression contribute to efficient storage utilization. ZFS is well-suited for applications demanding high reliability, scalability, and advanced storage features, making it a preferred choice in environments where data integrity is critical.

Hierarchical File System (HFS+) served as the default file system for Macintosh computers, offering a hierarchical structure for file organization. With features like journaling for improved reliability and support for larger file sizes, HFS+ was suitable for Mac users for an extended period. However, with the transition to Apple File System (APFS), designed for modern macOS versions, HFS+ is gradually being phased out. APFS introduces features such as native encryption, efficient snapshotting, and enhanced performance, aligning with the demands of Apple's evolving hardware and software ecosystem.

exFAT (Extended File Allocation Table) emerges as a specialized file system designed to overcome the limitations of FAT32, particularly concerning large file sizes and storage capacities. Introduced by Microsoft, exFAT prioritizes simplicity and interoperability across platforms. Its design makes it a popular choice for removable storage media, such as USB drives and memory cards, where compatibility with diverse operating systems is crucial. The elimination of file size restrictions in exFAT makes it suitable for scenarios involving large video files, high-resolution images, and other data-intensive content.

Network file systems play a pivotal role in facilitating shared storage across networks, with NFS (Network File System) and SMB (Server Message Block) representing prominent standards. NFS, developed by Sun Microsystems, enables file sharing and access between networked systems in Unix and Linux environments. It allows users and applications to interact with files as if they were local, fostering seamless collaboration. With multiple versions, including NFSv4 with enhanced security features, NFS remains a robust solution for networked file sharing.

SMB, also known as CIFS (Common Internet File System), is widely utilized in Windows environments for file and printer sharing across diverse operating systems. The SMB protocol allows for effective collaboration in mixed-platform environments, ensuring compatibility and seamless file access. Evolving through various versions, SMB3 introduces encryption, improved performance, and support for large file transfers, making it suitable for contemporary networked storage scenarios.

In a comparative context, these file systems exhibit distinct characteristics that align with specific use cases and requirements. FAT, with its simplicity and cross-platform compatibility, finds a niche in scenarios involving portable storage media. NTFS excels in Windows environments, especially in enterprise settings requiring robust security features and support for large volumes of data. ext4 caters to the Linux ecosystem, striking a balance between compatibility and modern storage needs.

Btrfs and ZFS emerge as modern file systems capable of handling data-intensive tasks, offering features like snapshots, compression, and efficient storage utilization. Their suitability spans from desktop use to server environments, where reliability, scalability, and advanced storage features are critical. APFS addresses the evolving needs of Apple's ecosystem, emphasizing native encryption, efficient snapshotting, and enhanced performance.

Specialized file systems like exFAT cater to scenarios where large file sizes and interoperability across platforms are paramount, making them suitable for removable storage media. Network file systems like NFS and SMB facilitate collaborative storage solutions across networks, each with its strengths in Unix/Linux and Windows environments, respectively.

In conclusion, the comparative analysis of file system characteristics and use cases underscores the importance of aligning storage solutions with specific requirements. The diversity of file systems reflects the varied demands of computing environments, from simplicity and cross-platform compatibility to advanced features, scalability, and security. The selection of an optimal file system depends on factors such as the operating environment, storage demands, and the nature of data-intensive tasks, highlighting the need for a nuanced approach in choosing the most suitable file system for a given scenario.

Chapter 2: Evolution of File Systems in Operating Systems

Tracing the evolution of file systems from early computing to modern operating systems.

The evolution of file systems traces a remarkable journey from the early days of computing to the sophisticated architectures of modern operating systems. In the nascent stages of computing, the concept of file systems emerged as a means to organize and manage data stored on magnetic tapes and later, disk drives. One of the earliest file systems was the IBM Generalized Information Retrieval and Listing System (GIRLS), developed in the 1950s for the IBM 704 computer. This system marked a departure from the manual handling of punched cards, introducing a hierarchical structure to organize files and directories.

As computing technologies progressed, the emergence of the first commercially successful minicomputer, the Digital Equipment Corporation's (DEC) PDP-8, in the 1960s brought forth the need for more advanced file systems. The DECtape file system allowed for sequential access to data on DECtapes, offering improved storage and retrieval capabilities. However, it lacked the hierarchical organization seen in later file systems.

The advent of time-sharing systems in the 1960s and 1970s, exemplified by the Multics project, brought about significant advancements in file system design. Multics introduced the notion of a hierarchical file structure with directories, paving the way for the organization of files into a tree-like hierarchy. This hierarchical approach facilitated more efficient data management and paved the way for the design principles that would become foundational in subsequent file systems.

The 1970s marked a pivotal moment in the evolution of file systems with the development of Unix at Bell Labs by Ken Thompson, Dennis Ritchie, and others. Unix introduced the File System Hierarchy Standard (FSHS), a hierarchical structure that organized files into directories such as /bin, /usr, and /etc. This innovative file system architecture contributed significantly to the widespread adoption of Unix and became a blueprint for subsequent file system designs.

The Berkeley Fast File System (FFS), developed in the late 1970s as an extension of Unix, brought about major improvements in performance and storage efficiency. FFS introduced concepts like cylinder groups and optimized block allocation, enhancing file access speed and reducing fragmentation. The principles laid out in FFS influenced many subsequent file system designs, including those used in other Unix-like operating systems.

The 1980s witnessed the rise of personal computing, and with it, the need for file systems that catered to the requirements of individual users. The File Allocation Table (FAT) file system, initially introduced in 1977 with the advent of MS-DOS, gained prominence during this era. FAT provided a simple and straightforward structure, suitable for the limited storage capacities and computing resources of early personal computers. It became a standard for IBM PC-compatible systems and persisted through subsequent iterations like FAT12, FAT16, and FAT32.

The introduction of the Macintosh in 1984 brought forth the Hierarchical File System (HFS), developed by Apple for its Macintosh operating system. HFS represented a departure from the hierarchical file structures of Unix, introducing a flat-file structure with a single directory containing files and folders. While not as prevalent in the broader computing landscape, HFS was a pioneering effort in user-friendly file organization and served as the default file system for Macintosh computers for many years.

The late 1980s and early 1990s saw the dominance of Microsoft's Windows operating systems, which initially relied on the FAT file system. However, with the release of Windows NT in 1993, Microsoft introduced the New Technology File System (NTFS). NTFS addressed the limitations of FAT, supporting larger file sizes, providing advanced security features through access control lists (ACLs), and implementing journaling for improved reliability. NTFS became the default file system for Windows, setting a new standard for file system capabilities in the Windows ecosystem.

In the realm of Unix and Linux, the 1990s witnessed the evolution of the Extended File System (ext) family. Ext2, introduced in 1993, brought forth innovations like the use of inodes to represent files and directories, improving metadata organization and storage efficiency. Ext3, introduced in the early 2000s, added journaling capabilities, enhancing fault tolerance and data recovery in case of system failures. Building upon these foundations, the introduction of ext4 in 2008 brought further improvements in performance, scalability, and support for larger file sizes.

The rise of networked computing in the late 20th century necessitated file systems capable of facilitating collaborative data sharing. The Network File System (NFS), developed by Sun Microsystems in the 1980s, became a standard for Unix and Linux environments. NFS allowed remote file access and sharing, enabling users to interact with files as if they were local, fostering seamless collaboration in networked environments. The evolution of NFS continues with subsequent versions introducing enhanced security features and performance improvements.

In the Windows environment, the Common Internet File System (CIFS), also known as the Server Message Block (SMB), became the standard for file and printer sharing. Developed by IBM and later adopted and extended by Microsoft, SMB enables cross-platform file sharing and collaboration, playing a crucial role in networking scenarios involving Windows-based systems.

The 21st century brought about a new era in file system design, characterized by the emergence of file systems with advanced features and capabilities. Btrfs (B-tree file system), introduced in 2007 for Linux, represented a departure from traditional file system structures. Btrfs employed a copy-on-write mechanism, allowing for efficient snapshots, improved fault tolerance, and support for large file systems. Btrfs aimed to address modern storage demands, offering features like subvolumes, transparent compression, and online resizing.

The Zettabyte File System (ZFS), developed by Sun Microsystems in the early 2000s, redefined the landscape of file systems. ZFS combined the functionalities of a file system and a volume manager, introducing features like data integrity checks with checksums, support for massive storage capacities, and advanced snapshot capabilities. ZFS's copy-on-write architecture ensured data consistency and made it a compelling choice for applications demanding high reliability, scalability, and storage efficiency.

As mobile computing became ubiquitous, the need for file systems compatible with flash storage and optimized for mobile devices became apparent. exFAT (Extended File Allocation Table), introduced by Microsoft in 2006, addressed these requirements. exFAT eliminated the file size restrictions of FAT32, making it suitable for scenarios involving large video files, high-resolution images, and other data-intensive content. exFAT became a common choice for removable storage media like USB drives and memory cards.

The transition to solid-state drives (SSDs) in the storage landscape prompted further innovation in file system design. The Apple File System (APFS), introduced by Apple in 2017, exemplified this trend. Developed specifically for macOS and iOS devices, APFS introduced features like native encryption, efficient snapshotting, and enhanced performance tailored to the characteristics of SSDs. APFS marked a departure from HFS+, aligning with Apple's commitment to modern storage technologies.

In summary, the evolution of file systems from early computing to modern operating systems reflects a continuous quest to address the changing landscape of computing environments, storage technologies, and user demands. From the rudimentary file structures of GIRLS and the hierarchical designs of Multics and Unix to the dominance of NTFS in Windows and the innovations brought forth by Btrfs, ZFS, exFAT, NFS, and SMB, each phase in this evolution has left an indelible mark on the way data is stored, accessed, and managed. The journey is marked by a commitment to simplicity, efficiency, reliability, and adaptability, demonstrating the pivotal role file systems play in the dynamic world of computing.

Key milestones and innovations in file system development.

The development of file systems has witnessed a series of key milestones and innovations, shaping the landscape of data storage and management throughout the history of computing. One of the earliest milestones can be traced back to the IBM Generalized Information Retrieval and Listing System (GIRLS), developed in the 1950s for the IBM 704 computer. While simple by modern standards, GIRLS introduced the concept of a hierarchical file structure, allowing for the organization of data on magnetic tapes and laying the groundwork for future file system designs.

In the 1960s and 1970s, the Multics project marked a significant milestone in file system development. Multics introduced the hierarchical file structure with directories, providing a more efficient means of organizing and accessing files. This innovation laid the foundation for subsequent file system designs and became a blueprint for the development of hierarchical structures in Unix and other operating systems.

The advent of Unix in the 1970s brought about another pivotal milestone. Unix introduced the File System Hierarchy Standard (FSHS), a hierarchical organization of directories that included /bin, /usr, and /etc. This standardized structure enhanced file organization and management, contributing to the widespread adoption of Unix and influencing the design of subsequent file systems.

In the late 1970s, the Berkeley Fast File System (FFS) represented a leap forward in file system performance and storage efficiency. FFS introduced concepts such as cylinder groups and optimized block allocation, significantly improving file access speed and reducing fragmentation. FFS became a standard in Unix-like operating systems and influenced many subsequent file system designs, setting a precedent for optimizing storage efficiency.

The 1980s saw the proliferation of personal computing, and with it, the need for file systems tailored to individual users. The File Allocation Table (FAT) file system, initially introduced in 1977 with MS-DOS, became a dominant file system for IBM PC-compatible systems. FAT's simplicity and compatibility made it a standard choice for early personal computers, marking a milestone in the evolution of file systems for individual users.

The introduction of the Macintosh in 1984 brought forth the Hierarchical File System (HFS), developed by Apple. HFS represented a milestone in user-friendly file organization, introducing a flat-file structure with a single directory containing files and folders. Although not as prevalent in broader computing, HFS set a precedent for designing file systems with a focus on user experience and ease of navigation.

The 1990s marked a crucial period with the dominance of Microsoft's Windows operating systems. The release of Windows NT in 1993 introduced the New Technology File System (NTFS). NTFS addressed the limitations of FAT, supporting larger file sizes, introducing advanced security features through access control lists

(ACLs), and implementing journaling for improved reliability. NTFS became the default file system for Windows, setting a new standard for capabilities in the Windows ecosystem.

In parallel, the development of Unix and Linux file systems continued with the evolution of the Extended File System (ext) family. Ext2, introduced in 1993, brought forth innovations like inodes for representing files and directories, improving metadata organization and storage efficiency. The introduction of ext3 in the early 2000s added journaling capabilities, enhancing fault tolerance and data recovery in case of system failures. Ext3 set the stage for the subsequent introduction of ext4 in 2008, which brought further improvements in performance, scalability, and support for larger file sizes.

The late 20th century also saw the emergence of networked computing, leading to the development of file systems capable of facilitating collaborative data sharing. The Network File System (NFS), developed by Sun Microsystems in the 1980s, became a standard for Unix and Linux environments. NFS enabled remote file access and sharing, allowing users to interact with files as if they were local, fostering seamless collaboration in networked environments.

In the Windows environment, the Common Internet File System (CIFS), also known as the Server Message Block (SMB), played a crucial role in file and printer sharing. Initially developed by IBM and later adopted and extended by Microsoft, SMB enabled cross-platform file sharing and collaboration. The continual evolution of NFS and SMB, with multiple versions introducing enhanced security features and performance improvements, marked milestones in networked file system development.

The 21st century brought about a new era in file system design with the introduction of innovative features and capabilities. Btrfs (B-tree file system), introduced in 2007 for Linux, marked a departure from traditional file system structures. Btrfs employed a copy-on-write mechanism, enabling efficient snapshots, improved fault tolerance, and support for large file systems. Btrfs aimed to address modern storage demands, offering features like subvolumes, transparent compression, and online resizing.

ZFS (Zettabyte File System), developed by Sun Microsystems in the early 2000s, redefined the landscape of file systems. ZFS combined the functionalities of a file system and a volume manager, introducing features like data integrity checks with checksums, support for massive storage capacities, and advanced snapshot capabilities. ZFS's copy-on-write architecture ensured data consistency and made it a compelling choice for applications demanding high reliability, scalability, and storage efficiency.

With the proliferation of mobile computing, file systems tailored for flash storage and optimized for mobile devices became essential. exFAT (Extended File Allocation Table), introduced by Microsoft in 2006, addressed these requirements. exFAT eliminated the file size restrictions of FAT32, making it suitable for scenarios involving large video files, high-resolution images, and other data-intensive content. exFAT became a common choice for removable storage media like USB drives and memory cards.

The transition to solid-state drives (SSDs) prompted further innovation in file system design. The Apple File System (APFS), introduced by Apple in 2017, exemplified this trend. Developed specifically for macOS and iOS devices, APFS introduced features like native encryption, efficient snapshotting, and enhanced performance tailored to the characteristics of SSDs. APFS marked a departure from HFS+, aligning with Apple's commitment to modern storage technologies.

In conclusion, the key milestones and innovations in file system development have been integral to the evolution of computing. From the early hierarchical structures of GIRLS and Multics to the dominance of NTFS in Windows and the advent of modern file systems like Btrfs, ZFS, exFAT, NFS, and SMB, each milestone has addressed specific needs and challenges of its time. The journey reflects a commitment to simplicity, efficiency, reliability, and adaptability, showcasing the pivotal role file systems play in shaping the dynamic world of computing.

Examining early file systems like FAT16 and FAT32.

The examination of early file systems, specifically FAT16 and FAT32, takes us back to a crucial period in the evolution of computing when storage capacities were relatively modest, and the need for efficient file organization and accessibility was paramount. The File Allocation Table (FAT) file system, initially introduced in 1977 with the advent of MS-DOS, played a pivotal role in shaping the landscape of file systems for IBM PC-compatible systems. FAT16, an early iteration, emerged as a significant milestone in the development of file systems, offering improvements over its predecessor, FAT12. FAT16, as the name suggests, utilized a 16-bit file allocation table entry, allowing for a more extensive range of cluster addresses and, consequently, accommodating larger storage volumes. This was particularly significant in an era where the average storage capacities of personal computers were escalating, and the limitations of FAT12 became apparent.

FAT16's file allocation table entries allowed for the addressing of up to 65,536 clusters, which equated to enhanced storage capacity compared to the 4,096 clusters that FAT12 could address. Each cluster represented a contiguous block of storage space on the disk, and with FAT16, the finer granularity in addressing clusters facilitated the management of larger files and storage volumes. The file allocation table served as a crucial index, mapping each file's clusters on the disk, enabling the operating system to locate and retrieve data efficiently. FAT16's compatibility and simplicity made it the de facto file system for early versions of MS-DOS and Windows.

However, as computing needs continued to evolve, the limitations of FAT16 became apparent. One of the notable constraints was the maximum volume size it could effectively support. With the 16-bit addressing scheme, FAT16 imposed a practical limit on the size of storage volumes it could manage. The maximum volume size was capped at 2 gigabytes (GB), which posed challenges as storage capacities continued to soar. In an era where the demand for larger storage volumes was becoming more prevalent, FAT16's limitations in accommodating these burgeoning requirements became a key factor driving the need for further advancements in file system technology.

This need for larger storage capacities and improved efficiency led to the development of FAT32, an extension and refinement of the FAT file system lineage. FAT32, introduced in 1996 with the release of Windows 95 OSR2, addressed the limitations of FAT16 by adopting a 32-bit file allocation table entry. This upgrade allowed for an even more extensive range of cluster addresses, resulting in significantly enhanced storage capacities. The maximum volume size supported by FAT32 skyrocketed to an impressive 2 terabytes (TB), representing a thousandfold increase from the constraints of FAT16. This transformative leap was particularly impactful, considering the increasing demand for storage space in the late 20th century.

The implementation of FAT32 brought about a paradigm shift in file system capabilities. The adoption of 32-bit addressing facilitated the efficient organization and management of large storage volumes, accommodating the ever-growing sizes of hard drives and other storage devices. The increased cluster addressing range allowed for more granular allocation of storage space, reducing wasted space and optimizing disk utilization. FAT32's enhanced compatibility with a wide range of operating systems and storage devices further solidified its status as a versatile and widely adopted file system during its era.

Moreover, FAT32 introduced improvements in file and directory management. The increased number of clusters enabled the allocation of larger files, and the enhanced directory structure support-ed more efficient organization of files and folders. FAT32 continued to rely on the concept of a file allocation table, which mapped the clusters assigned to each file. This table was crucial for the operating system to locate and retrieve data efficiently. The simplicity and straightforwardness of FAT32 made it suitable for various applications, from personal computers to removable storage media such as USB drives and memory cards.

Despite the notable advantages, FAT32 also had its set of limitations. One significant drawback was the inefficient utilization of storage space for small files. The fixed cluster size, even for small files that did not require the allocated space fully, led to a phenomenon known as "slack space," where portions of clusters remained unused. This inefficiency became more pronounced as storage capacities continued to increase, underscoring the need for file systems that could better optimize space utilization.

The era of FAT16 and FAT32 marked a crucial juncture in file system development, representing a time when computing was transitioning from its early stages to a more mature and sophisticated landscape. The adaptability of FAT16 and the transformative leap with FAT32 played vital roles in catering to the storage demands of their respective eras. These file systems became foundational in the history of personal computing, laying the groundwork for subsequent advancements and innovations in file system design. While the computing world has moved on to more advanced file systems, the legacy of FAT16 and FAT32 endures, reminding us of the evolutionary journey that has shaped the way we organize, store, and access data in the digital age.

Understanding the limitations and advantages of legacy file systems.

The exploration of legacy file systems reveals a complex interplay between advantages that paved the way for the digital landscape's early development and limitations that underscored the need for subsequent innovations. Legacy file systems, such as the File Allocation Table (FAT) system, including iterations like FAT12, FAT16, and FAT32, played a pivotal role in the formative years of personal computing. One of the advantages of these legacy systems was their simplicity. The straightforward design of FAT made it accessible and easy to implement, a crucial factor in the early days when computing technology was still in its infancy. This simplicity contributed to the widespread adoption of FAT in various operating systems, including MS-DOS and early versions of Windows. Users appreciated the ease with which they could organize files and directories in a hierarchical structure, facilitating straightforward file management.

However, as computing needs and storage capacities began to expand, the limitations of legacy file systems like FAT became increasingly apparent. One significant disadvantage was the lack of support for large storage volumes. FAT12, FAT16, and even FAT32, while representing advancements in their respective times, imposed practical limits on the size of storage volumes they could effectively manage. The maximum volume size for FAT16, for example, was capped at 2 gigabytes (GB), and though FAT32 extended this to 2 terabytes (TB), it remained a finite range that would prove insufficient as storage technologies continued to evolve.

Another notable limitation of legacy file systems was their suboptimal use of storage space, particularly for small files. The fixed cluster size employed by these systems meant that even the smallest file would occupy an entire cluster, leading to a phenomenon known as "slack space." This inefficiency in space utilization became more pronounced with the increasing prevalence of larger storage capacities. As a result, legacy file systems struggled to optimize storage use effectively, leading to wasted space on storage devices.

The lack of advanced features in legacy file systems was another drawback. Security and access control were rudimentary at best.

FAT, for instance, lacked robust mechanisms for file and directory permissions, leaving systems vulnerable to unauthorized access. This limitation became a critical concern as computing environments evolved, especially in enterprise settings where data security and user access control were of paramount importance. Additionally, the absence of journaling, a feature introduced in more modern file systems, meant that legacy file systems like FAT did not provide a built-in mechanism to recover from system crashes or power failures, potentially resulting in data corruption and loss.

Despite these limitations, legacy file systems possessed distinct advantages that contributed significantly to the early success of personal computing. The simplicity of FAT made it an ideal choice for early operating systems where computational resources were limited. The absence of complexity allowed for quick and efficient data access in an era when computational power was at a premium. Additionally, the compatibility of FAT across various operating systems, including MS-DOS and Windows, fostered interoperability and eased the transition for users moving between different computing environments.

The concept of drive letters, a characteristic feature of FAT-based systems, provided a familiar and intuitive means for users to navigate and access storage devices. This simplicity in drive letter assignments became a part of the user experience, influencing the way individuals interacted with their computers. The straightforward directory structure and file naming conventions further contributed to a user-friendly environment, enhancing accessibility for a broad user base.

Legacy file systems also demonstrated a level of versatility that allowed them to adapt to different storage media. FAT, in particular, found application in a range of devices, from hard drives and floppy disks to USB drives and memory cards. This adaptability contributed to the widespread use of FAT in various computing scenarios, establishing it as a standard for a significant period.

As computing needs grew more sophisticated, the limitations of legacy file systems became increasingly apparent, necessitating the development of more advanced alternatives. Newer file systems, such as the New Technology File System (NTFS) in the Windows environment and the Extended File System (ext) family in the Unix and Linux realm, sought to address these shortcomings. NTFS, for instance, introduced features like support for larger file sizes, advanced security mechanisms, and journaling, making it a more robust choice for modern computing environments.

The ext file systems, starting with ext2 and evolving to ext3 and ext4, brought improvements in performance, scalability, and reliability. These advancements addressed the inefficiencies of space utilization and enhanced the ability to manage larger storage volumes effectively. The inclusion of journaling in ext3 and ext4 improved fault tolerance, providing a safeguard against data corruption in the event of system crashes or power failures.

The shift to more modern file systems also brought about innovations such as Btrfs and ZFS. Btrfs, with its copy-on-write mechanism, offered features like snapshots, efficient space utilization, and support for large storage volumes. ZFS, combining file system and volume manager functionalities, introduced features like data integrity checks, support for massive storage capacities, and advanced snapshot capabilities.

In conclusion, the examination of legacy file systems like FAT reveals a nuanced landscape where advantages and limitations coexist. The simplicity and compatibility of these systems played a pivotal role in the early days of personal computing, fostering accessibility and ease of use. However, as computing environments evolved and storage demands increased, the constraints of legacy file systems became apparent, necessitating the development of more advanced alternatives. The transition to modern file systems brought about enhanced capabilities, improved space utilization, and robust security mechanisms. The legacy of file systems like FAT serves as a testament to the dynamic evolution of computing, where the strengths and weaknesses of earlier technologies laid the foundation for the sophisticated storage solutions in use today.

Exploring the shift towards 64-bit file systems for improved scalability.

The exploration of the shift towards 64-bit file systems represents a significant milestone in the evolution of computing, driven by the imperative for improved scalability in response to the escalating demands of modern computing environments. In the early years of computing, file systems operated within the constraints of 32-bit architectures, where memory addresses and data structures were limited to a 32-bit address space. This limitation imposed practical constraints on the size of files, storage volumes, and the overall scalability of file systems. As computational tasks became more complex and storage needs surged, the need for larger address spaces and increased scalability emerged as a critical consideration. The transition to 64-bit architectures was a logical progression, addressing the limitations inherent in their 32-bit counterparts.

One of the primary advantages of 64-bit architectures is the significantly expanded address space. In a 64-bit system, memory addresses are represented by 64 bits, providing an astronomical address range of 2^{64}, or approximately 18.4 million terabytes. This vast address space allows for the efficient management and organization of data on a scale previously unimaginable. In the realm of file systems, this expanded address space directly translates to the ability to handle much larger files and storage volumes. The shift towards 64-bit file systems was, therefore, a strategic response to the growing storage demands of contemporary computing environments where massive datasets, multimedia content, and complex applications are pervasive.

The improvement in scalability achieved through 64-bit file systems is particularly evident in the handling of large files. In a 32-bit file system, the maximum file size is constrained by the 32-bit address space, often capping at 4 gigabytes. This limitation posed significant challenges in the face of burgeoning file sizes, especially with the proliferation of high-definition multimedia content, scientific datasets, and other data-intensive applications. The transition to 64-bit file systems, such as those based on the NTFS (New Technology File System) in Windows or ext4 in Linux, removes this barrier, allowing for the creation and manipulation of files that can span exabytes in size. This newfound capacity aligns seamlessly with contemporary storage requirements, ensuring that file systems can accommodate the vast datasets generated by advanced applications and technologies.

Moreover, the scalability of 64-bit file systems extends beyond individual file sizes to encompass the management of storage volumes. In 32-bit file systems, the addressable space for the entire volume is also restricted to the 32-bit limit. This limitation imposed practical restrictions on the maximum size of storage volumes, impeding the scalability of file systems in the face of evolving storage technologies. With 64-bit file systems, the address space for storage volumes is vastly expanded, allowing for the creation of enormous volumes that can span thousands of petabytes. This scalability is crucial in environments where large-scale data storage and retrieval are integral, such as data centers, cloud computing infrastructure, and enterprise storage solutions.

The transition to 64-bit file systems has also introduced improvements in performance and efficiency. The larger address space enables file systems to more effectively manage and organize data structures, reducing the potential for fragmentation and optimizing data access. The enhanced scalability allows for the implementation of advanced caching mechanisms, improving read and write speeds for large files. These performance enhancements are particularly signifi-cant in scenarios where rapid data access is essential, such as in high-performance computing environments, scientific research, and real-time data processing applications.

Furthermore, the shift towards 64-bit file systems has facilitated advancements in metadata handling. Metadata, which includes in-formation about files and directories, plays a crucial role in file sys-tem operations. In 32-bit file systems, the limited address space for metadata could become a bottleneck, especially in scenarios with a vast number of files. With the expanded address space in 64-bit file systems, the capacity to manage extensive metadata grows propor-tionately. This is particularly advantageous in environments charac-terized by a high volume of small files, such as those encountered in web servers, databases, and content delivery networks, where effi-cient metadata handling is essential for optimal performance.

The adoption of 64-bit file systems has also addressed security considerations. In environments where data integrity and access con-trol are paramount, the expanded address space facilitates the im-plementation of more robust security mechanisms. Features such as access control lists (ACLs) and encryption, which are essential for safeguarding sensitive data, can be more effectively implemented in 64-bit file systems. This is especially relevant in enterprise settings, fi-nancial institutions, and other sectors where stringent security mea-sures are imperative.

While the advantages of 64-bit file systems are substantial, it is crucial to acknowledge the broader context of this shift and the challenges that come with it. Compatibility considerations are para-mount, particularly in heterogeneous computing environments where a mix of 32-bit and 64-bit systems may coexist. Interoperabili-ty between different architectures and file system types requires care-ful planning to ensure seamless data exchange and accessibility across diverse computing platforms. Additionally, the transition to 64-bit file systems necessitates updates to software applications and utilities to fully leverage the expanded capabilities. Legacy applications designed for 32-bit systems may need adaptation to harness the benefits of 64-bit architectures fully.

In conclusion, the exploration of the shift towards 64-bit file systems illuminates a transformative phase in the evolution of computing, driven by the imperative for improved scalability. The advantages of 64-bit architectures, including expanded address spaces, enhanced scalability for large files and storage volumes, improved performance, and robust security features, have positioned 64-bit file systems as essential components in addressing the demands of contemporary computing environments. The scalability achieved through 64-bit file systems aligns with the realities of a data-driven era, where massive datasets, high-performance computing, and diverse applications necessitate storage solutions that can efficiently scale to meet evolving needs. As technology continues to advance, the trajectory towards increasingly scalable and efficient file systems remains a critical aspect of ensuring the continued evolution and adaptability of computing infrastructure.

The impact of 64-bit architecture on file system design.

The advent of 64-bit architecture has ushered in a transformative era in file system design, profoundly impacting the way data is stored, accessed, and managed in modern computing environments. The shift to 64-bit architecture represents a departure from the limitations imposed by the earlier 32-bit counterparts, unlocking unprecedented possibilities for scalability, performance, and efficiency in file systems. At the core of this impact lies the substantially expanded address space provided by 64-bit architectures, where memory addresses are represented by 64 bits, resulting in an astronomical address range of 2^{64}. This monumental increase in addressable space has reverberated throughout file system design, addressing longstanding challenges associated with the limitations of 32-bit architectures.

One of the pivotal consequences of the 64-bit architecture on file system design is the ability to handle significantly larger files. In a 32-bit system, the addressable space limits the maximum size of a file to 4 gigabytes. This restriction became a formidable barrier as the demand for handling massive datasets, high-definition multimedia content, and complex applications burgeoned. With 64-bit architectures, the file size limitations are practically eliminated, and file systems can now accommodate files spanning exabytes, providing a seamless solution to the challenges posed by the exponential growth in data volume. This has profound implications for applications such as video editing, scientific simulations, and database management, where the manipulation of colossal files is essential.

The scalability afforded by 64-bit architecture extends beyond individual file sizes to encompass the management of entire storage volumes. In 32-bit file systems, the addressable space for the entire volume is constrained, limiting the maximum size of storage volumes. The transition to 64-bit architectures removes this constraint, allowing for the creation of enormous storage volumes that can span thousands of petabytes. This scalability is paramount in contemporary computing environments characterized by vast datasets, cloud computing infrastructures, and enterprise storage solutions, where the ability to efficiently manage and organize colossal volumes of data is essential.

The impact of 64-bit architecture on file system design is further manifested in improvements in performance and efficiency. The larger address space enables file systems to more effectively manage and organize data structures, reducing the potential for fragmentation and optimizing data access. This improved efficiency is particularly significant in scenarios where rapid data access is crucial, such as high-performance computing environments, real-time data processing applications, and scientific research, where computational efficiency directly correlates with overall system performance.

Additionally, the scalability of 64-bit file systems has led to advancements in metadata handling. Metadata, encompassing information about files and directories, is critical for file system operations. In 32-bit file systems, the limited address space for metadata could become a bottleneck, especially in scenarios with a vast number of files. With the expanded address space in 64-bit file systems, the capacity to manage extensive metadata grows proportionately. This is particularly advantageous in environments characterized by a high volume of small files, such as web servers, databases, and content delivery networks, where efficient metadata handling is essential for optimal performance.

The security landscape of file systems has also witnessed notable enhancements as a consequence of the transition to 64-bit architecture. In environments where data integrity and access control are paramount, the expanded address space facilitates the implementation of more robust security mechanisms. Features such as access control lists (ACLs), encryption, and advanced authentication protocols can be more effectively implemented in 64-bit file systems. This is especially relevant in enterprise settings, financial institutions, and other sectors where stringent security measures are imperative to protect sensitive data from unauthorized access or tampering.

Moreover, the impact of 64-bit architecture on file system design has catalyzed innovation in fault tolerance and data recovery mechanisms. The expanded address space allows for the implementation of advanced journaling systems, where changes to the file system are logged in a journal. In the event of a system crash or power failure, these journals enable file systems to recover to a consistent and reliable state, minimizing the risk of data corruption. Journaling, coupled with the enhanced scalability of 64-bit file systems, ensures a higher degree of resilience in the face of unforeseen events, reinforcing the reliability of modern file systems.

The transition to 64-bit architecture has also played a crucial role in supporting advanced features in file systems that were previously challenging to implement within the constraints of 32-bit architectures. Copy-on-write mechanisms, snapshots, and subvolumes are examples of sophisticated features that have become more prevalent in 64-bit file systems. Copy-on-write, for instance, enables efficient creation and management of snapshots without duplicating data unnecessarily. This not only contributes to improved storage efficiency but also facilitates enhanced data protection and versioning capabilities.

Furthermore, the impact of 64-bit architecture extends to the compatibility and interoperability of file systems across diverse computing environments. The larger address space allows for greater flexibility in handling mixed 32-bit and 64-bit environments, ensuring seamless data exchange and accessibility. This has significant implications for heterogeneous computing environments where a variety of systems with different architectures may coexist. The compatibility afforded by 64-bit file systems mitigates potential barriers to data interoperability and simplifies the integration of diverse computing platforms.

While the advantages of 64-bit architecture on file system design are substantial, it is imperative to acknowledge the challenges associated with this transition. Compatibility considerations are paramount, especially in environments where a mix of 32-bit and 64-bit systems may coexist. Interoperability between different architectures and file system types requires careful planning to ensure seamless data exchange and accessibility across diverse computing platforms. Additionally, the transition to 64-bit file systems necessitates updates to software applications and utilities to fully leverage the expanded capabilities. Legacy applications designed for 32-bit systems may need adaptation to harness the benefits of 64-bit architectures fully.

In conclusion, the impact of 64-bit architecture on file system design is multifaceted, reshaping the fundamental principles and capabilities of contemporary storage solutions. The transition to 64-bit architectures has elevated file systems to new heights of scalability, performance, and efficiency, addressing longstanding challenges posed by the limitations of 32-bit architectures. From handling massive files and storage volumes to improving metadata handling, enhancing security features, and enabling advanced functionalities, the influence of 64-bit architecture permeates every aspect of file system design. As technology continues to advance, the trajectory towards increasingly scalable and efficient file systems remains a pivotal aspect of ensuring the continued evolution and adaptability of computing infrastructure.

The emergence of networked file systems like NFS and SMB.

The emergence of networked file systems, exemplified by protocols like the Network File System (NFS) and Server Message Block (SMB), marks a transformative phase in the evolution of computing, fundamentally altering the landscape of data sharing and accessibility. This paradigm shift is rooted in the recognition that as computing environments evolved, the need for seamless collaboration, file sharing, and remote access became increasingly critical. NFS, developed by Sun Microsystems in the early 1980s, stands as one of the pioneering solutions in this realm. It introduced a revolutionary approach to file sharing, allowing remote access to files as if they were local, thus fostering a distributed and collaborative computing environment. NFS operates on a client-server model, where the server exports a directory that can be mounted by clients, providing transparent access to files over the network. This innovation laid the foundation for networked file systems, catalyzing a new era of interconnected computing.

The significance of networked file systems like NFS extends beyond their technical underpinnings; it lies in their ability to redefine the way users interact with data. NFS, in particular, prioritized simplicity and universality. Its design was agnostic to the underlying file systems on the server and client machines, fostering interoperability in heterogeneous computing environments. This universality contributed to the widespread adoption of NFS across various Unix and Linux distributions, establishing it as a de facto standard for networked file sharing in these ecosystems. NFS's open nature and straightforward design made it a favored choice in academic and research institutions, where collaborative projects and data sharing are integral to the research process.

Parallelly, the emergence of the Server Message Block (SMB) protocol, initially developed by IBM and later refined and extended by Microsoft, added another dimension to the realm of networked file systems. SMB, also known as CIFS (Common Internet File System), became the foundation for file and printer sharing in Windows environments. The advent of SMB allowed Windows-based computers to seamlessly share files and resources across local networks. SMB operates on a client-server model similar to NFS, with the server providing shared resources and the client accessing these resources over the network. The protocol's integration into the Windows operating system contributed to the ubiquity of SMB in corporate environments, shaping the way businesses manage and share information.

One of the defining characteristics of networked file systems like NFS and SMB is their ability to abstract the complexities of data storage and access, providing users with a unified and familiar interface. This abstraction is particularly evident in the concept of mounting in NFS or mapping network drives in SMB, where remote resources seamlessly integrate into the local file hierarchy. This transparent integration simplifies user interactions with files and directories, fostering a user experience that is agnostic to the physical location of data. The emergence of such networked file systems thus marked a departure from the traditional model of local file access, democratizing data and enabling a more flexible and collaborative computing paradigm.

The adoption of networked file systems also heralded a shift towards centralized data management. NFS and SMB facilitated the consolidation of data on dedicated file servers, which could be accessed by multiple clients across a network. This centralization offered advantages in terms of data security, backup, and resource management. File servers became the custodians of critical data, allowing for centralized administration, user access control, and the implementation of backup strategies. The move towards centralized data storage addressed challenges associated with the proliferation of data across individual machines, providing a more robust and scalable solution for managing information in networked environments.

The rise of networked file systems like NFS and SMB also played a crucial role in shaping the nascent stages of the internet. The standardization of protocols for remote file access laid the groundwork for the development of distributed file systems and paved the way for broader connectivity. The universality of NFS and SMB protocols enabled seamless file sharing not only within local area networks but also across wide-area networks and the emerging internet. This interconnectedness became foundational for collaborative efforts, remote access to data, and the creation of a globally distributed computing environment.

The universality and adoption of NFS and SMB were further propelled by their extensibility and adaptability. As computing environments continued to evolve, both protocols underwent iterations and enhancements to accommodate new requirements and technologies. NFS versions 2, 3, and 4 successively introduced improvements in performance, security, and features. Similarly, SMB evolved through various versions, each bringing refinements and additions to address the changing landscape of computing. These continuous developments ensured the relevance and longevity of NFS and SMB in the dynamic and evolving realm of networked file systems.

The security considerations of networked file systems became increasingly prominent as these protocols gained widespread adoption. NFS, in its early versions, had limited security mechanisms, relying on host-based authentication and lacking robust encryption. Recognizing the importance of enhancing security, NFS version 4 introduced significant improvements, including support for strong authentication mechanisms, integrity checking, and encryption. SMB also underwent security enhancements over its iterations, with features like encrypted communication, secure authentication protocols, and access control mechanisms. These advancements addressed concerns related to data integrity and confidentiality, making networked file systems more resilient to security threats in diverse computing environments.

The integration of networked file systems like NFS and SMB into operating systems and their role in facilitating cross-platform interoperability became increasingly evident in the expanding landscape of computing. The prevalence of mixed environments, where Unix-based systems coexisted with Windows machines, highlighted the importance of protocols that could bridge the gap between different operating systems. NFS, with its roots in the Unix ecosystem, and SMB, deeply integrated into Windows, became instrumental in fostering cross-platform compatibility. This interoperability enabled seamless collaboration in heterogeneous environments, allowing users on different systems to access and share files without being constrained by platform-specific limitations.

The impact of networked file systems extends beyond traditional desktop and server computing to encompass emerging technologies such as cloud computing. The principles established by NFS and SMB laid the groundwork for cloud-based file storage and sharing solutions. Cloud storage providers adopted similar paradigms, allowing users to mount cloud storage as if it were a local file system. This abstraction of remote storage resources aligns with the fundamental concepts introduced by networked file systems, contributing to the seamless integration of cloud storage into diverse computing environments.

In conclusion, the emergence of networked file systems, epitomized by protocols like NFS and SMB, represents a pivotal chapter in the evolution of computing. These protocols have transcended their initial roles as facilitators of file sharing to become integral components of collaborative, distributed, and interconnected computing environments. The universality, simplicity, and adaptability of NFS and SMB have not only shaped the way users interact with data but have also laid the foundation for broader connectivity, cross-platform interoperability, and the evolution of cloud-based storage solutions. The legacy of networked file systems endures, underscoring their foundational role in the dynamic landscape of modern computing.

Enabling file sharing and collaboration across distributed environments.

Enabling file sharing and collaboration across distributed environments represents a fundamental paradigm shift in the way individuals and organizations interact with data, fostering a dynamic and interconnected approach to information sharing. At the heart of this transformation lies the recognition that geographical boundaries and disparate computing environments should not be impediments to seamless collaboration. The evolution of technologies facilitating distributed file sharing and collaboration has been instrumental in shaping the modern landscape of interconnected computing.

Central to this evolution is the concept of networked file systems, which provide the foundation for enabling file sharing and collaboration in distributed environments. Protocols such as the Network File System (NFS) and Server Message Block (SMB) have played a pivotal role in democratizing data access by allowing users to share files as if they were local, transcending the limitations of physical proximity. NFS, originating in the Unix ecosystem, and SMB, deeply integrated into Windows environments, have become cornerstones in facilitating cross-platform collaboration. These protocols, operating on a client-server model, allow users to seamlessly access and share files over a network, laying the groundwork for collaborative computing across diverse operating systems.

The advent of distributed version control systems, exemplified by Git, has further revolutionized collaborative development practices in the realm of software engineering. Git's decentralized architecture allows developers to work on code collaboratively, irrespective of their physical locations. Each participant maintains a local copy of the entire repository, enabling them to make changes independently. Through mechanisms like branching and merging, Git ensures that collaboration is seamless, minimizing conflicts and providing a robust framework for distributed software development. Git has become integral not only to open-source projects but also to enterprise environments where distributed teams collaborate on software development across the globe.

Cloud computing has emerged as a transformative force in enabling distributed file sharing and collaboration. Cloud storage services, such as Dropbox, Google Drive, and Microsoft OneDrive, leverage the power of the cloud to provide users with centralized and accessible storage repositories. Users can upload, share, and collaborate on files in real-time, transcending the limitations of physical storage devices. These services synchronize files across devices, ensuring that collaborators have access to the most up-to-date versions of documents, fostering a collaborative environment that extends beyond traditional file sharing.

The rise of collaborative online platforms has redefined how teams collaborate across distributed environments. Tools like Google

Workspace (formerly G Suite) and Microsoft 365 provide a suite of applications, including document editors, spreadsheets, and presentation software, that operate in the cloud. These platforms facilitate real-time collaboration, allowing multiple users to edit documents simultaneously, leave comments, and track changes. The ability to collaborate in real-time, coupled with the convenience of cloud storage, empowers distributed teams to work cohesively and efficiently, regardless of their physical locations.

In the context of distributed scientific research, collaborative platforms and distributed file sharing mechanisms have become indispensable. Projects involving researchers from different institutions or even different countries require seamless data sharing and collaboration. Distributed file systems and collaborative platforms enable researchers to share datasets, analysis scripts, and research findings in a secure and efficient manner. This collaborative approach accelerates the pace of scientific discovery by fostering a global community of researchers who can build upon each other's work.

Blockchain technology has introduced novel paradigms for secure and decentralized file sharing. Blockchain, originally designed as the underlying technology for cryptocurrencies, has found applications in creating decentralized file storage solutions. Platforms like InterPlanetary File System (IPFS) and Filecoin leverage blockchain to create a distributed and incentivized network where users can store and retrieve files. The decentralized nature of these systems ensures data redundancy, security, and availability, making them suitable for scenarios where traditional centralized storage may be impractical or vulnerable.

The Internet of Things (IoT) has extended the scope of distributed file sharing and collaboration to include a myriad of connected devices. In smart homes, for example, IoT devices such as smart thermostats, cameras, and appliances generate data that needs to be shared and accessed across various devices. Distributed file systems and cloud-based solutions facilitate seamless integration and collaboration among IoT devices, enabling users to monitor and control their smart home environments from anywhere in the world.

The principles of edge computing, where data processing occurs closer to the source of data rather than relying on centralized cloud servers, have also influenced distributed file sharing and collaboration. Edge computing mitigates latency issues and enhances the efficiency of real-time collaboration in scenarios where immediate data processing is critical. File sharing protocols and collaborative platforms are adapting to support edge computing, ensuring that users can collaborate seamlessly even in edge-dominated environments.

Security considerations are paramount in the realm of distributed file sharing and collaboration. As data traverses networks and cloud services, ensuring the confidentiality, integrity, and availability of information becomes a critical concern. Encryption protocols, secure socket layers (SSL), and multi-factor authentication mechanisms are integral components of secure file sharing solutions. Additionally, compliance with data protection regulations and industry standards becomes essential, especially when handling sensitive information across distributed environments.

The evolution of application programming interfaces (APIs) has played a pivotal role in fostering integration and interoperability among disparate systems. APIs allow different software applications to communicate and share data seamlessly. In the context of distributed file sharing and collaboration, APIs facilitate the integration of diverse tools and platforms, creating a cohesive ecosystem where users can leverage the functionalities of multiple applications seamlessly. This integration is particularly crucial for distributed teams that rely on various tools for communication, project management, and collaboration.

The advent of artificial intelligence (AI) and machine learning (ML) has introduced new dimensions to collaborative data analysis in distributed environments. Collaborative platforms equipped with AI capabilities can analyze large datasets, identify patterns, and provide insights collaboratively. This collaborative AI-driven approach is transforming industries such as healthcare, finance, and research, where distributed teams leverage advanced analytics to make data-driven decisions.

In conclusion, the enablement of file sharing and collaboration across distributed environments has undergone a profound transformation, driven by advancements in networked file systems, version control systems, cloud computing, collaborative platforms, blockchain, IoT, edge computing, security mechanisms, APIs, and AI. The integration of these technologies has created a dynamic ecosystem where individuals and organizations can collaborate seamlessly, transcending geographical constraints and operating in a globally connected landscape. The continued evolution of these technologies promises further innovations, ensuring that the future of distributed collaboration remains vibrant and responsive to the evolving needs of the digital era.

The integration of file systems with cloud computing.

The integration of file systems with cloud computing signifies a transformative synergy that has redefined the landscape of data storage, access, and collaboration. Cloud computing, as a paradigm, introduces a fundamental shift by offering on-demand access to a pool of computing resources and services over the internet. This shift extends to the way file systems operate, ushering in a new era where traditional boundaries of storage are transcended, and data becomes fluid, accessible, and scalable. At the core of this integration lies the concept of cloud storage, where file systems are hosted and managed in the cloud, providing users with a versatile and resilient environment for storing, sharing, and collaborating on data.

Cloud file storage services, exemplified by platforms like Amazon S3, Microsoft Azure Blob Storage, and Google Cloud Storage, serve as the foundational elements of integrating file systems with cloud computing. These services leverage the principles of object storage, where files are treated as objects and stored with metadata, facilitating scalable and cost-effective storage solutions. The transition to cloud storage mitigates the limitations of traditional on-premises storage infrastructure, offering virtually limitless capacity that can scale on-demand based on the evolving needs of users and applications.

One of the transformative aspects of integrating file systems with cloud computing is the concept of ubiquitous access. Cloud file storage solutions allow users to access their data from any location with internet connectivity, breaking free from the constraints of physical hardware. This ubiquity is especially advantageous for distributed teams, remote workers, and organizations with global footprints, enabling seamless collaboration irrespective of geographical boundaries. Cloud file storage services ensure that users have consistent access to their files, fostering a collaborative environment that transcends traditional office settings.

The integration of file systems with cloud computing is synonymous with the paradigm of Infrastructure as a Service (IaaS), where cloud providers offer virtualized computing resources over the internet. In this context, file systems are deployed and managed as virtual instances in the cloud, providing users with the flexibility to configure and scale their storage infrastructure according to specific requirements. This approach eliminates the need for organizations to invest in and maintain physical hardware, shifting the focus to operational efficiency and resource optimization.

Cloud file storage solutions introduce a pay-as-you-go model, allowing users to pay only for the storage they consume and the operations they perform. This cost effective approach contrasts with traditional storage solutions, where organizations must invest in infrastructure upfront, often leading to overprovisioning and underutilization. The cloud's elasticity ensures that users can scale their storage needs dynamically, optimizing costs and aligning expenditures with actual usage. Additionally, cloud providers often offer tiered storage options, allowing users to choose storage classes based on performance, access frequency, and cost considerations.

The concept of serverless computing further accentuates the integration of file systems with cloud computing. Serverless architectures, epitomized by platforms like AWS Lambda and Azure Functions, abstract the underlying infrastructure, allowing users to focus solely on executing code without managing servers. In the realm of file systems, serverless computing enables the creation of applications that can interact with cloud file storage without the need for dedicated servers. This serverless approach streamlines development, reduces operational overhead, and aligns with the cloud's philosophy of resource efficiency.

The integration of file systems with cloud computing has given rise to innovative storage solutions that transcend the limitations of traditional file storage. Cloud-native file systems, such as Amazon EFS, Azure Files, and Google Cloud Filestore, are designed to seamlessly integrate with cloud environments, providing scalable and shared file storage. These services offer features like automatic scalability, high availability, and compatibility with cloud-native applications, making them well-suited for modern, dynamic workloads.

In addition to the advantages of scalability and flexibility, cloud file storage solutions introduce advanced features that enhance data management and security. Versioning, for instance, allows users to track changes to files over time, facilitating recovery from accidental deletions or modifications. Object-level access control and encryption mechanisms provide robust security measures, ensuring the confidentiality and integrity of stored data. Cloud providers often incorporate data redundancy and geographic replication, minimizing the risk of data loss due to hardware failures or unforeseen disasters.

Cloud-based collaborative platforms, exemplified by tools like Google Workspace, Microsoft 365, and Dropbox Business, leverage integrated file systems to provide a comprehensive environment for real-time collaboration. These platforms combine cloud storage, document editing, and communication tools, enabling users to collaborate seamlessly on files, spreadsheets, and presentations. The integration of file systems with collaboration platforms fosters a cohesive workspace where distributed teams can work cohesively, leveraging the power of the cloud for efficient document sharing, editing, and version control.

The advent of cloud computing has also led to the emergence of cloud-native applications that inherently leverage cloud file storage for data persistence. Microservices architectures, containerized applications, and serverless functions all rely on cloud file storage solutions for handling persistent data. The integration of file systems with cloud-native application development streamlines the deployment, scaling, and management of applications, aligning with the agility and efficiency goals of cloud computing.

The integration of file systems with cloud computing has not only transformed data storage but has also influenced the development of Big Data and analytics solutions. Cloud-based data lakes, powered by storage services like Amazon S3 and Azure Data Lake Storage, provide scalable repositories for storing vast amounts of structured and unstructured data. Analytical frameworks, such as Apache Hadoop and Apache Spark, seamlessly integrate with cloud file storage, enabling distributed and parallel processing of data for insights and decision-making.

The concept of hybrid cloud further extends the integration of file systems by providing a unified approach to data management across on-premises infrastructure and cloud environments. Hybrid cloud architectures allow organizations to leverage the benefits of cloud file storage while maintaining critical data on-premises for compliance, security, or latency considerations. This hybrid approach acknowledges the diversity of enterprise IT landscapes, offering a balanced solution that optimizes resource utilization and accommodates diverse storage needs.

The integration of file systems with cloud computing also aligns with the principles of edge computing, where data processing occurs closer to the data source rather than relying solely on centralized cloud servers. Edge file systems extend the benefits of cloud storage to edge devices, facilitating efficient data storage and retrieval in scenarios where low latency and immediate access are paramount. This integration ensures a seamless experience for applications that require real-time data processing, such as IoT devices and edge analytics solutions.

While the integration of file systems with cloud computing has brought about numerous benefits, it also introduces considerations related to data governance, compliance, and vendor lock-in. Organizations must carefully navigate these challenges, implementing robust policies for data management, ensuring compliance with regulations, and adopting strategies that mitigate the risks associated with dependence on specific cloud providers.

In conclusion, the integration of file systems with cloud computing represents a pivotal evolution in the way data is stored, accessed, and managed. Cloud file storage solutions, characterized by scalability, flexibility, and cost-effectiveness, have become foundational elements in modern computing environments. Whether through cloud-native file systems, collaborative platforms, serverless architectures, or hybrid cloud strategies, the integration of file systems with cloud computing continues to shape the digital landscape, providing organizations and users with a versatile and dynamic approach to data storage and collaboration.

How cloud-based file systems enhance storage and accessibility.

Cloud-based file systems have emerged as transformative solutions that redefine the paradigms of storage and accessibility, ushering in a new era of flexibility, scalability, and efficiency in handling digital assets. At the heart of this evolution lies the fundamental shift from traditional, on-premises storage infrastructure to the dynamic, distributed architecture of the cloud. These cloud-based file systems, exemplified by platforms such as Amazon S3, Microsoft Azure Blob Storage, and Google Cloud Storage, harness the power of the cloud to provide users with unprecedented capabilities to store, manage, and access their data.

One of the paramount advantages offered by cloud-based file systems is the remarkable scalability they afford. In contrast to traditional storage solutions that necessitate upfront investments in physical hardware and face limitations on capacity, cloud-based file systems operate on an elastic model, allowing users to scale their storage needs dynamically. This scalability is not constrained by the physical boundaries of hardware, enabling organizations to seamlessly expand their storage capacity as data volumes grow. The cloud's virtually limitless capacity ensures that users are no longer encumbered by concerns about running out of storage space, providing a responsive and scalable solution that adapts to the evolving needs of modern computing.

Furthermore, the concept of on-demand provisioning inherent in cloud-based file systems aligns with the principles of Infrastructure as a Service (IaaS). Users can create, modify, and delete storage resources as needed, optimizing resource allocation and operational efficiency. This agile approach contrasts with traditional storage infrastructure, where provisioning often involves complex processes and lead times. Cloud-based file systems empower users to provision storage instantaneously, accelerating deployment timelines and fostering a dynamic IT environment where storage resources can be aligned with business requirements in real-time.

The ubiquitous accessibility facilitated by cloud-based file systems represents a paradigm shift in the way users interact with their data. Geographical boundaries and physical locations are rendered inconsequential as users gain the ability to access their files from any device with internet connectivity. This democratization of data access is particularly advantageous for distributed teams, remote workers, and organizations with a global presence, fostering a collaborative environment that transcends traditional office settings. Cloud-based file systems ensure that users have consistent access to their files, promoting seamless collaboration and enabling a mobile and interconnected workforce.

Cost-effectiveness is a cornerstone of the appeal of cloud-based file systems. The pay-as-you-go pricing model, a hallmark of cloud computing, ensures that users only pay for the storage they consume and the operations they perform. This contrasts with traditional storage solutions, where organizations often make substantial upfront investments in hardware, regardless of actual usage. The cloud's cost-effective approach enables organizations to align their storage expenditures with actual consumption, eliminating the inefficiencies associated with overprovisioning. Additionally, cloud providers often offer tiered storage options, allowing users to choose storage classes based on performance, access frequency, and cost considerations.

The advent of cloud-native file systems, designed explicitly for seamless integration with cloud environments, further enhances storage and accessibility. Platforms such as Amazon EFS, Azure Files, and Google Cloud Filestore are architected to provide scalable and shared file storage within the cloud ecosystem. These services leverage the native capabilities of cloud providers, offering features like automatic scalability, high availability, and compatibility with cloud-native applications. Cloud-native file systems are well-suited for modern, dynamic workloads that demand the performance and flexibility required in contemporary computing environments.

The agility of cloud-based file systems extends to their compatibility with serverless computing, a paradigm that abstracts the underlying infrastructure, allowing users to focus solely on executing code without managing servers. In the context of file systems, serverless computing enables the creation of applications that can interact with cloud file storage without the need for dedicated servers. This serverless approach streamlines development, reduces operational overhead, and aligns with the cloud's philosophy of resource efficiency. Users can build applications that leverage the storage capabilities of the cloud without the complexity of managing underlying infrastructure.

Security considerations are paramount in the design and operation of cloud-based file systems. Cloud providers implement robust security measures to ensure the confidentiality, integrity, and availability of stored data. Encryption protocols safeguard data during transmission and at rest, protecting it from unauthorized access. Access control mechanisms enable granular control over who can access and manipulate files, reducing the risk of data breaches. Cloud providers often undergo rigorous security certifications and compliance audits, providing assurances to users regarding the robustness of the security measures in place. Cloud-based file systems thus offer a secure and trustworthy environment for storing sensitive and critical data.

Versioning, a feature prevalent in many cloud-based file systems, enhances data management capabilities by allowing users to track changes to files over time. This feature is invaluable in scenarios where collaboration is intensive, as it facilitates the recovery from accidental deletions or modifications. Users can roll back to previous versions of files, ensuring data integrity and providing a safety net against unintended changes. Versioning is particularly beneficial in collaborative environments, where multiple users may be concurrently working on shared files, minimizing the risk of conflicts and data loss.

Object-level access control mechanisms further contribute to the robust security posture of cloud-based file systems. Users can define fine-grained access policies for individual objects, specifying who can read, write, or delete specific files. This level of granularity ensures that access permissions align with organizational policies and compliance requirements. By implementing object-level access controls, cloud-based file systems empower users to enforce data governance and ensure that sensitive information is accessed only by authorized individuals.

The geographic redundancy and replication capabilities inherent in cloud-based file systems address concerns related to data availability and disaster recovery. Cloud providers often replicate data across multiple geographically dispersed data centers, minimizing the risk of data loss due to hardware failures or unforeseen disasters. In the event of a hardware failure or outage in one data center, users can seamlessly access their data from redundant copies in other locations. This resilience ensures continuous data availability, a critical factor in maintaining business continuity and minimizing disruptions.

Collaborative platforms that leverage cloud-based file systems exemplify the evolution of collaborative workflows in the digital era. Tools like Google Workspace, Microsoft 365, and Dropbox Business integrate cloud storage with document editing and communication tools, providing users with a comprehensive environment for real-time collaboration. Cloud-based collaborative platforms enable multiple users to edit documents simultaneously, leave comments, and track changes, fostering a cohesive workspace where distributed teams can work cohesively and efficiently. This integration reflects the changing nature of collaboration, where cloud-based file systems serve as the backbone of seamless and integrated workflows.

The integration of cloud-based file systems with collaborative platforms aligns with the principles of real-time collaboration, where distributed teams can work on shared documents concurrently. Cloud storage ensures that collaborators have access to the most up-to-date versions of files, eliminating the need for cumbersome file sharing and version control practices. This real-time collaboration extends beyond traditional document editing to encompass various forms of digital content, including spreadsheets, presentations, and multimedia files. The result is a collaborative environment where information flows seamlessly, and team members can contribute to projects in a fluid and dynamic manner.

The principles of cloud-based file systems have found applications beyond traditional office environments, influencing industries such as healthcare, finance, and research. In healthcare, for instance, cloud-based file systems facilitate the storage and sharing of medical records, images, and research data. The accessibility and scalability of the cloud are particularly beneficial in scenarios where rapid access to patient data and collaboration among healthcare professionals are paramount. Similarly, in finance, cloud-based file systems support the storage of vast datasets, transaction records, and analytical outputs, enabling financial institutions to leverage scalable storage solutions that align with regulatory requirements.

The integration of cloud-based file systems has also played a crucial role in the development of Big Data and analytics solutions. Cloud-based data lakes, powered by storage services like Amazon S3 and Azure Data Lake Storage, provide scalable repositories for storing vast amounts of structured and unstructured data. Analytical frameworks, such as Apache Hadoop and Apache Spark, seamlessly integrate with cloud file storage, enabling distributed and parallel processing of data for insights and decision-making. The scalability and performance characteristics of cloud-based file systems make them well-suited for the storage and processing requirements of Big Data applications.

The concept of edge computing further extends the influence of cloud-based file systems, particularly in scenarios where low latency and immediate access to data are critical. Edge file systems bring the advantages of cloud storage closer to the data source, facilitating efficient storage and retrieval in edge-dominated environments. This is particularly relevant in the context of Internet of Things (IoT) devices, where edge computing minimizes the round-trip time for data processing and storage. Cloud-based file systems enable seamless integration with edge devices, ensuring a consistent and responsive experience for applications that demand real-time data processing.

The integration of cloud-based file systems is not without its challenges and considerations. Data governance, compliance with regulatory frameworks, and the potential for vendor lock-in require careful attention. Organizations must formulate robust strategies for managing and securing their data in the cloud, ensuring that policies align with industry regulations and internal standards. Additionally, considerations related to data egress costs, data transfer speeds, and the evolving landscape of cloud providers necessitate a nuanced approach to cloud adoption.

In conclusion, the integration of cloud-based file systems represents a transformative force in the realms of storage and accessibility. These systems embody a paradigm shift, enabling users and organizations to break free from the constraints of traditional storage infrastructure and embrace a dynamic, scalable, and ubiquitous approach to data management. From seamless collaboration and real-time access to cost-effective scalability and security, the benefits of cloud-based file systems permeate diverse industries and use cases. As the digital landscape continues to evolve, the integration of cloud-based file systems stands as a testament to the pivotal role they play in shaping the future of data storage and accessibility.

Chapter 3: Critical Components: Anatomy of File Systems

Breaking down the architecture of file systems into layers. The architecture of file systems is a multifaceted construct that comprises several layers, each serving distinct functions and contributing to the overall organization, management, and access of data. At its core, file system architecture is designed to provide a structured and efficient means of storing and retrieving files, ensuring seamless interactions between the operating system, applications, and the underlying storage media. The layered architecture of file systems can be conceptualized into several key components, each playing a crucial role in the complex orchestration of file operations.

The first layer in the architecture of file systems is the physical storage layer. This layer encompasses the actual storage media, which could be hard disk drives (HDDs), solid-state drives (SSDs), network-attached storage (NAS), or any other storage technology. The physical storage layer is responsible for storing data in a persistent manner, and it serves as the foundational level upon which the entire file system architecture is built. The choice of storage media impacts factors such as access speed, durability, and overall system performance. The physical storage layer interfaces with the higher layers of the file system, translating logical file operations into the physical read and write operations on the storage device.

Above the physical storage layer is the block layer, which acts as an intermediary between the physical storage and the higher-level file system components. This layer deals with the storage and retrieval of data in fixed-sized blocks, typically called sectors or clusters. The block layer abstracts the details of the underlying storage device, providing a consistent interface for higher-level file operations. It manages issues such as block allocation, deallocation, and the mapping of logical addresses to physical locations on the storage media. The block layer plays a pivotal role in optimizing data access, ensuring efficient use of storage space, and handling low-level storage intricacies.

On top of the block layer is the logical file system layer, often referred to as the file system proper. This layer is responsible for organizing and managing files and directories in a hierarchical structure, providing a logical representation of data storage. The logical file system layer abstracts the complexities of the physical storage and block layers, presenting users and applications with a familiar file and directory hierarchy. It defines file attributes, such as permissions, timestamps, and file size, and manages metadata associated with files and directories. The logical file system layer also includes data structures like file allocation tables (FAT), inode tables, or other mechanisms for tracking the location of data on the storage media.

Within the logical file system layer, a critical component is the directory management subsystem. This subsystem is responsible for maintaining the hierarchical organization of files and directories. Directories serve as containers for files and subdirectories, and the directory management subsystem facilitates the creation, deletion, and traversal of these organizational structures. It manages the metadata associated with directories, such as the list of files they contain, their permissions, and timestamps. The directory management subsystem is crucial for efficient file organization and retrieval, enabling users and applications to navigate the file system and locate specific files.

A key aspect of the logical file system layer is the file access layer, which handles the translation between logical file operations initiated by applications or users and the corresponding physical operations on the storage media. This layer interprets high-level file operations, such as opening, reading, writing, and closing files, and translates them into the appropriate block-level operations. The file access layer also enforces file permissions and security policies, ensuring that only authorized users or processes can perform specific operations on files. It acts as a bridge between the logical file system and the lower layers, facilitating seamless communication between applications and the underlying storage.

The caching layer constitutes another vital component in the file system architecture. This layer introduces a cache, a temporary storage area that holds frequently accessed data to expedite future access. Caching enhances performance by reducing the need to retrieve data directly from the slower, persistent storage media. The caching layer operates at multiple levels, including block-level caching, where frequently accessed blocks are retained in memory, and metadata caching, where information about files and directories is temporarily stored. Caching strategies vary and may involve techniques such as read-ahead caching, write-behind caching, and adaptive algorithms to optimize the use of available memory.

Sitting above the logical file system layer is the file interface layer, which serves as the bridge between the file system and applications or user-level processes. This layer provides a set of system calls or application programming interfaces (APIs) that applications use to interact with files. Common file-related system calls include open, read, write, close, and others that enable applications to perform file operations. The file interface layer abstracts the complexities of lower-level file system operations, presenting a standardized interface that applications can use regardless of the underlying file system implementation. This abstraction fosters portability, allowing applications to work seamlessly across different file system types.

An integral aspect of the file interface layer is the virtual file system (VFS). The VFS is an abstraction layer that allows multiple file systems to coexist within an operating system. It provides a common interface to applications, irrespective of the underlying file system. This abstraction enables the implementation of various file systems, such as FAT, NTFS, ext4, and others, to be seamlessly integrated into the operating system. The VFS translates generic file operations initiated by applications into specific calls to the appropriate file system, ensuring compatibility and interoperability.

Security considerations are embedded within the file system architecture, spanning multiple layers. The access control layer, situated within the logical file system, is responsible for enforcing file permissions and managing user access to files and directories. Access control mechanisms define who can read, write, execute, or modify files, contributing to the overall security posture of the file system. Additionally, encryption and authentication mechanisms may be integrated into various layers to safeguard data integrity and confidentiality, especially in scenarios where sensitive information is stored.

In summary, the architecture of file systems is intricately layered, encompassing physical storage, block management, logical file systems, directory organization, file access, caching, file interfaces, and virtual file systems. Each layer plays a specialized role in facilitating the storage, retrieval, and management of data within a computing environment. The seamless integration of these layers ensures that users and applications can interact with files in a consistent, efficient, and secure manner, regardless of the underlying storage technology or file system implementation. The layered architecture of file systems remains a cornerstone in providing a structured and reliable framework for organizing and accessing data in the digital landscape.

Understanding the interaction between the kernel, file system drivers, and user space.

The interaction between the kernel, file system drivers, and user space constitutes a critical nexus in the operation of an operating system, orchestrating the seamless flow of data between storage devices and user-level applications. At the heart of this intricate interaction is the kernel, the core component of the operating system that manages system resources and provides essential services. The kernel plays a central role in mediating communication between user space and file system drivers, acting as an intermediary that facilitates file operations, ensures data integrity, and enforces security policies.

Within the kernel, the file system layer is a pivotal component responsible for implementing file-related operations and managing the underlying storage. File system drivers, also known as file system modules, are kernel-level components that bridge the gap between the generic file system layer and the specific characteristics of different storage devices or file system types. These drivers translate high-level file system requests into low-level operations that interact directly with storage media, whether they be traditional hard disk drives, solid-state drives, or network-attached storage.

The interaction begins with user space, where applications or user-level processes initiate file-related operations such as reading, writing, creating, or deleting files. These applications communicate their intent through system calls, which are requests for services provided by the kernel. Common file-related system calls include open, read, write, and close. When an application requests to open a file, for example, the corresponding system call is directed to the kernel.

The kernel, acting as the arbiter between user space and the underlying hardware, performs several crucial functions in handling file system requests. It verifies the validity of the request, checking permissions and ensuring that the user or process making the request has the necessary rights to perform the operation. The kernel then translates the abstract file operation into a series of low-level commands understood by the specific file system driver associated with the storage device.

File system drivers play a key role in the interaction, serving as the link between the generic file system layer and the idiosyncrasies of different storage systems. These drivers are responsible for implementing file system-specific operations, managing data structures such as inodes or file allocation tables, and communicating with the storage device to perform read and write operations. Each file system driver is tailored to the characteristics and requirements of a particular file system type, whether it be FAT, NTFS, ext4, or others.

The kernel's file system layer, encompassing the Virtual File System (VFS), further enriches the interaction by providing a unified interface for various file systems. The VFS abstracts the details of specific file systems, allowing the kernel to support multiple file system types concurrently. This abstraction enables the kernel to seamlessly switch between different file systems based on the storage media in use. When an application makes a file-related system call, the VFS determines the appropriate file system driver to handle the request, allowing for a versatile and extensible file system framework.

As the file system driver interacts with the storage device, it translates logical file system requests into physical operations at the block level. This involves reading or writing data in fixed-size blocks, often referred to as sectors or clusters, on the storage media. The block-level interactions are crucial for ensuring data consistency, optimizing data access patterns, and managing the allocation of storage space.

Caching mechanisms further enhance the efficiency of the interaction between the kernel, file system drivers, and user space. Caching involves the temporary storage of frequently accessed data in memory, reducing the need to retrieve data directly from the slower, persistent storage media. Both the kernel and file system drivers implement caching strategies to expedite read and write operations, improving overall system performance. Cache management involves decisions on when to update the cache, evict stale data, and synchronize changes between the cache and the underlying storage.

The security considerations within this interaction are paramount, as the kernel must enforce file permissions, access controls, and other security policies to protect the integrity and confidentiality of data. The kernel verifies the identity and permissions of the user or process making file-related requests, ensuring that only authorized operations are executed. Encryption mechanisms may also be employed to secure data during transmission or when stored on the storage media.

In the context of multi-user systems, where multiple users or processes may concurrently access files, the kernel plays a crucial role in preventing conflicts and ensuring data consistency. File locks, implemented by the kernel, allow processes to coordinate access to shared files, preventing simultaneous modifications that could lead to data corruption. The kernel's coordination of file access is vital for maintaining the integrity of shared data and avoiding race conditions.

The communication between the kernel, file system drivers, and user space is bidirectional, allowing for feedback and error handling. When a file operation is completed, the kernel communicates the result back to user space, indicating success or providing error codes in case of failures. This feedback loop is essential for applications to respond appropriately to the outcome of their file-related requests.

User space, representing the realm of applications and user-level processes, is where the impact of the interaction becomes most apparent. Applications interact with files through standard interfaces provided by the kernel, oblivious to the intricacies of the underlying file system or storage device. This abstraction shields applications from the complexities of managing storage at the hardware level and promotes portability, enabling applications to work across different file systems without modification.

In the context of networking and distributed file systems, the interaction extends beyond a single machine. Network file system protocols, such as NFS (Network File System) or SMB (Server Message Block), allow for file access over a network. The kernel and file system drivers incorporate networking protocols to facilitate remote file operations, enabling seamless file sharing and collaboration across machines.

In summary, the interaction between the kernel, file system drivers, and user space represents a fundamental aspect of operating system functionality, shaping the user experience and ensuring the reliable and secure management of data. The kernel serves as the mediator, interpreting high-level file system requests, enforcing security policies, and coordinating with file system drivers to perform the necessary low-level operations on storage devices. File system drivers bridge the gap between the generic file system layer and the specifics of different storage media or file system types. User space, where applications reside, interacts with files through system calls, leveraging the abstraction provided by the kernel to access and manage data without being burdened by the intricacies of storage management. This tripartite interaction underscores the robustness and adaptability of modern file systems, supporting a diverse range of storage technologies and providing a foundation for the efficient and secure handling of data in computing environments.

The role of inodes and file allocation tables in file system structures.

In the intricate tapestry of file system structures, the role of inodes and file allocation tables (FAT) stands as a foundational and indispensable component, providing the organizational framework and metadata management necessary for the efficient storage and retrieval of files. Inodes, short for index nodes, are data structures at the core of many file systems, including Unix-like systems such as ext4, while file allocation tables are a key feature of file systems like FAT16 and FAT32, prevalent in earlier Microsoft operating systems.

Together, they contribute to the organization, tracking, and retrieval of data on storage media.

Inodes, often associated with Unix-based file systems, are data structures that store metadata about files and directories. The metadata encapsulated by inodes includes critical information such as file permissions, ownership details, timestamps indicating when a file was created or modified, and the size of the file. Importantly, inodes also store pointers to the data blocks on the storage device where the actual content of the file is stored. This separation of metadata and data storage allows for greater flexibility and efficiency in managing files. When a file is created, an inode is assigned to it, acting as a reference point that the file system uses to locate and manage the associated data blocks.

The hierarchical organization of directories and subdirectories within a file system is facilitated by inodes. Each directory is essentially a file that contains entries pointing to the inodes of the files or subdirectories it encompasses. This hierarchical structure enables the systematic arrangement of files and directories, providing users and applications with an intuitive means of navigating and accessing stored data. Inodes, being critical to file system functionality, are allocated dynamically as files and directories are created, allowing for the efficient use of storage space.

In the context of Unix-like file systems, such as ext4, the allocation of storage space for files is achieved through the use of blocks. These blocks, which can be of varying sizes, represent the units of storage assigned to files. Inodes store pointers to these blocks, specifying the location of the data on the storage media. The allocation of blocks for a file is dynamic, with additional blocks being assigned as the file grows in size. This dynamic allocation mechanism ensures optimal utilization of storage space while accommodating the varying sizes of files.

File allocation tables, on the other hand, are a distinctive feature of file systems like FAT16 and FAT32, which were widely employed in earlier Microsoft operating systems. The file allocation table is a data structure that serves as a map or index, indicating the allocation status of each cluster on the storage device. A cluster is a grouping of sectors, the smallest addressable storage unit on a disk. The file allocation table records which clusters are in use, which are available, and how clusters are linked together to form files.

In FAT file systems, each file is composed of a series of clusters, and the file allocation table tracks the sequence of clusters that constitute a file. When a file is created or modified, the file allocation table is updated to reflect the allocation status of clusters. This table-based approach simplifies file management and reduces fragmentation, as the file system can easily locate the next available cluster in the file allocation table when extending a file. However, it also poses limitations on the maximum size of individual files and the overall file system due to the finite size of the file allocation table.

The file allocation table provides a straightforward method for managing storage space, but it introduces challenges in terms of scalability and performance, particularly as storage media capacities have increased over time. To address these limitations, more modern file systems, such as NTFS (New Technology File System), have moved away from the simple structure of file allocation tables and adopted more advanced data structures, including a master file table (MFT) that functions similarly to inodes.

In contrast to the dynamic allocation of blocks in Unix-like file systems, where inodes point directly to data blocks, FAT file systems use a chain-like structure to link clusters. The file allocation table specifies the sequence of cluster numbers, and each cluster contains data as well as a pointer to the next cluster in the file. This sequential linking mechanism enables the file system to navigate through clusters efficiently.

The role of inodes and file allocation tables extends beyond the mere storage and retrieval of files; they are crucial for the overall performance, organization, and integrity of a file system. Inodes, with their metadata-rich structure, enable efficient file management, supporting features like file permissions, timestamps, and ownership details that contribute to the security and accessibility of data. The hierarchical arrangement facilitated by inodes enhances the user experience by providing an organized and navigable structure for stored data.

File allocation tables, while simpler in structure, provide a systematic means of tracking and managing clusters, ensuring that files can be easily extended without excessive fragmentation. This simplicity comes with trade-offs, such as limitations on file size and scalability, but for certain use cases and historical contexts, FAT file systems have proven to be effective and straightforward.

As file systems have evolved, there has been a shift towards more sophisticated and adaptable structures. For example, NTFS, the file system introduced by Microsoft to replace FAT, employs a master file table that bears conceptual similarities to inodes. The master file table stores metadata for each file, including attributes, security descriptors, and pointers to data extents. This more advanced approach addresses the limitations of file allocation tables and aligns with the requirements of modern storage systems.

In conclusion, the role of inodes and file allocation tables in file system structures is nuanced, with each serving as a linchpin for the organization, storage, and retrieval of data. Inodes, prevalent in Unix-like file systems, provide a metadata-rich representation of files and directories, enabling hierarchical organization and efficient data access. On the other hand, file allocation tables, characteristic of file systems like FAT, offer a simple yet effective means of tracking clusters and managing file storage. The evolution of file systems has seen a transition from the straightforward structures of file allocation tables to more sophisticated approaches, as exemplified by the master file table in NTFS. Understanding the intricacies of inodes and file allocation tables sheds light on the design principles that underlie file systems, illuminating the trade-offs and considerations inherent in the architecture of storage management systems.

How these components manage and track file information and storage allocation.

The management and tracking of file information and storage allocation within a file system are intricate processes orchestrated by various components, each playing a specialized role in ensuring the organization, accessibility, and integrity of stored data. At the heart of these operations are the inodes and file allocation tables (FAT), two fundamental components that exemplify different strategies for managing file information and storage allocation. Understanding how these components interplay provides insights into the nuanced mechanisms employed by file systems to handle the complexities of data storage.

Inodes, prevalent in Unix-like file systems such as ext4, are central to the management of file information. Each file or directory in these systems is associated with an inode, a data structure that serves as a repository for essential metadata. This metadata encompasses a wealth of information crucial for effective file management, including file permissions, ownership details, timestamps indicating when a file was created or modified, and the size of the file. The inode also contains pointers to the data blocks on the storage device where the actual content of the file is stored.

One of the key roles of inodes is to facilitate the hierarchical organization of files and directories within the file system. Directories themselves are essentially files that contain entries pointing to the inodes of the files or subdirectories they encapsulate. This hierarchical structure provides users and applications with an intuitive means of navigating and accessing stored data. Inodes, serving as reference points for files, allow the file system to efficiently locate and manage the associated data blocks. The dynamic allocation of inodes as files and directories are created ensures that the file system adapts to changing storage requirements, providing flexibility and efficient use of storage space.

The organization of data within Unix-like file systems involves the allocation of storage space in units known as blocks. Inodes play a critical role in this process by storing pointers to these blocks, specifying the location of the data on the storage media. The allocation of blocks for a file is dynamic, with additional blocks being assigned as the file grows in size. This dynamic allocation mechanism ensures optimal utilization of storage space and accommodates the varying sizes of files. In essence, inodes act as navigational aids for the file system, guiding the efficient retrieval and storage of data.

File allocation tables, on the other hand, present a distinct approach to managing file information and storage allocation, as exemplified in file systems like FAT16 and FAT32, common in earlier Microsoft operating systems. The file allocation table is a structured map or index that outlines the allocation status of each cluster on the storage device. In the context of FAT file systems, a cluster represents a grouping of sectors, the smallest addressable storage unit on a disk.

Clusters are the building blocks of files in FAT file systems, and the file allocation table records the status of each cluster, indicating whether it is in use, available, or linked to the next cluster in a file. This sequential linking of clusters is fundamental to the structure of FAT file systems. When a file is created or modified, the file allocation table is updated to reflect the allocation status of clusters. This table-based approach simplifies file management, as the file system can readily locate the next available cluster in the file allocation table when extending a file.

The allocation status recorded in the file allocation table serves as a reference point for the file system to understand the layout of clusters and the composition of files. This method of organization is particularly efficient for sequential access patterns, as the file system can easily traverse clusters in sequence. However, it introduces limitations, such as constraints on the maximum size of individual files and the overall scalability of the file system due to the finite size of the file allocation table.

The role of inodes and file allocation tables extends beyond mere storage and retrieval; they are integral components for maintaining the integrity, security, and accessibility of a file system. Inodes, with their metadata-rich structure, enable the file system to support features like file permissions, timestamps, and ownership details that contribute to the security and reliability of stored data. They encapsulate a comprehensive set of attributes that empower the file system to enforce access controls and provide a foundation for auditing and tracking file-related activities.

In contrast, the simplicity of file allocation tables in FAT file systems contributes to their efficiency and ease of implementation. The straightforward structure allows for rapid access to cluster information, facilitating quick file operations and minimizing overhead. This simplicity, however, comes with trade-offs, including limitations on file size and scalability, making FAT file systems more suitable for specific use cases where simplicity and compatibility are paramount.

The evolution of file systems has seen a transition towards more sophisticated structures, as exemplified by file systems like NTFS, which introduces concepts such as the master file table (MFT). The MFT, akin to inodes, stores metadata for each file, including attributes, security descriptors, and pointers to data extents. This approach addresses the limitations of file allocation tables and aligns with the requirements of modern storage systems, allowing for more flexibility, scalability, and advanced features.

The management and tracking of file information and storage allocation are intricately tied to the efficiency and performance of a file system. Inodes and file allocation tables represent distinct strategies that underscore the trade-offs and considerations inherent in the design of storage management systems. Inodes, with their rich metadata and hierarchical organization, offer a robust foundation for Unix-like file systems, supporting features essential for modern computing environments. On the other hand, file allocation tables, with their simplicity and efficiency, cater to specific use cases where a streamlined approach is preferred.

In conclusion, the interplay between inodes and file allocation tables reflects the diverse strategies employed by file systems to manage and track file information and storage allocation. The evolution of file systems continues to be shaped by the need for efficiency, scalability, and advanced features, paving the way for innovative approaches that meet the demands of contemporary computing landscapes. Understanding the intricacies of these components provides a deeper appreciation for the design principles that underlie file systems and the nuanced considerations involved in storing and retrieving data in the digital age.

Explaining the concept of journaling for file system integrity.

Journaling, a fundamental concept in file system design, stands as a robust mechanism to ensure the integrity and consistency of stored data. At its core, journaling is a technique that provides a systematic and recoverable approach to handle potential disruptions, such as power failures or system crashes, which can compromise the stability of a file system. The concept of journaling revolves around the creation and maintenance of a transaction log, often referred to as a journal, that records changes to the file system before they are applied to the main data structures. This proactive approach minimizes the risk of data corruption and facilitates swift recovery in the event of an unexpected interruption.

In the absence of journaling, traditional file systems face challenges in maintaining data consistency during abrupt shutdowns or failures. When a file system operation is initiated, such as creating, modifying, or deleting a file, the changes are directly applied to the file system's data structures. If an interruption occurs mid-operation, the file system may be left in an inconsistent state, with some changes applied and others pending. This inconsistency can lead to data corruption, making it challenging to recover the file system to a coherent and reliable state.

Journaling addresses these challenges by introducing a layer of indirection between file system operations and the actual modification of data structures. The journal serves as a temporary repository for changes, capturing the intended modifications before they are executed on the main file system structures. This journal contains a chronological record of transactions, each encapsulating a set of changes related to file system operations. These transactions are logged in a manner that ensures atomicity, consistency, isolation, and durability – collectively known as the ACID properties – even in the face of unexpected interruptions.

The structure of the journal itself is designed for resilience and reliability. Typically, journals are implemented as circular buffers, where new transactions are appended to the end of the journal. As the journal reaches its capacity, older transactions are discarded or archived, creating a continuous loop. This circular design ensures that the journal remains a manageable size while retaining a record of recent changes. The journal is stored in a location separate from the main file system data structures, often on a dedicated portion of the storage media.

When a file system operation is initiated, the changes are first recorded in the journal before being applied to the main file system structures. This two-step process provides a safeguard against interruptions during the application of changes. In the event of an unexpected interruption, the file system can consult the journal during the recovery process. By replaying the transactions stored in the journal, the file system can reapply the intended changes to the main data structures, bringing the file system back to a consistent and recoverable state.

There are several types of journaling strategies, each offering a nuanced approach to balancing performance and reliability. The most common types include write-ahead logging (WAL), ordered journaling, and copy-on-write (COW) journaling. Write-ahead logging involves recording changes to the journal before modifying the main data structures, ensuring that the journal always reflects the most recent state of the file system. Ordered journaling maintains a specific order for recording changes, prioritizing metadata updates to maintain file system consistency. Copy-on-write journaling creates a new copy of modified data structures in the journal, preserving the original state until the changes are confirmed.

The benefits of journaling extend beyond recovery from unexpected interruptions. Journaling also enhances the efficiency of routine file system operations. By separating the logging of transactions from the actual modification of data structures, journaling reduces the number of disk writes required for each operation. This optimization contributes to improved performance and longevity of the storage media.

However, the implementation of journaling introduces considerations related to performance overhead and storage utilization. The continuous logging of transactions incurs additional write operations to the storage media, impacting overall system performance. To mitigate this overhead, various optimizations, such as journal compression and batched logging, have been employed. Additionally, the storage space allocated for the journal needs to be carefully managed to ensure that it is sufficient for storing the expected volume of transactions while not consuming excessive resources.

The concept of journaling is not limited to a specific file system type and has been widely adopted across various file systems, including ext4, NTFS, and HFS+. Each file system may implement journaling with its own set of optimizations and considerations, but the underlying principle remains consistent – maintaining a transaction log to ensure data consistency and recoverability. As technology has advanced, innovations such as journal checksums and journaling on non-volatile memory (NVM) have been introduced to further enhance the reliability and performance of journaling mechanisms.

In conclusion, the concept of journaling represents a pivotal advancement in file system design, offering a robust solution to address the challenges of data consistency and integrity in the face of unexpected interruptions. By introducing a transaction log or journal, file systems can proactively capture changes before applying them to the main data structures, enabling a swift and reliable recovery process. The various journaling strategies, from write-ahead logging to copy-on-write journaling, provide flexibility in balancing performance and reliability based on the specific requirements of the file system and the underlying storage technology. As computing environments continue to evolve, the concept of journaling stands as a cornerstone in the quest for resilient and dependable file systems that can withstand the uncertainties of the digital landscape.

How logging mechanisms facilitate error recovery and system stability.

Logging mechanisms play a pivotal role in facilitating error recovery and ensuring system stability within the complex realm of computing environments. At their essence, logging mechanisms are structured frameworks that systematically record events, activities, and changes in a chronological manner. These logs serve as indispensable tools for diagnosing errors, understanding system behavior, and, critically, for recovering from unexpected faults or disruptions that could jeopardize the stability and integrity of a system.

One of the fundamental functions of logging mechanisms is to provide a detailed record of events occurring within a system. This historical perspective allows system administrators, developers, and operators to trace the sequence of activities leading up to an error or system failure. These logs act as a digital trail, offering insights into the conditions and events that might have triggered an unexpected outcome. By examining the log entries, stakeholders can gain a comprehensive understanding of the system's state and the sequence of actions leading to the occurrence of errors or faults.

In the context of error recovery, logging mechanisms enable a proactive and reactive approach to addressing issues that may compromise system stability. Proactively, logs capture routine events, warnings, and error messages during normal system operation. This proactive logging allows administrators to identify potential issues before they escalate into critical errors. For instance, warning messages related to low disk space or high system loads can serve as early indicators of impending issues, providing an opportunity to address them before they lead to system instability.

Reactive error recovery hinges on the detailed information captured in logs during unexpected events or failures. When an error occurs, logs can be instrumental in post-mortem analysis, aiding in the identification of root causes and contributing factors. Armed with this information, system administrators can formulate effective strategies for resolving the issues and preventing recurrence. The chronological order of log entries is particularly valuable in reconstructing the sequence of events that led to a failure, offering a roadmap for diagnosing and rectifying the underlying problems.

Logging mechanisms contribute significantly to system stability by facilitating the detection and resolution of various types of errors. This includes software bugs, hardware failures, configuration issues, and environmental factors. Software bugs, for instance, may manifest as unexpected behaviors or crashes. Detailed logs that capture the context surrounding these anomalies aid developers in pinpointing the source code responsible for the error, expediting the debugging process and enhancing the stability of software applications.

Hardware failures, a common challenge in computing environments, can also be effectively addressed through logging. When hardware components exhibit signs of malfunction, logs record error messages and alerts generated by the system or hardware devices. These logs not only assist in identifying the failing hardware but also aid in predicting potential failures through the analysis of patterns and trends in error messages.

Configuration issues, arising from misconfigurations or changes to system settings, can introduce instability. Logging mechanisms document configuration changes and their timestamps, allowing administrators to correlate configuration adjustments with system behavior. This correlation is invaluable in diagnosing issues related to misconfigurations and ensuring that systems operate within intended parameters.

Environmental factors, such as power outages, network disruptions, or adverse conditions, can also impact system stability. Logs capture events triggered by these external factors, offering a comprehensive view of the system's response during adverse situations. In the event of a power outage, for instance, logs may reveal how the system gracefully shut down or abruptly terminated processes, aiding in recovery efforts upon power restoration.

Furthermore, logging mechanisms play a critical role in the context of security and compliance. Security-related events, such as unauthorized access attempts, malware activities, or system breaches, leave distinct traces in logs. Security logs, often referred to as audit logs or event logs, record details about authentication attempts, resource access, and security policy violations. In the event of a security incident, these logs serve as forensic tools, providing crucial information for incident response and remediation.

The stability of a system is inherently linked to its ability to recover gracefully from errors and disruptions. Logging mechanisms contribute to this resilience by capturing not only error messages but also contextual information surrounding events. This contextual information includes details about the state of the system, the sequence of actions leading to an error, and any external factors influencing system behavior. Armed with this contextual data, administrators can make informed decisions during the error recovery process, mitigating the impact of disruptions on system stability.

Logging mechanisms are further enhanced by incorporating levels of severity or importance into log entries. Commonly used log levels include INFO, DEBUG, WARN, ERROR, and FATAL. Each level corresponds to the significance of the logged event, ranging from informational messages to critical errors. This hierarchical structure allows administrators to filter and prioritize log entries based on their severity, focusing attention on the most critical issues affecting system stability.

In distributed or networked environments, logging mechanisms extend their reach to facilitate error recovery and ensure stability across interconnected systems. Centralized logging solutions consolidate logs from multiple systems into a centralized repository, providing a unified view of events across the entire network. This centralized approach simplifies the process of error detection, recovery, and analysis, especially in scenarios where multiple systems contribute to a shared workload or service.

As the scale and complexity of computing environments continue to evolve, logging mechanisms have adapted to meet the demands of modern systems. Machine learning and artificial intelligence techniques are increasingly being applied to log analysis, enabling automated anomaly detection and predictive maintenance. These advanced analytics capabilities enhance the proactive aspect of logging, allowing systems to anticipate potential issues before they manifest as critical errors.

However, the effectiveness of logging mechanisms is contingent on prudent design, configuration, and management. An excess of verbose logging, capturing every minutiae of system activity, can lead to information overload and hinder effective analysis. Conversely, inadequate logging may result in critical events going unnoticed. Striking the right balance requires a thoughtful approach to log configuration, defining what events to log, setting appropriate log levels, and implementing mechanisms for log rotation to manage log file sizes over time.

In conclusion, logging mechanisms serve as linchpins for error recovery and system stability in the dynamic landscape of computing. By capturing a comprehensive record of events, errors, and activities, logs empower administrators and operators with the insights needed to diagnose, mitigate, and prevent issues that could compromise system stability. Whether proactively identifying potential challenges or reactively recovering from unexpected disruptions, logging mechanisms contribute to the resilience and reliability of computing systems. The integration of advanced analytics further augments the capabilities of logging, ushering in an era where systems can not only recover from errors but also anticipate and mitigate potential issues before they impact stability. As computing environments continue to evolve, logging mechanisms stand as indispensable tools, providing a transparent window into the inner workings of systems and bolstering their ability to navigate the complexities of the digital landscape.

Various directory structures, such as tree-structured and hash-based.

Directory structures form the organizational backbone of file systems, shaping how files and directories are arranged and accessed. Among the multitude of directory structures, two prominent paradigms stand out: tree-structured directories and hash-based directories. These structures underpin the hierarchical organization of files, facilitating efficient navigation, retrieval, and management within a file system.

The tree-structured directory, a classic and widely adopted model, mirrors the hierarchical nature of file systems. This structure establishes a tree-like hierarchy where directories or folders are arranged in a parent-child relationship. At the pinnacle of the hierarchy is the root directory, acting as the starting point for the entire file system. Subdirectories emanate from the root, forming branches that further bifurcate into additional levels of subdirectories. Files are located at the terminal nodes or leaves of these branches, making it a straightforward and intuitive model for users and applications to navigate and organize their data.

Each directory in the tree structure can contain both files and subdirectories, creating a nested arrangement that reflects the user's logical organization of information. This hierarchical organization provides a clear and intuitive means of accessing files, as the path to a file corresponds to its location within the directory tree. For example, in a Unix-like file system, the path "/home/user/documents/file.txt" signifies that "file.txt" is located in the "documents" subdirectory, which is nested within the "user" directory, and so forth.

The tree structure's simplicity and ease of navigation make it a prevalent choice in various operating systems, including Unix-based systems (such as Linux and macOS) and Microsoft Windows. Users are accustomed to interacting with directories and files in a tree-like fashion, whether through command-line interfaces or graphical file explorers. Additionally, the tree structure aligns with the hierarchical organization of information in many real-world scenarios, further contributing to its widespread adoption.

While the tree structure excels in its intuitiveness, it may encounter challenges in scenarios with a massive number of files or directories at a single level. The linear traversal of directories in a tree structure can become computationally expensive in such cases, potentially impacting performance. To address this limitation, hash-based directory structures offer an alternative approach.

Hash-based directory structures leverage mathematical functions, known as hash functions, to distribute files across directories in a manner that avoids the pitfalls of linear traversal. In these structures, the names of files or directories undergo a hashing process, generating a unique hash value. This hash value then determines the location or directory where the file or directory will be stored. The essence of this approach is to achieve a uniform distribution of files, preventing the accumulation of a disproportionately large number of entries in a single directory.

One popular implementation of hash-based directory structures is the hash table. In this model, the hash function transforms the file or directory name into an index, and each index corresponds to a location in the hash table. The actual storage may involve a linked list or another data structure to accommodate multiple entries sharing the same index, a phenomenon known as a collision. By distributing files based on their hashed values, hash-based structures minimize the likelihood of collisions and provide a more balanced distribution, promoting efficient access and retrieval.

The hash-based approach is particularly advantageous in scenarios where the number of files is expected to be substantial, as it helps maintain a relatively uniform distribution of entries across directories. This is especially relevant in large-scale storage systems, databases, or distributed file systems where optimizing access times and avoiding bottlenecks are paramount considerations.

However, hash-based directory structures introduce challenges in terms of human readability and predictability. Unlike the tree structure, where the path to a file reflects its logical organization, hash-based structures do not inherently convey any semantic meaning through the file's location. This lack of human-readable organization can make it challenging for users to intuitively understand the layout and relationships between files and directories.

Moreover, hash-based structures might encounter issues when dealing with dynamic systems where file additions and deletions are frequent. Reshuffling files or directories due to changes in the hash values can disrupt the predictability of file locations, potentially impacting applications or users relying on specific organizational patterns.

In summary, tree-structured and hash-based directory structures represent two fundamental approaches to organizing files and directories within a file system. The tree structure, with its intuitive hierarchy and familiar traversal patterns, remains a prevalent choice in various operating systems. Its simplicity aligns with users' mental models and facilitates straightforward navigation. On the other hand, hash-based structures leverage mathematical hashing functions to achieve a more uniform distribution of files, optimizing access times and minimizing potential performance bottlenecks, especially in large-scale storage scenarios. However, this efficiency comes at the cost of sacrificing the human-readable organization inherent in tree structures. The choice between these structures often hinges on the specific requirements and characteristics of the system or application in question, balancing factors such as user experience, performance, and scalability.

How directory structures impact file retrieval and organization.

Directory structures, the organizational frameworks that dictate how files are arranged within a file system, play a pivotal role in shaping the landscape of file retrieval and organization. The impact of directory structures extends beyond mere storage; it permeates the user experience, system performance, and the efficiency of file management. Two primary paradigms, tree-structured directories and hash-based directories, embody distinct approaches to organizing files, each influencing the dynamics of file retrieval and organization in unique ways.

The tree-structured directory, a venerable and widely adopted model, constructs a hierarchical arrangement reminiscent of an inverted tree. At its apex lies the root directory, serving as the starting point for the entire file system. Subdirectories branch out from the root, creating a nested and intuitive hierarchy. This hierarchical model mirrors the way users naturally organize information, providing a clear and familiar structure for file retrieval and organization. Users navigate through directories using a path that reflects the hierarchical relationship, making it easy to locate and retrieve files based on their logical organization within the directory tree.

In a tree structure, directories act as containers for both files and additional subdirectories, creating a nested arrangement that mirrors real-world organizational paradigms. This hierarchy aligns with users' mental models, facilitating a straightforward and intuitive approach to organizing and retrieving files. The tree structure fosters a sense of order and predictability, allowing users to navigate through directories with ease. For example, in a Unix-like file system, the path "/home/user/documents/file.txt" delineates a clear route: the file "file.txt" resides within the "documents" subdirectory, itself located within the "user" directory, and so forth.

One of the key advantages of the tree structure lies in its simplicity and human-friendly organization. Users can easily conceptualize the hierarchical arrangement, making it an approachable model for a wide range of applications and operating systems. Additionally, the hierarchical nature of the tree structure aligns seamlessly with common file management tasks, such as creating, moving, and deleting files, providing an intuitive interface that supports the day-to-day activities of users and applications.

However, as the volume of files and directories within a single level increases, the linear traversal of the tree structure can introduce performance challenges. The need to navigate through numerous levels of subdirectories may result in slower file retrieval times, especially in scenarios where directories become densely populated. To address this limitation, hash-based directory structures emerge as an alternative approach, leveraging mathematical functions to distribute files in a manner that enhances retrieval efficiency.

Hash-based directory structures, notably prevalent in scenarios with large-scale storage systems, databases, or distributed file systems, depart from the tree model's hierarchical simplicity. Instead, these structures employ hash functions to generate unique hash values for file or directory names. These hash values then determine the location or directory where the file or directory will be stored. This approach aims to achieve a uniform distribution of files across directories, minimizing the likelihood of performance bottlenecks associated with linear traversal.

In the context of file retrieval and organization, the hash-based approach offers advantages in scenarios with a massive number of files, as it ensures a relatively balanced distribution of entries across directories. This balanced distribution optimizes access times and avoids the potential accumulation of an excessive number of entries in a single directory. As a result, hash-based structures are particularly beneficial in large-scale storage systems where rapid access to files and efficient management of vast datasets are essential considerations.

While hash-based structures excel in optimizing access times and preventing performance bottlenecks, they introduce challenges related to human readability and predictability. Unlike the tree structure, where the path to a file reflects its logical organization, hash-based structures do not inherently convey any semantic meaning through the file's location. The lack of a discernible hierarchy can make it challenging for users to intuitively understand the layout and relationships between files and directories, impacting the user experience and usability of the file system.

Moreover, hash-based structures might encounter issues in dynamic systems where file additions and deletions are frequent. Reshuffling files or directories due to changes in the hash values can disrupt the predictability of file locations, potentially impacting applications or users relying on specific organizational patterns. This dynamic reshuffling introduces a level of unpredictability that contrasts with the stable and deterministic nature of tree-structured directories.

In the broader context of file organization, both tree-structured and hash-based directory structures contribute to the efficiency and effectiveness of file management. The choice between these structures often hinges on the specific requirements and characteristics of the system or application in question, balancing factors such as user experience, performance, and scalability.

The impact of directory structures on file retrieval and organization extends beyond the theoretical realm, profoundly influencing the daily experiences of users and the performance characteristics of file systems. The tree structure, with its intuitive hierarchy and familiar traversal patterns, aligns seamlessly with users' mental models, fostering a sense of order and predictability. It provides a straightforward and human-friendly interface for file organization and retrieval, supporting a diverse array of applications and operating systems.

Conversely, hash-based directory structures, with their emphasis on efficient access times and balanced distribution of files, cater to scenarios where large-scale storage systems demand optimized performance and scalability. While sacrificing some of the human-readable organization inherent in tree structures, hash-based approaches excel in scenarios where rapid and efficient access to files is paramount. The trade-offs between these structures underscore the nuanced considerations involved in designing file systems that meet the diverse needs of users and applications across a spectrum of computing environments.

In conclusion, the impact of directory structures on file retrieval and organization is profound, shaping the user experience and performance characteristics of file systems. The choice between tree-structured and hash-based approaches reflects a delicate balance between human-friendly organization and optimized access times. As computing environments continue to evolve, directory structures remain central to the quest for file systems that seamlessly integrate with user expectations while delivering the performance and scalability demanded by modern applications.

Understanding the importance of metadata in file systems.

Metadata, the unsung hero of file systems, constitutes a critical layer that transcends the mere storage of data, providing the essential context and structure necessary for effective file management. At its core, metadata refers to the data about data – a set of descriptors and attributes that characterize files and directories within a file system. This layer of information serves as a silent orchestrator, playing a pivotal role in the organization, accessibility, and integrity of stored data.

In the realm of file systems, metadata encapsulates a diverse array of attributes, offering a rich tapestry of information that goes beyond the binary contents of files. Among the fundamental metadata elements are file names, extensions, creation dates, and modification timestamps. These attributes provide the basic framework for identifying and tracking files within the file system, forming the foundation for subsequent layers of metadata that contribute to a more nuanced understanding of stored data.

File permissions, a cornerstone of metadata, wield significant influence over the security and access control mechanisms within a file system. Through metadata, file systems enforce policies that regulate who can read, write, or execute a given file, safeguarding sensitive data from unauthorized access and manipulation. This aspect of metadata, often expressed through symbolic or numeric representations, empowers administrators to define access privileges for users and groups, establishing a hierarchical structure of permissions that mirrors the organizational hierarchy of the file system.

Ownership details, another facet of metadata, shed light on the provenance and accountability associated with files. Through metadata attributes such as user and group identifiers, file systems attribute ownership to specific users and groups, facilitating the tracking of changes, audits, and accountability. The attribution of ownership enhances the transparency and traceability of file-related activities, allowing administrators to ascertain who created, modified, or deleted a file, thereby contributing to the broader landscape of data governance and compliance.

In the digital age, where data proliferates at an unprecedented pace, metadata emerges as a linchpin for effective search and retrieval mechanisms within file systems. Descriptive metadata, encompassing attributes like file type, size, and format, empowers users to search for and identify specific files based on their characteristics. This aspect of metadata transforms file systems from mere repositories into intelligent information systems, facilitating rapid and targeted retrieval of relevant data. In essence, metadata acts as a cataloging system that enhances the discoverability and accessibility of files, transcending the boundaries of traditional hierarchical file organization.

Timestamps, an integral component of metadata, chronicle the temporal aspects of file existence, reflecting when files were created, modified, or accessed. These temporal markers contribute to version control, backup strategies, and forensic analysis, offering a temporal dimension to the understanding of file system activities. By leveraging metadata timestamps, file systems enable users to track the evolution of files, recover previous versions, and establish temporal patterns in data access and modification.

The hierarchical organization of files within directories, facilitated by metadata, defines the structural integrity of file systems. Directories themselves are a manifestation of metadata, serving as containers that encapsulate files and subdirectories. The hierarchical arrangement, guided by metadata attributes such as parent-child relationships, ensures a logical and navigable structure that aligns with users' mental models. This hierarchical metadata-driven organization is a fundamental pillar of file systems, providing a framework that supports the intuitive navigation and organization of data.

Moreover, metadata contributes to the efficiency of file systems by optimizing storage allocation and utilization. Through attributes like file size and allocation unit details, metadata allows file systems to manage storage space effectively. File systems can allocate storage in units that match the underlying characteristics of the storage media, reducing fragmentation and enhancing the overall efficiency of data storage. Metadata-driven storage management ensures that files are stored in contiguous blocks whenever possible, minimizing storage wastage and optimizing data retrieval times.

The importance of metadata extends beyond the confines of individual file systems, playing a pivotal role in interoperability and data exchange across diverse computing environments. Standardized metadata conventions, such as those defined by file system specifications and protocols, facilitate seamless communication and data interchange between heterogeneous systems. These conventions ensure that metadata attributes are universally understood and interpreted, enabling the smooth exchange of files and information between different platforms, applications, and file systems.

The advent of extended attributes represents a progressive evolution in the landscape of file system metadata. Extended attributes provide a flexible and extensible framework for associating additional information with files, beyond the traditional set of attributes. This extension of metadata enables file systems to adapt to the evolving needs of modern computing environments, accommodating diverse requirements such as tagging, classification, and custom metadata attributes. Extended attributes empower users and applications to attach contextual information to files, enhancing the richness and contextuality of metadata in the digital realm.

In the context of data preservation and archival, metadata emerges as a guardian of long-term accessibility and comprehensibility. Metadata attributes like file formats, encoding details, and preservation metadata contribute to the documentation and preservation of digital assets. This metadata layer ensures that future generations, applications, or systems can interpret and understand the characteristics of archived files, mitigating the risks of obsolescence and ensuring the enduring accessibility of digital content.

The significance of metadata is particularly pronounced in the landscape of cloud computing and distributed file systems. In these environments, where data is dispersed across diverse storage nodes and accessed from various locations, metadata becomes a unifying force that harmonizes the disparate elements of a distributed file system. Through consistent metadata management, distributed file systems provide a cohesive view of data, enabling seamless collaboration, data sharing, and synchronization across geographically dispersed entities.

The evolving landscape of artificial intelligence and machine learning further amplifies the role of metadata as an enabler of intelligent data processing. Metadata attributes, augmented by semantic annotations and context-rich information, empower machine learning algorithms to understand, categorize, and derive insights from data. The synergy between metadata and machine learning augments the analytical capabilities of file systems, transforming them into intelligent information platforms capable of automated categorization, content recognition, and contextual understanding.

Despite its fundamental importance, metadata faces challenges and considerations that merit attention. The sheer volume of metadata associated with a burgeoning influx of data necessitates efficient management strategies to prevent metadata sprawl and ensure optimal system performance. Balancing the granularity of metadata with performance considerations becomes a delicate endeavor, requiring thoughtful design choices to strike a harmonious equilibrium.

Security considerations also loom large in the metadata landscape. Sensitivity surrounding metadata attributes, such as ownership details and access permissions, demands robust security measures to safeguard against unauthorized access or tampering. Metadata security is paramount in scenarios where compliance, data privacy, and confidentiality are non-negotiable requirements.

In conclusion, the importance of metadata in file systems transcends its role as a supplementary layer of information; it is the silent architect that imbues order, accessibility, and intelligence to the digital landscape. Metadata transforms file systems from inert storage repositories into dynamic and intelligent information platforms, shaping the user experience, facilitating efficient data retrieval, and providing the context necessary for meaningful interpretation and analysis. As computing environments continue to evolve, the role of metadata remains central to the quest for resilient, adaptive, and intelligent file systems that can navigate the complexities of the digital era.

How metadata stores information about files, permissions, and attributes.

Metadata serves as the silent custodian of crucial information about files within a file system, encapsulating a diverse array of details that go beyond the binary contents of the files themselves. One of the foundational roles of metadata is to store information about the identity and characteristics of files, starting with the basic attributes such as file names and extensions. These descriptors provide the essential framework for identifying and distinguishing one file from another within the file system. File names, often human-readable, serve as labels that facilitate user understanding and interaction, while extensions convey information about the file's format or type, guiding applications on how to interpret and process the file's contents.

In the realm of file permissions, metadata becomes a guardian of access control and security. Permissions, a critical aspect of metadata, determine who can read, write, or execute a given file. Through metadata attributes related to permissions, file systems enforce policies that regulate access, safeguarding sensitive data from unauthorized manipulation or disclosure. The ownership details associated with files, including user and group identifiers, contribute to the fabric of metadata. This ownership metadata, expressed through numeric identifiers, allows file systems to attribute specific files to particular users and groups, enabling administrators to define a hierarchical structure of permissions that mirrors the organizational hierarchy of the file system.

Ownership details are pivotal components of metadata that go beyond mere identification; they offer insights into the provenance and accountability associated with files. By storing information about the user or group that owns a file, metadata enhances the transparency and traceability of file-related activities. This aspect of metadata becomes particularly crucial in scenarios where tracking changes, audits, and establishing accountability are essential requirements, contributing to the broader landscape of data governance, compliance, and security.

Descriptive metadata constitutes another layer within the metadata framework, storing information about the characteristics and attributes of files that extend beyond their binary content. File size, an attribute within descriptive metadata, provides insights into the volume of data a file occupies, influencing storage allocation and retrieval efficiency. File type, often discerned through metadata, guides applications on how to interpret and present the file's content, whether it be a text document, image, audio file, or another format. This descriptive metadata empowers users and applications to search for and identify specific files based on their attributes, transforming file systems into intelligent information systems capable of nuanced data retrieval.

Timestamps, integral components of metadata, chronicle the temporal aspects of a file's existence. Metadata timestamps, including creation, modification, and access times, offer a temporal dimension to the understanding of file system activities. Creation timestamps reveal when a file was first introduced into the file system, providing insights into its origin. Modification timestamps track when a file's content was last altered, aiding version control, backup strategies, and forensic analysis. Access timestamps capture when a file was last read or otherwise accessed, contributing to the broader temporal context of data interactions within the file system.

The hierarchical organization of files within directories, facilitated by metadata, defines the structural integrity of file systems. Directories themselves are a manifestation of metadata, serving as containers that encapsulate files and subdirectories. Metadata attributes related to parent-child relationships guide the hierarchical arrangement, ensuring a logical and navigable structure that aligns with users' mental models. This hierarchical metadata-driven organization is a fundamental pillar of file systems, providing a framework that supports the intuitive navigation and organization of data.

Moreover, metadata contributes to the efficiency of file systems by optimizing storage allocation and utilization. Through attributes like file size and allocation unit details, metadata enables file systems to manage storage space effectively. File systems can allocate storage in units that match the underlying characteristics of the storage media, reducing fragmentation and enhancing the overall efficiency of data storage. Metadata-driven storage management ensures that files are stored in contiguous blocks whenever possible, minimizing storage wastage and optimizing data retrieval times.

In the context of file systems that support extended attributes, metadata becomes an even more versatile repository. Extended attributes offer an extensible framework for associating additional information with files beyond the traditional set of attributes. This extension of metadata enables file systems to adapt to the evolving needs of modern computing environments, accommodating diverse requirements such as tagging, classification, and custom metadata attributes. Extended attributes empower users and applications to attach contextual information to files, enhancing the richness and contextuality of metadata in the digital realm.

Security considerations loom large in the metadata landscape, particularly concerning sensitivity surrounding attributes like ownership details and access permissions. Robust security measures are crucial to safeguard against unauthorized access or tampering of metadata, ensuring the integrity and confidentiality of sensitive information. The security of metadata becomes paramount in scenarios where compliance, data privacy, and confidentiality are non-negotiable requirements, reinforcing the role of metadata as a guardian of secure and accountable file management.

In the broader context of data preservation and archival, metadata attributes such as file formats, encoding details, and preservation metadata become custodians of long-term accessibility and comprehensibility. Preservation metadata captures essential information about the conditions and strategies employed to preserve digital assets. This metadata layer ensures that future generations, applications, or systems can interpret and understand the characteristics of archived files, mitigating the risks of obsolescence and ensuring the enduring accessibility of digital content.

The significance of metadata extends beyond individual file systems to the landscape of cloud computing and distributed file systems. In these environments, where data is dispersed across diverse storage nodes and accessed from various locations, metadata becomes a unifying force that harmonizes the disparate elements of a distributed file system. Consistent metadata management ensures that distributed file systems provide a cohesive view of data, enabling seamless collaboration, data sharing, and synchronization across geographically dispersed entities.

The evolving landscape of artificial intelligence and machine learning further amplifies the role of metadata as an enabler of intelligent data processing. Metadata attributes, augmented by semantic annotations and context-rich information, empower machine learning algorithms to understand, categorize, and derive insights from data. The synergy between metadata and machine learning augments the analytical capabilities of file systems, transforming them into intelligent information platforms capable of automated categorization, content recognition, and contextual understanding.

Despite its fundamental importance, metadata faces challenges and considerations that merit attention. The sheer volume of metadata associated with a burgeoning influx of data necessitates efficient management strategies to prevent metadata sprawl and ensure optimal system performance. Balancing the granularity of metadata with performance considerations becomes a delicate endeavor, requiring thoughtful design choices to strike a harmonious equilibrium.

In conclusion, metadata is a multifaceted and indispensable layer within file systems that stores information about files, permissions, and attributes. It transcends the realm of mere data storage, offering a nuanced understanding of the files it encapsulates. Metadata weaves together the fabric of file systems, providing the context, security, and structure necessary for effective file management. As computing environments continue to evolve, the role of metadata remains central to the quest for resilient, adaptive, and intelligent file systems that can navigate the complexities of the digital era.

Chapter 4: Efficiency and Performance Tuning in File Systems

Defining key performance metrics, including throughput, latency, and IOPS.

Key performance metrics, the yardsticks by which the efficiency and effectiveness of computing systems are gauged, encompass a spectrum of parameters that collectively illuminate the performance landscape. One of the fundamental metrics is throughput, a measure of the rate at which a system or component can process and transfer data. Expressed in units such as bytes per second or transactions per second, throughput quantifies the system's capacity to handle data, offering insights into its overall efficiency. In the context of networks, it signifies the volume of data transmitted successfully over a specified period, providing a vital indicator of network efficiency. Throughput, therefore, serves as a foundational metric for assessing the capacity and data-handling capabilities of diverse computing elements, ranging from storage devices to network infrastructure.

Latency, a metric intricately linked to responsiveness, denotes the time it takes for a system to respond to a given stimulus or input. In the realm of computing, latency encompasses various facets, including data access, processing, and network communication. Storage latency, for instance, measures the time it takes for a storage system to fulfill a read or write request. Similarly, network latency captures the time delay in data transmission between networked devices. Low latency is often synonymous with high responsiveness, crucial in applications where real-time interactions or rapid data access are paramount. Latency, expressed in milliseconds or microseconds, becomes especially critical in scenarios such as online gaming, financial transactions, and interactive multimedia streaming, where delays can have tangible impacts on user experience and system effectiveness.

IOPS, or Input/Output Operations Per Second, stands as a pivotal metric in the domain of storage performance. IOPS quantifies the number of read and write operations a storage system can perform in one second. It serves as a cornerstone for evaluating the responsiveness and efficiency of storage devices, including hard disk drives (HDDs), solid-state drives (SSDs), and other storage mediums. IOPS becomes particularly significant in scenarios where rapid data access is a primary concern, such as database operations, virtualization environments, and high-performance computing. The metric offers a tangible measure of a storage system's ability to handle concurrent input and output requests, serving as a key parameter for architects and administrators seeking to optimize storage performance based on specific workload requirements.

Throughput, latency, and IOPS collectively form a triad of interrelated performance metrics that holistically characterize the efficiency and responsiveness of computing systems. Throughput, as a measure of data processing capacity, provides a macroscopic view of a system's ability to handle data in bulk. It is especially relevant in scenarios where large datasets need to be efficiently transferred or processed, such as in data storage and network communication. Latency, on the other hand, zooms in on the temporal aspects of performance, scrutinizing the time it takes for individual operations to be executed. In latency-sensitive applications, like online transactions or real-time data processing, minimizing delays is paramount for ensuring a seamless user experience. IOPS, with its focus on input and output operations, delves into the granular details of storage performance, capturing the speed at which data can be retrieved or written.

The significance of these metrics extends across diverse computing environments, from traditional data centers to cloud infrastructures and edge computing deployments. In storage systems, optimizing throughput, minimizing latency, and maximizing IOPS are perennial challenges that demand careful consideration of hardware configurations, data access patterns, and workload characteristics. Achieving a balance between these metrics becomes particularly crucial in scenarios where specific performance objectives, such as meeting service level agreements (SLAs) or supporting high-performance applications, are imperative.

In the context of networked systems, throughput assumes a central role in determining the efficiency of data transfer. Network throughput, often measured in bits per second (bps) or its derivatives like kilobits per second (Kbps) or gigabits per second (Gbps), gauges the capacity of a network to transmit data between connected devices. High network throughput is desirable for scenarios involving large-scale data transfers, multimedia streaming, and distributed computing. The trade-off between network throughput and latency is a classic consideration; while high throughput signifies a robust data-carrying capacity, minimizing latency ensures that the transmitted data reaches its destination swiftly.

Latency, in networking, encapsulates the time taken for data packets to traverse the network from source to destination. It includes various components such as propagation delay, transmission delay, queuing delay, and processing delay. Minimizing network latency is crucial for applications demanding real-time responsiveness, such as video conferencing, online gaming, and financial trading platforms. Throughput and latency often exhibit an inverse relationship in networking; as throughput increases, latency may rise due to potential congestion or processing overhead. Striking an optimal balance between these metrics is pivotal to designing networks that cater to diverse communication needs while meeting performance expectations.

In storage systems, IOPS assumes a position of paramount importance, especially as organizations grapple with escalating data volumes and increasingly complex workloads. IOPS directly influences the speed at which data can be read or written to storage media, a critical consideration for applications ranging from databases to virtualized environments. Solid-state drives (SSDs) often shine in the realm of IOPS compared to traditional hard disk drives (HDDs), making them preferred choices for scenarios where rapid data access is a priority. Storage architectures, caching mechanisms, and RAID configurations play pivotal roles in influencing IOPS, with administrators tailoring configurations based on specific application demands and performance objectives.

The intricacies of these performance metrics become even more pronounced in virtualized environments, where multiple virtual machines (VMs) contend for shared resources. In such settings, optimizing throughput, minimizing latency, and balancing IOPS are intricate tasks that demand a nuanced understanding of virtualization technologies, hypervisor configurations, and workload characteristics. Ensuring that each VM receives its fair share of resources while maintaining overall system efficiency is a delicate balancing act that administrators navigate through meticulous resource allocation and performance tuning.

Cloud computing, with its inherent emphasis on resource scalability and on-demand provisioning, places a premium on performance metrics to deliver reliable and responsive services. Throughput, in the context of cloud storage and networking, underpins the ability of cloud platforms to cater to diverse workloads and data access patterns. Cloud providers often tout their network throughput capabilities as a key differentiator, particularly in scenarios where high-performance computing or data-intensive applications are prevalent.

Latency, in the cloud, acquires additional dimensions as data traverses through distributed and virtualized environments. The geographic dispersion of cloud data centers introduces considerations related to the physical distance between users and data, influencing round-trip times and user experience. Cloud providers strategically position their data centers to minimize latency and enhance responsiveness, acknowledging the critical role this metric plays in user satisfaction and the overall efficacy of cloud services.

IOPS, in the cloud context, becomes a focal point for organizations migrating workloads to virtual machines or cloud storage solutions. The ability to scale IOPS based on changing workload demands is a key feature offered by many cloud providers, allowing users to dynamically adjust storage performance to match application requirements. This flexibility is particularly valuable in cloud environments characterized by variable workloads, providing a cost-effective approach to meeting performance objectives without over-provisioning resources.

The intersection of these performance metrics gains further complexity in edge computing, where computing resources are distributed closer to the devices generating or consuming data. Edge computing environments, characterized by a diverse array of devices and connectivity options, place unique demands on throughput, latency, and IOPS. Minimizing latency becomes a critical consideration in scenarios where real-time data processing at the edge is pivotal, such as in industrial IoT applications or autonomous vehicles. Throughput considerations in edge computing often revolve around optimizing data transfers between edge devices and central data repositories, ensuring that the distributed nature of edge environments doesn't compromise overall system efficiency.

In conclusion, key performance metrics – throughput, latency, and IOPS – form the cornerstone of evaluating and optimizing the efficiency of computing systems across diverse environments. These metrics collectively paint a comprehensive picture of a system's capabilities, encompassing data handling capacity, responsiveness, and storage performance. Striking a delicate balance between these metrics is a perpetual challenge for architects and administrators, necessitating a nuanced understanding of workload characteristics, hardware configurations, and the unique demands of each computing environment. As technology continues to evolve, these performance metrics remain pivotal in guiding the design, deployment, and optimization of computing systems that meet the ever-growing expectations of users and applications.

Evaluating the impact of file system design on overall system performance.

The impact of file system design on overall system performance is a multifaceted and intricate interplay that resonates across the entire computing landscape. At the heart of this dynamic lies the fundamental role of file systems in organizing, storing, and retrieving data – a mission-critical function that reverberates through every facet of computing operations. The choice of file system design, whether it be a traditional hierarchical structure or a more modern, distributed model, profoundly shapes the efficiency, reliability, and scalability of the overall system.

One of the primary dimensions through which file system design influences performance is data access speed. The architectural decisions governing how files are organized, indexed, and retrieved directly impact the speed at which applications can read or write data. In traditional tree-structured file systems, the hierarchy of directories and subdirectories introduces a predictable path for data retrieval, aligning with users' mental models and fostering ease of navigation. However, as the volume of files within a single level of the hierarchy increases, the linear traversal inherent in this structure can introduce performance bottlenecks, leading to slower access times.

Conversely, modern file systems often leverage hash-based or distributed approaches to enhance data access speed, especially in scenarios with large-scale storage systems or distributed computing environments. Hash-based structures distribute files across directories using mathematical functions, promoting a more balanced distribution and reducing the likelihood of performance degradation associated with linear traversal. This distributed approach is particularly advantageous in scenarios where rapid access to vast datasets is crucial, such as in big data analytics or cloud-based storage systems.

The impact of file system design extends beyond mere data access speed to encompass storage efficiency. The organization of data within storage media, influenced by file system design choices, directly affects how efficiently storage space is utilized. Traditional file systems, particularly those associated with legacy technologies, may exhibit fragmentation issues, where files are scattered across non-contiguous blocks on storage media. This fragmentation can result in suboptimal storage efficiency, as it may lead to wasted space and slower data retrieval times due to increased seek operations.

Modern file systems often integrate mechanisms to mitigate fragmentation and optimize storage efficiency. Techniques like advanced allocation strategies, including delayed allocation and extents, seek to allocate storage in a manner that minimizes fragmentation and enhances overall efficiency. These design considerations are particularly relevant in scenarios where large files or frequent data modifications are commonplace, such as in video editing applications or database systems. By addressing fragmentation and optimizing storage allocation, file system designs can significantly impact the overall utilization of storage resources, contributing to improved performance and responsiveness.

Moreover, the scalability of file systems, a critical consideration in contemporary computing environments, is intricately tied to design choices. As the volume of data grows and computing systems expand, the file system must adapt to accommodate increasing demands without sacrificing performance. The hierarchical nature of traditional file systems may pose challenges in scalability, especially when dealing with a massive number of files or directories at a single level. The linear traversal required to navigate through the hierarchy can introduce bottlenecks, limiting the system's ability to scale seamlessly.

Distributed and scalable file system designs, on the other hand, aim to overcome these limitations by embracing parallelism and decentralization. File systems like Hadoop Distributed File System (HDFS) or Google File System (GFS) distribute data across multiple nodes, enabling parallel processing and efficient handling of large-scale datasets. These distributed designs are well-suited for environments where scalability is paramount, such as in cloud computing infrastructures or data-intensive scientific research. The ability of a file system to gracefully scale with the growth of data and computing demands is a testament to the foresight embedded in its design.

Security considerations also come to the forefront when evaluating the impact of file system design on overall system performance. File systems play a pivotal role in enforcing access control policies, safeguarding sensitive data from unauthorized access or manipulation. Traditional file systems often rely on discretionary access control models, where the owner of a file or directory has significant control over access permissions. While this model offers flexibility, it may also lead to security vulnerabilities if not configured and managed judiciously.

Modern file systems incorporate advanced security features, such as access control lists (ACLs) and mandatory access control (MAC) mechanisms, to provide more fine-grained control over permissions.

These enhancements empower administrators to enforce stricter access policies, reducing the risk of unauthorized access or data breaches. In scenarios where data security is of utmost importance, such as in financial institutions or healthcare organizations, the security features embedded in file system design become critical determinants of overall system performance.

The resilience of file systems in the face of failures or data corruption is another facet deeply influenced by design considerations. Traditional file systems may lack robust mechanisms for data integrity and recovery, making them susceptible to issues like data loss or file corruption in the event of hardware failures or unexpected shutdowns. Modern file systems often integrate features like journaling or copy-on-write mechanisms, which provide enhanced protection against data corruption and enable efficient recovery after system crashes.

The choice of file system design also impacts the overall system's ability to support advanced features like snapshots, which allow the creation of point-in-time copies of the file system. Snapshots are invaluable in scenarios where data consistency and backup strategies are paramount, providing a mechanism to revert to a known state in case of errors or data corruption. By incorporating such features, file system designs contribute to the system's overall reliability and resilience, influencing performance in terms of data integrity and recovery.

Interactions between file systems and applications also bear significant weight in evaluating overall system performance. The design of file systems dictates how applications interact with stored data, influencing the efficiency of common file operations like create, read, update, and delete (CRUD). Traditional file systems may impose limitations on the speed and efficiency of these operations, especially in scenarios where large datasets or concurrent access are prevalent. Modern file systems often optimize these operations through techniques like data caching, write-ahead logging, and efficient metadata management, enhancing the overall responsiveness of applications.

The impact of file system design on overall system performance is further underscored by its role in supporting advanced functionalities like data deduplication and compression. These features, integrated into the design of modern file systems, contribute to more efficient storage utilization by eliminating redundant data and reducing storage footprints. In environments where data storage costs are a critical consideration, such as in enterprise data centers or cloud storage services, the ability of a file system to leverage deduplication and compression becomes instrumental in optimizing performance and resource utilization.

Furthermore, the emergence of file systems tailored for specific use cases, such as high-performance computing (HPC) or real-time data processing, emphasizes the specialization that design choices can bring. File systems optimized for parallel access, distributed processing, or low-latency requirements cater to the unique demands of these specialized domains. The efficiency of file system designs in aligning with the specific needs of diverse applications contributes to the overall performance and effectiveness of computing systems in these targeted environments.

In conclusion, the impact of file system design on overall system performance is a nuanced interplay of architectural choices that reverberate through every layer of the computing stack. From influencing data access speed and storage efficiency to shaping scalability, security, and resilience, the design of file systems serves as a linchpin in the quest for optimal system performance. Modern file system designs, with their emphasis on distributed, scalable, and secure architectures, exemplify the evolving landscape of computing environments. As technology continues to advance, the careful consideration of file system design will remain pivotal in orchestrating computing systems that seamlessly balance performance, reliability, and adaptability to meet the diverse needs of users and applications.

Strategies for optimizing file access speed and reducing latency.

Optimizing file access speed and reducing latency are paramount objectives in the realm of computing, essential for ensuring responsive and efficient interactions between applications and data. A multifaceted approach, encompassing both hardware and software considerations, underpins strategies for achieving these goals. One foundational aspect involves leveraging advancements in storage technologies. The adoption of solid-state drives (SSDs) over traditional hard disk drives (HDDs) stands out as a transformative strategy. SSDs, with their lack of moving parts and faster read and write speeds, significantly enhance file access speed and reduce latency, especially in scenarios where rapid data retrieval is critical.

File system design plays a pivotal role in dictating access speed and latency. The traditional hierarchical file system structures, while intuitive, can introduce inefficiencies as the volume of files within a single directory grows. Hash-based or distributed file system designs, on the other hand, distribute files across directories using mathematical functions, mitigating the linear traversal bottleneck and reducing latency. Such design choices are particularly beneficial in large-scale storage systems or distributed computing environments, offering a more balanced distribution of data and facilitating faster data access.

Caching mechanisms constitute another powerful strategy for optimizing file access speed. By maintaining a cache of frequently accessed data in faster storage tiers, such as RAM, file systems can expedite read operations and reduce latency. Caching is especially effective for applications with predictable access patterns, ensuring that commonly accessed data is readily available. Write-ahead caching, where write operations are initially buffered in the cache before being committed to the storage medium, further enhances the efficiency of file systems by decoupling write speed from the speed of the underlying storage.

Parallelization emerges as a crucial strategy in optimizing file access speed, particularly in the context of large datasets and high-performance computing environments. Parallel file systems, designed to support concurrent access from multiple nodes, leverage parallel I/O operations to enhance both read and write speeds. This approach is particularly relevant in scientific computing, data analytics, and simulations where massive datasets are processed concurrently. The parallelization of file access operations can significantly reduce latency, enabling applications to harness the collective capabilities of multiple nodes for faster data processing.

Furthermore, the adoption of advanced file allocation strategies contributes to optimizing access speed and reducing latency. Techniques such as delayed allocation and extents aim to allocate storage in a manner that minimizes fragmentation and enhances overall efficiency. By intelligently managing how data is stored on storage media, file systems can streamline access patterns, reducing the need for extensive seek operations and enhancing overall data access speed. These strategies are especially relevant in scenarios where large files or frequent data modifications are commonplace.

The introduction of optimized protocols for file access, such as the Network File System (NFS) or the Server Message Block (SMB), plays a pivotal role in networked environments. These protocols facilitate efficient communication between client and server, minimizing latency in file access operations over a network. Tuning and optimizing these protocols for specific use cases, such as adjusting buffer sizes or employing compression, can further enhance file access speed and reduce latency, especially in scenarios where network performance is a critical factor.

Efficient metadata management is a cornerstone strategy for improving file access speed and reducing latency. Metadata, which includes information about files, directories, and permissions, is crucial for navigating and accessing data. Modern file systems employ techniques like B-trees and indexing to organize and retrieve metadata swiftly, minimizing the time required for file system operations. Additionally, file systems supporting extended attributes provide a flexible framework for associating additional metadata with files, enabling richer contextual information that can be leveraged to optimize access patterns.

Minimizing the impact of seek times, especially in traditional HDDs, is an enduring challenge in file access optimization. Techniques like prefetching, where data is proactively loaded into cache before it is actually needed, aim to reduce the latency associated with seek operations. Predictive algorithms that anticipate access patterns and preload relevant data contribute to smoother file access experiences, particularly in scenarios where repetitive data access patterns can be identified and leveraged for optimization.

The adoption of tiered storage architectures introduces another layer of sophistication in optimizing file access speed. By strategically organizing data across different storage tiers based on access patterns and priority, tiered storage allows frequently accessed data to reside in faster, more expensive storage mediums, while less accessed or archival data is stored in slower, cost-effective tiers. Automated data movement between tiers, driven by access patterns and policies, ensures that data is dynamically placed where it can be accessed most efficiently, contributing to optimized file access speed.

In the realm of networked file systems, the strategic placement of file servers and the optimization of network configurations are instrumental in reducing latency. Geographic considerations play a pivotal role, and the strategic deployment of file servers closer to end-users or applications can significantly minimize the round-trip times for data access. Load balancing mechanisms that distribute access requests evenly across multiple servers further contribute to reducing latency, ensuring that no single server becomes a bottleneck in file access operations.

The use of parallel processing and distributed computing frameworks aligns with strategies for optimizing file access speed, especially in the context of data-intensive applications. Technologies like Apache Hadoop and Apache Spark facilitate parallelized data processing, allowing applications to distribute file access operations across multiple nodes. This distributed approach not only accelerates data retrieval but also reduces latency by harnessing the collective computational power of a cluster of nodes.

Intelligent use of data compression and deduplication techniques can contribute to optimizing file access speed and reducing latency by minimizing the volume of data that needs to be transferred. Compression reduces the size of data during storage and transmission, leading to faster read and write speeds, while deduplication eliminates redundant data, further enhancing storage efficiency. These techniques are particularly beneficial in scenarios where network bandwidth is a limiting factor or where storage costs are a significant consideration.

Moreover, advancements in file system monitoring and performance tuning tools play a crucial role in the ongoing effort to optimize file access speed. Real-time monitoring of file system activities, combined with the ability to dynamically adjust configurations based on performance metrics, allows administrators to fine-tune file systems for optimal efficiency. Proactive identification of performance bottlenecks, whether related to storage, network, or file system design, enables timely interventions to address issues and enhance overall file access speed.

In conclusion, strategies for optimizing file access speed and reducing latency span a diverse spectrum of hardware and software considerations. From embracing advancements in storage technologies like SSDs to leveraging sophisticated file system designs, caching mechanisms, and parallel processing, each strategy contributes to a comprehensive approach aimed at enhancing the efficiency of file access operations. The evolution of network protocols, metadata management techniques, and tiered storage architectures further exemplifies the multifaceted nature of these strategies. As computing environments continue to evolve, the pursuit of faster and more responsive file access remains a central theme, driving innovation and prompting a continuous exploration of new strategies to meet the ever-growing demands of modern applications and users.

Cache management and prefetching techniques for enhanced efficiency.

Cache management and prefetching techniques constitute integral components in the quest for enhanced computational efficiency, playing pivotal roles in optimizing data access speed and reducing latency. Caches, acting as high-speed intermediate storage between the processor and main memory, are essential for minimizing the time-consuming process of fetching data directly from the slower main memory. Effective cache management strategies involve decisions on how to organize, allocate, and replace data in the cache to maximize its utilization and impact on overall system performance.

One fundamental cache management approach is the Least Recently Used (LRU) algorithm, which prioritizes retaining in the cache the data that has been least recently accessed. The LRU algorithm leverages the principle that recently accessed data is more likely to be accessed again in the near future. While conceptually straightforward, the implementation of LRU can be resource-intensive, as it requires tracking the access history of each cache line. In contrast, other algorithms like the Random or First-In-First-Out (FIFO) approaches provide simpler alternatives, but they may not always yield optimal cache performance.

Prefetching techniques represent another dimension of cache optimization, focusing on proactively loading data into the cache before it is explicitly requested. Prefetching aims to mitigate the latency associated with cache misses by anticipating future data needs and bringing relevant information into the cache preemptively. Various prefetching strategies exist, ranging from hardware-based mechanisms that automatically predict access patterns to software-controlled approaches where programmers provide hints or directives to guide prefetching decisions.

Hardware-based prefetching mechanisms often rely on sophisticated algorithms and heuristics to predict which data should be prefetched into the cache. For example, the Stream Prefetching technique identifies sequential access patterns and preloads consecutive data into the cache. Stride Prefetching, another hardware-centric strategy, focuses on predicting regular patterns in memory access and prefetching data at fixed intervals. These mechanisms, embedded in modern processors, are designed to adapt dynamically to varying access patterns, thereby optimizing cache utilization without requiring explicit programmer intervention.

On the software side, explicit or compiler-directed prefetching allows programmers to provide hints to the system about the expected access patterns of their code. Compiler directives, such as those in OpenMP or pragma directives in languages like C or Fortran, offer a means to guide prefetching decisions. By providing insights into the anticipated memory usage patterns, programmers can influence the prefetching strategy employed by the system. However, this approach necessitates a deeper understanding of the underlying hardware architecture and may require fine-tuning for different target platforms.

Temporal and spatial locality principles are foundational concepts guiding both cache management and prefetching strategies. Temporal locality refers to the tendency of a program to access the same memory locations repeatedly over a short period. Spatial locality, on the other hand, highlights the likelihood that adjacent memory locations will be accessed together. Both principles inform cache management algorithms, ensuring that frequently accessed data and its neighbors are efficiently retained in the cache.

Cache hierarchies, featuring multiple levels of caches with varying sizes and speeds, present additional complexity in cache management. The interaction between these cache levels requires careful coordination to maximize the benefits of each cache tier. L1 caches, closer to the processor cores, often prioritize smaller sizes with lower latency, focusing on critical data for immediate execution. L2 and L3 caches, situated further from the cores but with larger capacities, serve as additional layers to capture a broader scope of data and reduce the likelihood of cache misses.

Cache coherence, a crucial consideration in multiprocessor systems, ensures that each processor in a system has a consistent view of shared data. Protocols like MESI (Modified, Exclusive, Shared, Invalid) or MOESI (Modified, Owned, Exclusive, Shared, Invalid) manage cache coherence by tracking the state of cache lines and coordinating updates. Maintaining cache coherence is essential for preventing inconsistencies in shared data, but it introduces challenges in terms of synchronization and potential performance overhead.

Furthermore, the efficiency of cache management and prefetching techniques is influenced by the memory hierarchy and the characteristics of the underlying storage medium. The effectiveness of caching strategies varies between systems with traditional hard disk drives (HDDs) and those with solid-state drives (SSDs). While caching is instrumental in mitigating the high latency of HDDs, the inherently faster access times of SSDs impact the relevance and impact of certain prefetching and caching mechanisms. Adaptive approaches that dynamically adjust caching and prefetching strategies based on the specific characteristics of the storage medium contribute to optimal performance.

Cache-conscious programming practices emphasize aligning code with the principles of cache optimization. Data-oriented design, which organizes data structures to enhance spatial and temporal locality, aligns with cache-friendly programming. Techniques like loop unrolling and loop blocking aim to optimize memory access patterns, reducing cache misses and improving overall program performance. However, cache-conscious programming requires a delicate balance, as overly aggressive optimizations may lead to increased code complexity or hinder maintainability.

The trade-off between computation and communication costs guides decisions in cache management and prefetching. While prefetching aims to reduce latency by proactively loading data into the cache, it introduces overhead in terms of bandwidth and computational resources. Striking the right balance involves considering the cost of prefetching against the potential benefits in terms of reduced cache misses and improved overall execution time. As computing systems evolve, the interplay between computation and communication costs remains a crucial aspect in refining cache management and prefetching strategies.

In conclusion, cache management and prefetching techniques constitute essential elements in the pursuit of enhanced computational efficiency. The intricacies of cache design, ranging from algorithms and coherence protocols to the impact of hardware and storage characteristics, underscore the multifaceted nature of cache optimization. Prefetching strategies, whether hardware-driven or guided by programmer directives, contribute to minimizing latency by anticipating and proactively addressing data access needs. The principles of temporal and spatial locality, cache hierarchies, and cache-conscious programming practices collectively shape the landscape of cache optimization. As computing environments continue to evolve, the refinement of these techniques remains a dynamic area of research and implementation, driven by the ongoing quest for faster, more efficient, and responsive computing systems.

The importance of proper disk partitioning for optimal file system performance.

Proper disk partitioning stands as a foundational element in the quest for optimal file system performance, wielding a significant impact on the efficiency, reliability, and organization of data within a storage system. The partitioning process involves dividing a physical storage device into distinct, isolated sections or partitions, each of which can be independently managed and formatted with its own file system. The importance of this seemingly straightforward task becomes apparent when delving into its implications for storage optimization, data organization, and system management.

One of the key considerations in disk partitioning is the creation of distinct areas for the operating system, application software, and user data. Allocating a dedicated partition for the operating system ensures that it is isolated from user data, reducing the risk of data corruption or system instability in the event of software issues or crashes. This separation fosters a modular and organized storage environment, simplifying system maintenance, updates, and backups. By compartmentalizing the OS from user data, partitioning contributes to enhanced system stability and ease of management.

Beyond the isolation of the operating system, proper disk partitioning allows for the segregation of application software from both the OS and user data. Allocating a specific partition for applications facilitates efficient management, updates, and maintenance of software components. It also ensures that changes to the operating system or user data do not inadvertently impact application installations. This organizational structure not only streamlines system administration but also aids in troubleshooting and recovery efforts, as issues within one partition are less likely to cascade into others.

Disk partitioning is integral to optimizing storage space and ensuring that available capacity is used judiciously. By creating separate partitions for the operating system, applications, and user data, administrators can allocate appropriate amounts of space based on the specific needs of each component. This approach prevents scenarios where a runaway process or excessive data growth in one area consumes all available disk space, potentially leading to system crashes or performance degradation. Effective space management through partitioning supports a more predictable and controlled storage environment.

Moreover, disk partitioning plays a pivotal role in supporting different file system types and optimizing their performance characteristics. Different file systems are tailored for specific use cases, and proper partitioning allows for the selection of the most suitable file system for each partition based on factors such as data access patterns, reliability requirements, and scalability. For example, a partition hosting a database with high write-intensive operations might benefit from a file system optimized for transactional workloads, while a partition containing archival data may utilize a file system focused on data integrity and longevity. Tailoring file system choices through partitioning contributes to optimal performance and longevity for diverse storage needs.

The practice of proper disk partitioning extends its significance to the realm of security and data protection. By isolating user data in dedicated partitions, administrators can implement more granular access controls and encryption measures. This segregation enhances data security by limiting the potential impact of security breaches or unauthorized access to specific partitions. Furthermore, in scenarios where multi-boot configurations are employed (such as having multiple operating systems installed on a single machine), partitioning enables distinct areas for each OS, reducing the risk of cross-contamination and potential conflicts.

Efficient backup and recovery processes hinge on the proper partitioning of storage devices. Isolating user data in dedicated partitions simplifies backup procedures, allowing administrators to focus on preserving critical data without unnecessary redundancy. Additionally, when a backup is required, partition-specific restoration can be performed, minimizing downtime and reducing the complexity of recovery efforts. This targeted approach to backup and recovery is particularly valuable in large-scale environments where rapid data restoration is essential.

The role of disk partitioning in optimizing file system performance is closely intertwined with considerations of storage fragmentation. Fragmentation occurs when files are divided into non-contiguous blocks on storage media, leading to increased seek times and reduced data access speeds. Proper partitioning, in conjunction with intelligent file system design, helps mitigate fragmentation issues. By creating appropriately sized partitions and implementing file allocation strategies that minimize fragmentation, administrators can ensure that file data is stored contiguously, enhancing overall file system performance.

Furthermore, disk partitioning supports the implementation of advanced file system features such as journaling and snapshot capabilities. Journaling, a mechanism that records changes to a file system in a log or journal, enhances data integrity and aids in faster recovery from system crashes. Snapshots, point-in-time copies of a file system, provide a means to capture a consistent view of data for backup or recovery purposes. Properly partitioned storage devices facilitate the effective implementation of these features, contributing to enhanced reliability and resilience in the face of unforeseen events.

The performance benefits of disk partitioning extend to the realm of scalability and adaptability. As storage needs evolve, administrators can adjust the sizes of existing partitions or create new ones to accommodate changing requirements. This flexibility allows for the seamless expansion of storage capacity without disrupting existing configurations. In scenarios where dynamic allocation of resources is critical, such as in cloud computing environments or virtualized infrastructures, the ability to adapt partition sizes ensures that storage resources align with the evolving demands of applications and data workloads.

In summary, the importance of proper disk partitioning for optimal file system performance spans a spectrum of considerations, encompassing stability, organization, space management, file system optimization, security, backup efficiency, and adaptability. The careful allocation of partitions for the operating system, applications, and user data fosters a modular and organized storage environment. This approach not only enhances system stability and ease of management but also contributes to efficient space utilization and optimal performance. As storage technologies continue to evolve, the foundational principles of disk partitioning remain essential in orchestrating storage environments that meet the diverse and evolving needs of modern computing systems.

Techniques for aligning partitions to improve data access speed.

Aligning partitions is a critical technique in the pursuit of optimizing data access speed, particularly in the context of modern storage technologies. This practice addresses the underlying physical structure of storage devices and their interaction with file systems, aiming to align data in a manner that aligns with the characteristics of the storage medium. The significance of this alignment becomes evident when considering the impact on input/output (I/O) operations, storage efficiency, and overall system performance.

At the core of partition alignment is the concept of the Advanced Format (AF), which has become increasingly relevant with the prevalence of modern hard disk drives (HDDs) and solid-state drives (SSDs). AF refers to a storage format that utilizes larger physical sectors compared to traditional storage formats. Aligning partitions to the appropriate boundaries of these larger sectors ensures that data structures, such as file system clusters or pages, align with the physical structure of the storage device. This alignment minimizes the potential for misalignment-related performance penalties, often referred to as the "4K sector issue," which can occur when data structures cross physical sector boundaries, leading to additional I/O operations and decreased efficiency.

For mechanical HDDs, aligning partitions to the physical geometry of the disk is crucial to optimize data access speed. Traditional hard drives have a physical structure where data is stored in sectors, and aligning partitions to start and end at sector boundaries minimizes the need for multiple I/O operations to retrieve or write data that spans sectors. Misalignment in HDDs can result in additional rotational delays and seek times, leading to suboptimal performance. Aligning partitions to the inherent structure of HDDs reduces the likelihood of these inefficiencies, contributing to faster data access and improved overall system responsiveness.

The alignment of partitions gains even more significance in the context of solid-state drives (SSDs), where the internal architecture differs significantly from traditional HDDs. SSDs, based on NAND flash memory, have their own set of considerations regarding alignment. Aligning partitions to the page and block boundaries of the SSD is crucial to optimize performance and extend the lifespan of the drive. The concept of aligning partitions to the optimal size of the SSD's erase block ensures that data can be written and erased efficiently, minimizing write amplification and prolonging the longevity of the SSD.

Partition alignment is intimately connected with the choice of file system, as different file systems have varying requirements for optimal alignment. File systems like NTFS and FAT traditionally used default alignment values that may not align with the underlying storage device's physical structure. In contrast, modern file systems, such as ext4 or those designed explicitly for SSDs, often feature alignment settings that align with the native characteristics of contemporary storage devices. Aligning partitions based on the specific file system requirements ensures that the file system structures align seamlessly with the storage medium, reducing access latencies and enhancing overall performance.

Moreover, the practice of aligning partitions plays a crucial role in optimizing the efficiency of storage clusters or blocks, which are the basic units of data allocation in file systems. When clusters align with the physical storage structure, it minimizes the chances of partial I/O operations that might occur when a cluster spans multiple physical sectors. For example, in scenarios where misalignment results in a cluster crossing two physical sectors, a read or write operation might necessitate accessing both sectors, introducing additional latency. Aligning partitions to cluster boundaries mitigates such inefficiencies, promoting more efficient I/O operations and enhancing data access speed.

Advanced techniques, such as partition alignment tools and alignment-aware file system creation utilities, have emerged to simplify the alignment process. These tools often provide options to align partitions according to specific storage device characteristics or alignment requirements of the chosen file system. They automate the alignment process, reducing the likelihood of misalignment issues caused by manual partitioning. This automation is particularly valuable in environments where a large number of storage devices need to be aligned consistently, ensuring optimal performance across the entire storage infrastructure.

The significance of aligning partitions extends to scenarios where storage devices are utilized in RAID (Redundant Array of Independent Disks) configurations. RAID setups involve combining multiple storage devices for enhanced performance, reliability, or a combination of both. Aligning partitions in a RAID array is critical to ensure that data striping, parity, or mirroring aligns efficiently with the physical structure of each disk in the array. Misalignment in RAID configurations can lead to suboptimal performance and negate the advantages of RAID setups. Properly aligned partitions in RAID arrays contribute to balanced I/O distribution and improved overall system throughput.

Cloud computing environments, characterized by virtualized storage and diverse underlying hardware configurations, further underscore the importance of partition alignment. In virtualized environments, where storage resources are abstracted from physical devices, aligning virtual partitions with the characteristics of the underlying storage infrastructure remains crucial. Misalignment in virtual environments can introduce inefficiencies not only in the virtual machines themselves but also in the underlying physical storage systems. Aligning partitions in virtualized environments ensures that the benefits of partition alignment extend seamlessly from the physical to the virtual layer.

The advent of more sophisticated storage technologies, such as Non-Volatile Memory Express (NVMe), introduces new considerations for partition alignment. NVMe, designed to leverage the high-speed characteristics of solid-state storage, requires specific alignment practices to maximize performance. Aligning partitions to the optimal boundaries of NVMe devices ensures that data access patterns align with the device's architecture, reducing latency and fully capitalizing on the speed advantages offered by NVMe technology.

In conclusion, the techniques for aligning partitions represent a fundamental practice in the pursuit of optimizing data access speed across a spectrum of storage technologies. From traditional HDDs to modern SSDs and NVMe devices, the benefits of aligning partitions extend to improved I/O efficiency, reduced latency, and enhanced overall system performance. This practice is intimately tied to considerations of file system alignment, storage cluster efficiency, and RAID configurations. As storage technologies continue to evolve, the meticulous alignment of partitions remains a cornerstone in the design and deployment of storage solutions that deliver optimal performance and responsiveness in diverse computing environments.

Exploring the use of compression and deduplication in file systems.

The utilization of compression and deduplication in file systems represents a sophisticated approach to storage optimization, addressing the ever-growing challenge of managing and maximizing the efficiency of data storage. Compression, a process that reduces the size of files or data by encoding them in a more efficient representation, serves as a fundamental technique for conserving storage space. This is achieved by eliminating redundancy and encoding patterns within the data, resulting in smaller file sizes without compromising the integrity or usability of the stored information. By reducing the physical space occupied by files, compression contributes to the economical use of storage resources, a critical consideration in today's data-intensive computing environments.

File systems employ various compression algorithms, each with its own trade-offs in terms of compression ratios, processing overhead, and suitability for specific types of data. Common compression algorithms include Lempel-Ziv variants like gzip and zlib, as well as more recent advancements such as LZ4 and Zstandard. These algorithms use different techniques, such as dictionary-based encoding and entropy coding, to achieve compression. The choice of compression algorithm depends on factors like the nature of the data, the desired compression ratio, and the available processing resources. In scenarios where computational resources are abundant, file systems may opt for algorithms that provide higher compression ratios but demand more processing power.

Deduplication, on the other hand, addresses the issue of redundancy within a storage system by identifying and eliminating duplicate copies of data. This process involves analyzing the stored data and identifying identical blocks or segments, regardless of their location within the file system. Once duplicates are identified, only a single copy of each unique block is retained, and subsequent references to that data point to the original copy. Deduplication is particularly effective in environments where multiple instances of the same data exist, such as in backup systems, virtual machine images, or file repositories with a high degree of redundancy.

The implementation of deduplication introduces mechanisms for tracking and managing the metadata associated with duplicate data. This metadata, often stored in a deduplication index, maintains records of unique data blocks and their locations. As new data is added or modified, the deduplication process examines the incoming data to identify whether it matches existing content. If a match is found, the system references the existing copy, reducing the need for additional physical storage. Deduplication can be applied at various levels, including file-level, block-level, or even within variable-sized chunks, providing flexibility to adapt to diverse storage scenarios.

When compression and deduplication are combined, the result is a potent synergy that optimizes storage efficiency even further. The complementary nature of these techniques lies in their ability to target different aspects of data redundancy. Compression focuses on eliminating redundancy within individual files by encoding them in a more compact form, while deduplication operates at a broader level, identifying and removing redundancies across multiple files or data sets. This combination results in a more comprehensive approach to storage optimization, leveraging both intra-file and inter-file redundancy reduction strategies.

The benefits of compression and deduplication extend beyond mere storage space savings. Reduced storage requirements translate into lower costs, particularly in environments where storage capacity is a significant factor, such as in data centers or cloud storage services. Additionally, the minimized physical footprint of compressed and deduplicated data contributes to improved data transfer speeds and responsiveness. In scenarios where data needs to be transferred over networks or stored on devices with limited capacity, the reduced size of compressed and deduplicated data accelerates these operations, optimizing overall system performance.

Moreover, the adoption of compression and deduplication aligns with sustainability efforts in the realm of information technology. By minimizing the physical storage footprint of data, these techniques contribute to reduced power consumption, lower cooling requirements, and a smaller environmental impact. This is particularly pertinent in large-scale data centers where energy efficiency and environmental considerations have become integral components of operational strategies. The ability to store and manage data more efficiently aligns with the broader goal of creating sustainable and eco-friendly computing infrastructures.

While the advantages of compression and deduplication are evident, their application requires a nuanced consideration of the trade-offs involved. Compression, for instance, introduces processing overhead during the encoding and decoding phases. The extent of this overhead depends on factors such as the complexity of the chosen compression algorithm, the computational resources available, and the frequency of data access. In scenarios where computational resources are constrained or where data is frequently accessed, the potential trade-off between storage savings and processing overhead must be carefully evaluated.

Similarly, deduplication introduces challenges related to maintaining the integrity and availability of data. The reliance on metadata indexes to track duplicates necessitates robust mechanisms for ensuring data consistency, especially in the event of hardware failures or system crashes. The management of metadata and the deduplication index becomes crucial, requiring careful design and implementation to avoid potential risks associated with data corruption or loss. Additionally, the effectiveness of deduplication is contingent on the prevalence of duplicate data within the storage system; in scenarios with minimal redundancy, the benefits of deduplication may be limited.

File systems that incorporate compression and deduplication often provide configurable settings, allowing administrators to tailor these techniques to the specific requirements and characteristics of the data being stored. Compression ratios, deduplication policies, and the level of granularity at which these processes are applied can be adjusted based on the nature of the workload and the desired balance between storage efficiency and computational overhead. This configurability ensures that organizations can adapt these storage optimization techniques to their unique needs and use cases.

The integration of compression and deduplication in modern file systems aligns with the evolving landscape of storage technologies. As data volumes continue to escalate and the demand for efficient storage solutions intensifies, these techniques play a pivotal role in mitigating the challenges associated with data redundancy, space constraints, and environmental impact. The evolution of compression algorithms, deduplication methodologies, and their seamless integration into file systems exemplifies the ongoing quest for storage solutions that not only accommodate the burgeoning volumes of data but also do so in a manner that is resource-efficient, sustainable, and responsive to the dynamic needs of contemporary computing environments.

Balancing storage savings with processing overhead.

Balancing storage savings with processing overhead is a delicate equilibrium at the heart of storage optimization strategies, representing a dynamic trade-off that organizations must navigate to achieve an optimal solution tailored to their specific needs. The pursuit of storage efficiency involves implementing techniques such as compression and deduplication, which aim to reduce the physical footprint of stored data. However, the benefits of these strategies come with associated computational costs, introducing processing overhead during both the compression and decompression of data, as well as the identification and management of duplicates in deduplication processes.

Compression, a fundamental technique in storage optimization, revolves around encoding data in a more compact form to conserve storage space. The compression process, however, is not without its computational demands. Various compression algorithms, each with distinct characteristics and trade-offs, introduce different levels of processing overhead. Balancing storage savings with processing overhead entails selecting compression algorithms that align with the specific requirements of the data and the available computational resources. While algorithms like LZ4 prioritize speed with lower compression ratios, others such as gzip or zlib achieve higher compression ratios at the cost of increased computational demands. Striking the right balance requires careful consideration of the trade-off between storage space conservation and the computational capacity available for compression and decompression tasks.

Similarly, deduplication, a technique that identifies and eliminates redundant copies of data, introduces processing overhead in exchange for reduced storage requirements. The identification of duplicate data involves intricate algorithms and the maintenance of metadata indexes to track unique data blocks. Balancing storage savings with processing overhead in deduplication necessitates thoughtful consideration of the overhead introduced by maintaining these indexes and the computational complexity of the deduplication process itself. Organizations must evaluate the prevalence of duplicate data within their storage environment and weigh the benefits of reduced storage against the computational costs of deduplication, especially in scenarios where hardware resources may be constrained.

The challenge of balancing storage savings with processing overhead extends to scenarios where both compression and deduplication are employed concurrently. While the combined use of these techniques offers a potent strategy for storage optimization, it amplifies the computational demands on storage systems. The intricacies of this balance require a nuanced approach, considering factors such as the nature of the data, the types of workloads, and the underlying storage infrastructure. Organizations must determine the optimal configuration, including compression algorithms, deduplication policies, and the level of granularity at which these processes are applied, aligning them with the available computational resources to achieve an equilibrium that maximizes storage efficiency without unduly compromising system performance.

The choice of compression and deduplication settings is intrinsically linked to the broader context of the organization's storage requirements. In environments where storage capacity is a premium and computational resources are abundant, a more aggressive compression algorithm with higher computational overhead may be justified to achieve significant storage savings. Conversely, in scenarios where processing resources are constrained or where rapid data access is imperative, a more lightweight compression algorithm may be preferable, striking a balance that prioritizes computational efficiency over maximal compression ratios.

The impact of balancing storage savings with processing overhead is particularly pronounced in cloud computing environments, where storage optimization strategies directly influence operational costs. Cloud service providers offer a spectrum of storage options with varying performance characteristics and associated costs. Organizations must carefully calibrate their use of compression and deduplication in the cloud, factoring in both the financial implications and the computational constraints imposed by the chosen cloud service model. Achieving an optimal balance becomes crucial in cloud environments where resource utilization directly influences the operational expenses incurred.

Moreover, the dynamic nature of data workloads further complicates the balancing act. In scenarios where the characteristics of data and workloads fluctuate, the trade-off between storage savings and processing overhead becomes a moving target. Adaptive strategies that dynamically adjust compression settings or deduplication policies based on workload patterns and resource availability can provide a more responsive approach to maintaining the delicate equilibrium. This adaptability allows organizations to optimize storage efficiency in real-time, responding to changing demands without compromising system performance.

The evolution of hardware architectures, including advancements in processing power and storage technologies, introduces new dimensions to the interplay between storage savings and processing overhead. Modern processors with multiple cores and advanced instruction sets offer opportunities to parallelize compression and deduplication tasks, potentially mitigating the impact on overall system performance. Storage technologies, such as solid-state drives (SSDs) and Non-Volatile Memory Express (NVMe) devices, bring about improvements in data access speeds, influencing the calculus of the trade-off by potentially reducing the relative impact of processing overhead.

Additionally, advancements in specialized hardware accelerators, such as Graphics Processing Units (GPUs) or Field-Programmable Gate Arrays (FPGAs), provide avenues to offload and accelerate compression and deduplication tasks. Leveraging such accelerators can reshape the balance between storage savings and processing overhead, allowing organizations to achieve higher levels of storage efficiency without unduly burdening general-purpose processors. However, the integration of specialized hardware introduces its own considerations, including compatibility, cost-effectiveness, and the need for optimized software implementations.

In conclusion, the delicate balance between storage savings and processing overhead lies at the heart of storage optimization strategies, where techniques like compression and deduplication play pivotal roles. Achieving this balance requires a nuanced understanding of the organization's storage requirements, the characteristics of the data, and the capabilities of the underlying computational infrastructure. The trade-off involves making informed decisions about compression algorithms, deduplication policies, and the level of computational resources allocated to these tasks. Cloud computing environments, the dynamic nature of data workloads, and the evolution of hardware architectures introduce additional dimensions to this intricate equilibrium. As storage technologies continue to evolve, organizations must navigate this delicate balance with agility and foresight, optimizing storage efficiency without compromising the responsiveness and overall performance of their computing systems.

Addressing challenges related to concurrent file access.

Addressing challenges related to concurrent file access is a multifaceted endeavor that delves into the intricacies of file system design, data synchronization, and the management of shared resources in computing environments where multiple processes or users may simultaneously access the same files. This scenario is particularly pertinent in modern computing landscapes, ranging from multi-user systems to distributed file systems and cloud storage platforms. The challenges associated with concurrent file access revolve around ensuring data consistency, preventing race conditions, optimizing performance, and balancing the trade-offs between data integrity and system responsiveness.

One of the foremost challenges in concurrent file access is maintaining data consistency, especially in environments where multiple processes or users may attempt to read from or write to the same file concurrently. Ensuring that the file remains in a coherent state, free from inconsistencies resulting from overlapping operations, is paramount. Traditional file systems typically employ locking mechanisms to address this challenge. Locks can be either advisory or mandatory, with advisory locks providing a signal to other processes about the intent to access a file exclusively and mandatory locks enforcing exclusive access. However, the use of locks introduces potential bottlenecks and contention for resources, particularly in scenarios with high levels of concurrent access.

Another challenge stems from the potential occurrence of race conditions, where the interleaving of operations from multiple processes leads to unexpected and undesirable outcomes. For instance, if two processes concurrently read and modify the same file without proper synchronization, the result may be data corruption or inconsistencies. Implementing strategies like atomic operations or transactional file system features helps mitigate race conditions by ensuring that a sequence of operations either completes entirely or leaves the file system in a consistent state. Atomicity is crucial in preventing partial updates that could lead to data corruption, safeguarding the integrity of the shared file during concurrent access.

Optimizing performance in the context of concurrent file access involves striking a delicate balance between parallelism and the potential for contention. While the concurrent execution of read and write operations can enhance throughput, excessive contention for locks or resources may hinder performance. Strategies such as fine-grained locking, where locks are applied to specific portions of a file rather than the entire file, or lock-free data structures can alleviate contention by allowing multiple processes to operate on distinct sections of a file concurrently. However, the complexity of implementing and managing fine-grained locking introduces challenges related to correctness, as developers must carefully orchestrate lock acquisition and release to prevent deadlocks or data corruption.

The introduction of distributed file systems and cloud storage exacerbates the challenges of concurrent file access, bringing forth issues of consistency across distributed nodes and the need for synchronization mechanisms that operate seamlessly in distributed environments. Distributed file systems often adopt techniques such as distributed locking or consensus algorithms to coordinate access among multiple nodes. Consistency models, including strong consistency, eventual consistency, and causal consistency, provide a framework for managing data consistency across distributed systems. Striking the right balance between consistency and availability is a central challenge, as strong consistency may lead to increased latency or reduced availability in distributed scenarios.

Concurrency control mechanisms, such as optimistic concurrency control, offer an alternative approach by allowing multiple processes to perform operations independently and resolving conflicts at the point of data modification. However, this approach requires careful conflict resolution strategies and introduces the risk of inconsistent states if conflicts are not adequately managed. Additionally, achieving fault tolerance and resilience in distributed file systems involves addressing challenges related to network partitions, node failures, and ensuring that concurrent access does not compromise data durability or availability.

Furthermore, the use of caching and buffering mechanisms introduces complexities in the context of concurrent file access. Caches at different layers, including the operating system level, file system level, and application level, aim to improve performance by reducing the need for repeated disk I/O operations. However, concurrent access introduces challenges related to cache coherence, where updates made by one process may not be immediately reflected in the caches of other processes. Cache invalidation strategies, such as write-through or write-back policies, impact the visibility of changes across concurrent access scenarios and influence the trade-off between consistency and performance.

Concurrency challenges are also prevalent in scenarios where file systems interact with databases or other storage systems. Coordinating concurrent access between a file system and a database requires synchronization mechanisms to maintain consistency and prevent conflicts. Implementing transactional semantics that span both file system and database operations ensures that modifications to shared data occur atomically, preserving data integrity across the entire storage infrastructure.

In the realm of networked file systems, where clients access files over a network, challenges related to latency, bandwidth, and distributed synchronization come to the forefront. Network File System (NFS) and Server Message Block (SMB) protocols, commonly used for networked file access, employ mechanisms like file locking and opportunistic locks to manage concurrent access. The intricacies of managing concurrent access over a network add an additional layer of complexity, requiring robust error handling, network resilience, and strategies for handling disconnections or intermittent connectivity.

The evolution of cloud computing and containerization introduces new challenges in the context of concurrent file access. Containerized applications, often orchestrated by platforms like Kubernetes, may scale dynamically based on demand, leading to increased instances of concurrent file access. Coordinating file access across containerized environments involves addressing challenges related to inter-container communication, shared storage volumes, and synchronization mechanisms that operate seamlessly in container orchestration platforms.

In conclusion, addressing challenges related to concurrent file access encompasses a multifaceted approach, considering data consistency, race conditions, performance optimization, and the unique characteristics of diverse computing environments. The complexities of modern computing landscapes, with distributed file systems, cloud storage, and containerized architectures, amplify the intricacies of managing concurrent access. Strategies such as locking mechanisms, transactional semantics, distributed coordination, and cache management play pivotal roles in mitigating these challenges. Achieving an optimal balance between data consistency and system responsiveness requires a nuanced understanding of the specific requirements of the application, the characteristics of the data, and the underlying storage infrastructure. As computing environments continue to evolve, the effective management of concurrent file access remains a crucial aspect of designing robust and scalable storage systems that meet the demands of contemporary computing scenarios.

Scalability considerations for file systems in growing environments.

Scalability considerations for file systems in growing environments form a critical facet of designing robust storage solutions that can seamlessly accommodate the expanding demands of modern computing. As organizations experience an ever-increasing influx of data and diverse workloads, the ability of file systems to scale efficiently becomes paramount. Scalability encompasses various dimensions, including capacity scalability, performance scalability, and the capacity to handle growing numbers of users, files, or concurrent access scenarios. These considerations span hardware, software, and architectural aspects, shaping the trajectory of file system development to align with the evolving requirements of dynamic and expanding computing environments.

Capacity scalability, addressing the ability of a file system to handle a growing volume of data, is foundational to meeting the relentless increase in data generation. Traditional file systems often faced limitations in terms of maximum storage capacity or file count, necessitating careful planning and potential disruptions during capacity expansions. Modern file systems employ techniques such as distributed storage, where data is spread across multiple nodes or devices, to achieve seamless capacity scalability. Distributed file systems like the Hadoop Distributed File System (HDFS) or Ceph leverage a distributed architecture to distribute data across nodes, enabling organizations to scale storage capacity horizontally by adding more nodes to the cluster. This horizontal scalability allows systems to accommodate massive datasets without compromising performance or encountering capacity constraints.

Performance scalability, or the ability of a file system to sustain or enhance performance as the workload increases, is equally crucial in growing environments. As data volumes surge and the complexity of workloads intensifies, traditional file systems might struggle to provide consistent and responsive performance. Scalable file systems adopt parallelism and distributed computing principles to enhance performance. Techniques such as parallel I/O operations, distributed file caching, and load balancing contribute to improved performance scalability. In distributed file systems, parallel processing allows multiple nodes to handle concurrent read and write operations, mitigating bottlenecks and ensuring optimal performance, even in the face of escalating workloads.

The scaling of file systems in response to growing numbers of users, files, or concurrent access scenarios necessitates robust mechanisms for managing metadata and file structures. Traditional file systems often faced challenges when dealing with a large number of files in a single directory or accommodating numerous users concurrently accessing the same files. Modern file systems introduce hierarchical directory structures, distributed metadata management, and advanced indexing techniques to navigate and organize large file counts efficiently. Technologies like the General Parallel File System (GPFS) or Lustre adopt distributed metadata architectures, allowing for efficient scaling in the number of files and directories while maintaining rapid access times.

In distributed and networked file systems, scalability considerations extend to handling a growing number of users and ensuring equitable access to resources. Scalable file systems incorporate access control mechanisms, distributed authentication, and load balancing to manage increasing user numbers. Technologies like Network File System (NFS) or Server Message Block (SMB) implement access control lists (ACLs) and distributed authentication protocols, ensuring that access privileges can be efficiently managed across a diverse and expanding user base. Load balancing mechanisms distribute user requests across multiple servers, preventing individual nodes from becoming bottlenecks and enabling seamless scalability as the user population grows.

The evolution of cloud computing introduces unique challenges and opportunities in the realm of file system scalability. Cloud-based file systems need to adapt to the dynamic nature of cloud environments, where workloads can scale up or down rapidly based on demand. Scalable cloud file systems leverage elastic storage solutions, allowing organizations to adjust their storage capacity on-demand without significant disruptions. Cloud-native file systems like Amazon S3 or Azure Blob Storage provide scalable and durable object storage services, catering to the needs of cloud-native applications and facilitating seamless scaling in response to changing requirements.

Moreover, the emergence of containerization and orchestration platforms like Kubernetes has spurred the development of scalable file systems that align with the principles of containerized environments. Containerized applications often require shared storage volumes that can scale dynamically as the number of containers or instances grows. Scalable container storage solutions, such as Kubernetes Persistent Volumes or distributed storage systems integrated with container orchestration platforms, ensure that file systems can scale seamlessly with the proliferation of containerized workloads.

Scalability considerations extend beyond storage capacity and performance to encompass data access patterns and retrieval efficiency. In environments with diverse workloads and varied access patterns, file systems need to adapt to provide optimal access speed for different types of data. Scalable file systems leverage techniques such as tiered storage, where frequently accessed data is stored on high-performance storage tiers, while less frequently accessed data is migrated to lower-cost, high-capacity tiers. This tiered approach optimizes both performance and cost, aligning with the varying access needs of different data sets in growing environments.

The choice of file system architecture plays a pivotal role in addressing scalability considerations. Monolithic file systems, where a single server manages all aspects of file storage and retrieval, may face limitations in handling large-scale, distributed workloads. Scalable file systems often adopt a distributed architecture, where data is distributed across multiple nodes or servers. Distributed file systems like Google File System (GFS) or Hadoop Distributed File System (HDFS) are designed to scale horizontally by adding more nodes to the cluster, ensuring that both storage capacity and processing power can be expanded seamlessly as demands grow.

Additionally, the integration of parallel file processing capabilities contributes to performance scalability in growing environments. Scalable file systems incorporate parallel file processing techniques, enabling the concurrent execution of read and write operations across multiple nodes. This parallelism ensures that performance scales linearly with the addition of more processing nodes, providing an efficient and responsive solution for workloads characterized by large-scale data processing or analytics.

Scalability considerations also intersect with fault tolerance and reliability, especially in distributed or networked file systems. As the number of nodes increases, the probability of node failures or network disruptions rises. Scalable file systems implement strategies for data redundancy, data replication, and fault tolerance mechanisms to ensure data durability and availability in the face of hardware or network failures. Technologies like RAID (Redundant Array of Independent Disks) or distributed file systems with replication features enhance reliability and maintain data integrity even in the event of node failures.

Furthermore, the adaptability of file systems to emerging storage technologies contributes to scalability in growing environments. The evolution from traditional hard disk drives (HDDs) to solid-state drives (SSDs) and Non-Volatile Memory Express (NVMe) devices introduces opportunities for enhanced performance and scalability. Scalable file systems leverage the characteristics of these advanced storage technologies, optimizing data access patterns and taking advantage of the increased speed and throughput offered by SSDs and NVMe devices.

In conclusion, scalability considerations for file systems in growing environments encompass a spectrum of dimensions, ranging from capacity and performance scalability to handling increasing numbers of users, files, or concurrent access scenarios. Modern file systems adopt distributed architectures, parallel processing capabilities, and adaptive storage strategies to seamlessly scale in response to evolving demands. The challenges and opportunities presented by cloud computing, containerization, and advanced storage technologies further influence the landscape of file system scalability. As organizations navigate the complexities of managing expanding data volumes and diverse workloads, the design and deployment of scalable file systems stand as a cornerstone in building resilient, efficient, and responsive storage solutions for the dynamic computing environments of the future.

Chapter 5: Security Measures: Safeguarding File Systems

Overview of access control lists (ACLs) and permissions in file systems.

An access control list (ACL) and permissions in file systems form the bedrock of security measures, dictating how resources are accessed and manipulated within a computing environment. At their core, ACLs and permissions regulate the level of access granted to users or groups, safeguarding sensitive data and system integrity. Permissions, intrinsic to file systems, are the basic building blocks, determining who can read, write, or execute files and directories. The trio of permissions—read, write, and execute—correspond to different actions users can perform on a file. Read permission allows viewing the file's content, write permission permits modification, and execute permission enables the execution of a file if it is a program or script. These permissions are assigned separately for the file owner, the group associated with the file, and others, providing a granular level of control.

ACLs, while extending the foundational principles of permissions, introduce a more nuanced and flexible approach to access control. ACLs are a mechanism for specifying fine-grained access rights for users or groups beyond the standard owner-group-others paradigm. They empower administrators with the ability to tailor access permissions for specific individuals or subsets of users, facilitating a more sophisticated security model. In addition to the traditional read, write, and execute permissions, ACLs often include additional permissions such as delete, change permissions, and take ownership, affording administrators an expansive toolkit for crafting precise access policies.

The interplay between permissions and ACLs manifests in scenarios where complex access requirements arise. For instance, a file containing sensitive financial information may necessitate restricted access to a subset of users within a department, while allowing broader read-only access to others. Here, traditional permissions might prove inadequate, and ACLs step in to provide a supplementary layer of control. ACLs are associated with specific files or directories, augmenting or refining the permissions assigned at the standard level. This duality offers a versatile solution, accommodating both straightforward access scenarios and more intricate access management needs within the same file system.

Understanding the mechanics of permissions and ACLs involves recognizing the hierarchical structure inherent in file systems. At the top of this hierarchy is the superuser or root, who wields absolute control over the system and its resources. Below, each file or directory has an owner, a designated group, and a category of 'others' or the rest of the world. The owner, often the creator of the file, is bestowed with primary control and can delegate specific access rights to others. The group provides a means of organizing users with shared access needs, streamlining permission assignments. Meanwhile, the 'others' category encompasses all users who don't fall into the owner or group designation.

Assigning permissions within this hierarchical framework involves manipulating the access modes of a file using symbolic or octal notation. Symbolic notation employs letters to represent the permission types (r, w, x) and the characters u (user), g (group), and o (others) to specify the target. Octal notation condenses this information into a three-digit number, with each digit representing the sum of permissions for the owner, group, and others, respectively.

This numerical approach simplifies permission assignments but lacks the specificity that symbolic notation affords, especially when dealing with ACLs.

ACLs bring a degree of nuance by introducing named users and groups into the access control equation. Each entry in an ACL consists of a user or group identifier paired with a set of permissions, allowing for more detailed access management. These entries can be associated with specific users or groups, extending the scope of control beyond the traditional owner, group, and others framework. In this way, ACLs empower administrators to refine access rights based on organizational structures, project teams, or other criteria, fostering a more tailored and adaptable security posture.

The collaborative nature of modern computing environments necessitates effective control over shared resources, and ACLs shine in scenarios where collaboration intersects with nuanced access requirements. For instance, a shared project directory may require different levels of access for team members, with some having read-only permissions and others having write or delete capabilities. In such cases, ACLs enable the precise delineation of access privileges, ensuring that each user or group interacts with the shared resource according to their role or responsibilities.

While ACLs offer enhanced granularity, their effective deployment requires careful consideration. The potential for complexity arises as multiple ACL entries can coexist, each specifying distinct access rights for different users or groups. In situations where conflicts or ambiguities arise, file systems typically follow a set of rules to resolve these issues, with some systems prioritizing specific entries over others. Administrators must navigate these intricacies to construct ACLs that align with organizational policies and security best practices.

Additionally, the concept of inheritance plays a crucial role in ACLs, dictating how permissions propagate down the directory hierarchy. Inherited ACLs simplify the management of access control by allowing permissions assigned to a higher-level directory to automatically apply to its subdirectories and files. This hierarchical inheritance streamlines access management, ensuring consistency and reducing administrative overhead. However, administrators must exercise caution, as indiscriminate inheritance may lead to unintended consequences or potential security vulnerabilities. A nuanced understanding of how ACL inheritance operates is imperative for crafting robust access control policies.

As file systems have evolved, so too have the tools and interfaces for managing permissions and ACLs. Command-line utilities like chmod, chown, and setfacl provide administrators with the means to modify access rights and ACLs. Graphical interfaces, integrated into modern file browsers or system administration tools, offer a more user-friendly approach for those less familiar with command-line operations. These interfaces often present visual representations of permissions and ACLs, making it easier to comprehend and manage access control settings.

In the realm of networked file systems, such as those utilizing NFS or SMB protocols, the interplay between permissions, ACLs, and network-based access introduces additional considerations. Networked file systems must contend with issues of authentication, authorization, and secure data transmission. The seamless integration of ACLs into networked environments enables organizations to extend their access control policies across distributed systems, ensuring that users connecting remotely adhere to the same access rules as those accessing resources locally.

Ultimately, the robust implementation of permissions and ACLs is indispensable for maintaining the confidentiality, integrity, and availability of data in file systems. These access control mechanisms, while distinct, complement each other to create a comprehensive security framework. Permissions, rooted in the traditional Unix-style model, lay the groundwork with simplicity and universality. ACLs, offering a more intricate and adaptable approach, cater to the multifaceted access requirements of contemporary computing environments. Together, they empower administrators to tailor access control policies, balancing the imperative for security with the practicalities of collaborative and dynamic computing landscapes.

How file systems regulate user and group access to files and directories.

File systems serve as the gatekeepers of data access in computing environments, employing a multifaceted approach to regulate user and group access to files and directories. At the heart of this regulatory framework lies a set of permissions, a fundamental concept deeply ingrained in the architecture of file systems. Permissions, a legacy of Unix-style file systems, define the actions users and groups can perform on files and directories—reading, writing, and executing. This triad of permissions constitutes the bedrock of user and group access control, dictating the level of interaction with file system resources. Each file or directory, at its most basic level, is associated with three sets of permissions: one for the owner, another for the group to which it belongs, and a third for all other users. This tripartite structure provides a hierarchical and granular approach to access control, enabling administrators to tailor permissions according to the principles of least privilege, where users are granted only the minimum access necessary for their tasks.

For the owner of a file or directory, permissions translate into a degree of control commensurate with the role of creator or primary custodian. The owner is granted the ability to read the file's content, modify its contents, and execute it if it is a program or script. This level of control aligns with the owner's inherent responsibility for the data or processes encapsulated within the file. Whether crafting a document, compiling code, or generating logs, the owner exercises a certain dominion over the file, shaping its content and functionality.

This ownership extends beyond mere possession; it embodies a stewardship role, as the owner is entrusted with the integrity and security of the file.

The second tier of permissions pertains to the group associated with the file or directory. Groups offer a mechanism for organizing users with shared access requirements, streamlining permission assignments and fostering collaboration. The group permissions mirror those of the owner, encompassing read, write, and execute capabilities. This symmetry allows for a unified access model within the group, simplifying the task of managing permissions for a set of users with common needs. Consequently, group membership becomes a pivotal factor in shaping access rights. Group permissions are particularly potent in scenarios where multiple users collaborate on shared projects or share common data repositories, providing a means to enforce consistency in access control within a specific subset of users.

The third and final layer of permissions applies to all other users, constituting the remainder of the computing environment beyond the file owner and associated group. Often referred to as 'others,' this category encapsulates users who do not fall within the owner or group designations. The permissions assigned to others determine the access rights of anyone outside the owner or group affiliation. Here, the principles of openness and inclusivity come into play. Permissions for others may be configured to allow or restrict access based on the specific requirements of the file or directory. In a read-only scenario, others can view the file's content, but any modifications or executions are curtailed, preserving the file's integrity and functionality.

The orchestration of these permissions relies on a triad of symbols—r (read), w (write), and x (execute)—conjoined to delineate access rights. The symbolic notation is applied to the owner, group, and others in a sequential fashion, encapsulating the permission settings for each category. For instance, a permission setting of 'rwr—r—' signifies that the owner has read and write permissions, the group has read-only access, and others possess read-only access as well. This symbolic notation serves as a concise representation of the access matrix, offering a quick and standardized method for conveying permission settings.

While the traditional Unix-style permissions provide a robust foundation for access control, the evolving landscape of computing environments demands additional flexibility and nuance. Enter the concept of Access Control Lists (ACLs), an augmentation of the conventional permissions model. ACLs introduce a more sophisticated mechanism for specifying fine-grained access rights, accommodating scenarios where the standard owner-group-others paradigm falls short. ACLs extend beyond the simplicity of the traditional model by allowing administrators to assign specific access rights to individual users or groups on a per-file or per-directory basis.

The interplay between standard permissions and ACLs unfolds in situations where nuanced access requirements surface. For example, a file containing sensitive financial information may necessitate restricted access to a subset of users within a department, while allowing broader read-only access to others. In such instances, standard permissions alone might prove insufficient, and ACLs step in to provide an additional layer of control. ACLs are associated with specific files or directories, supplementing or refining the permissions assigned at the standard level. This tandem approach offers a versatile solution, accommodating both straightforward access scenarios and more intricate access management needs within the same file system.

The mechanics of ACLs introduce the concept of named users and groups into the access control equation, deviating from the numerical identifiers employed in standard permissions. Each entry in an ACL consists of a user or group identifier paired with a set of permissions, allowing for more detailed access management. These entries can be associated with specific users or groups, expanding the scope of control beyond the traditional owner, group, and others framework. In this way, ACLs empower administrators to craft access policies that align with organizational structures, project teams, or other criteria, fostering a more tailored and adaptable security posture.

ACLs, by design, exhibit a higher degree of granularity, reflecting the increasing complexity of access control needs in modern computing environments. Their deployment requires careful consideration, as multiple ACL entries can coexist, each specifying distinct access rights for different users or groups. Conflicts or ambiguities may arise, necessitating adherence to a set of rules to resolve these issues. While the complexity of ACLs introduces challenges, the benefits of enhanced access control precision and adaptability outweigh the inherent intricacies, especially in environments where diverse access scenarios abound.

Understanding the hierarchical structure inherent in file systems illuminates the intricate dance between permissions and ACLs. At the pinnacle of this hierarchy is the superuser or root, an entity endowed with absolute control over the system and its resources. Below, each file or directory assumes an identity with an owner, a designated group, and a category of 'others' or the rest of the world. This hierarchical arrangement permeates the fabric of access control, dictating the relationships and interactions among users and groups within the file system.

The hierarchical nature extends beyond individual files to encompass entire directory structures, introducing the concept of inheritance. Inherited permissions simplify access management by allowing permissions assigned to a higher-level directory to automatically apply to its subdirectories and files. This hierarchical inheritance ensures consistency and reduces administrative overhead, as changes made at the top propagate down the directory tree. However, administrators must exercise caution, as indiscriminate inheritance may lead to unintended consequences or potential security vulnerabilities. A nuanced understanding of how permissions and ACL inheritance operate is imperative for constructing robust access control policies.

The tools and interfaces for managing permissions and ACLs have evolved in tandem with the sophistication of file systems. Command-line utilities like chmod, chown, and setfacl provide administrators with the means to modify access rights and ACLs, offering granular control over the file system's security posture. Graphical interfaces, integrated into modern file browsers or system administration tools, present visual representations of permissions and ACLs, simplifying the comprehension and management of access control settings. These interfaces empower a broader spectrum of users, including those less familiar with command-line operations, to participate in access control decisions.

In the realm of networked file systems, where collaborative computing scenarios abound, the principles of user and group access regulation intertwine with issues of authentication, authorization, and secure data transmission. Networked file systems, leveraging protocols such as NFS or SMB, extend access control policies across distributed systems, ensuring that users connecting remotely adhere to the same access rules as those accessing resources locally. The seamless integration of permissions and ACLs into networked environments underscores their universality and adaptability, fostering a cohesive access control paradigm irrespective of the physical or geographical distribution of resources.

As computing environments continue to evolve, user and group access regulation remains a cornerstone in the design of secure and collaborative systems. The fusion of traditional permissions with the nuanced capabilities of ACLs reflects a commitment to adaptability, enabling file systems to accommodate the diverse access control needs of modern organizations. The triad of owner, group, and others, augmented by the flexibility of ACLs, provides a versatile and scalable framework for shaping access policies in response to the ever-changing landscape of data, collaboration, and security in contemporary computing.

Implementing encryption to secure data at rest.

Implementing encryption to secure data at rest is a critical measure in safeguarding sensitive information stored on various storage devices, ranging from hard drives and solid-state drives to external drives and cloud storage solutions. At its core, data at rest encryption is designed to protect data when it is stored and not actively being used, mitigating the risks associated with unauthorized access, theft, or compromise. The implementation of encryption involves converting plaintext data into ciphertext using cryptographic algorithms, rendering it unreadable without the appropriate decryption key. This process establishes a robust layer of defense, ensuring that even if physical access to the storage medium is obtained, the data remains unintelligible to unauthorized entities.

One of the prevalent methodologies for implementing data at rest encryption is Full Disk Encryption (FDE), a comprehensive approach that encrypts an entire storage device. FDE ensures that all data, including the operating system, applications, and user files, is encrypted seamlessly, without necessitating individual file or folder selection. Operating system integration facilitates a transparent encryption process, with users typically prompted to enter a decryption key or password during the system's boot-up sequence. FDE protects against various threats, including theft of the physical device or unauthorized access in case the device is repurposed or discarded, ensuring the confidentiality and integrity of the entire storage medium.

Another approach to data at rest encryption involves encrypting specific volumes or partitions on a storage device rather than the entire disk. This method, known as Volume Encryption, offers a more granular control over encryption policies, allowing users to select specific volumes or partitions to secure. Volume encryption is particularly useful in scenarios where certain data needs heightened protection, and the overhead of encrypting the entire disk is deemed unnecessary. It provides a balance between security and flexibility, allowing organizations to tailor encryption strategies based on the sensitivity of data stored in different volumes.

File-level encryption is yet another approach, focusing on encrypting individual files or directories rather than entire volumes or disks. This method offers the highest level of granularity, permitting users to select specific files or folders for encryption. Each encrypted file or directory is protected independently, providing a level of flexibility suitable for environments where specific files contain highly sensitive information. File-level encryption is often implemented through software-based solutions or integrated into applications, enabling users to encrypt and decrypt files seamlessly within their normal workflow.

Within the realm of data at rest encryption, the choice of encryption algorithms is paramount. Modern encryption standards, such as Advanced Encryption Standard (AES), are widely adopted for their robustness and resilience against cryptographic attacks. AES, in particular, supports key lengths of 128, 192, or 256 bits, with longer key lengths providing higher levels of security. The selection of an appropriate key length is a crucial aspect of encryption implementation, striking a balance between security and computational efficiency. Organizations must also consider compliance requirements and industry standards when choosing encryption algorithms, ensuring alignment with best practices and regulatory frameworks.

Key management is a central component of data at rest encryption, encompassing the generation, distribution, storage, and protection of encryption keys. Encryption keys are the linchpin of the encryption process, with the encryption key used to encrypt the data and the corresponding decryption key used to revert the data to its original form. Effective key management ensures the secure storage and transmission of keys, guarding against unauthorized access and potential vulnerabilities. Key management systems may involve hardware-based security modules (HSMs), secure key vaults, or cryptographic key management services, providing a secure repository for encryption keys and enforcing access controls to prevent unauthorized usage.

The concept of a Trusted Platform Module (TPM) adds an additional layer of security to data at rest encryption by providing a secure enclave for storing encryption keys. TPM is a hardware-based security feature embedded in modern computers that enables secure generation and storage of cryptographic keys. It ensures that encryption keys are tied to specific hardware, preventing unauthorized access even if the storage device is physically moved to another system. TPM enhances the overall security posture of data at rest encryption by safeguarding against key extraction or compromise, adding a hardware-rooted layer of trust.

The integration of hardware-based encryption accelerators or self-encrypting drives (SEDs) further enhances the performance and security of data at rest encryption. Hardware-based encryption offloads the encryption and decryption processes from the main processor to specialized components, minimizing the impact on system performance. SEDs, on the other hand, are storage devices with embedded encryption capabilities, ensuring that all data written to the drive is automatically encrypted, and only accessible with the correct authentication credentials. These hardware-centric approaches contribute to a seamless and efficient implementation of data at rest encryption, offering robust protection without compromising system responsiveness.

In cloud computing environments, the dynamics of data at rest encryption are further nuanced. Cloud Storage Providers (CSPs) typically offer encryption options to secure data stored in their infrastructure. Server-Side Encryption (SSE) is a common approach, wherein the CSP is responsible for encrypting and decrypting data on behalf of the user. SSE may involve the use of CSP-managed keys or customer-managed keys, providing users with varying degrees of control over the encryption process. Client-Side Encryption, on the other hand, empowers users to encrypt data locally before uploading it to the cloud. This approach ensures that the data remains encrypted throughout its journey to the cloud and is only decrypted when accessed by the user with the appropriate credentials.

While data at rest encryption provides robust protection against unauthorized access, its effectiveness hinges on secure and well-managed cryptographic keys. Key rotation, the periodic replacement of encryption keys, is a crucial practice to mitigate the impact of potential key compromises. Key rotation ensures that even if a key is compromised, its lifespan is limited, reducing the window of vulnerability. Robust key management policies also encompass secure key storage, backup procedures, and access controls, safeguarding keys against loss or unauthorized disclosure.

Audit trails and logging mechanisms play a pivotal role in monitoring and validating the effectiveness of data at rest encryption implementations. Comprehensive logging practices capture events related to key management, encryption, and access attempts, providing administrators with visibility into the security posture of encrypted data. Regular audits of these logs aid in identifying anomalous activities, potential security incidents, or deviations from established policies. The integration of encryption status indicators within system monitoring tools contributes to a proactive approach, allowing administrators to promptly address any issues related to the encryption of data at rest.

The implementation of data at rest encryption also intersects with regulatory compliance requirements, with various industry standards mandating the use of encryption to protect sensitive information. Regulations such as the Health Insurance Portability and Accountability Act (HIPAA) in healthcare, the Payment Card Industry Data Security Standard (PCI DSS) in financial transactions, and the General Data Protection Regulation (GDPR) in the European Union emphasize the importance of encryption as a fundamental security measure. Organizations operating within regulated environments must align their data at rest encryption practices with the specific requirements stipulated by relevant compliance frameworks.

In conclusion, the implementation of encryption to secure data at rest is a multifaceted endeavor that encompasses diverse approaches, ranging from Full Disk Encryption to Volume Encryption and File-Level Encryption. The selection of encryption algorithms, key management strategies, and integration with hardware-based security features significantly influences the efficacy and resilience of data at rest encryption. The evolving landscape of cloud computing introduces additional considerations, with CSPs offering encryption options that demand careful evaluation. Key rotation, audit trails, and compliance alignment further contribute to the holistic approach required to establish a robust and effective data at rest encryption strategy. As organizations navigate the complex terrain of securing sensitive information, the conscientious implementation of encryption at rest stands as a cornerstone in fortifying the confidentiality and integrity of stored data against a myriad of potential threats.

File-level and disk-level encryption techniques.

File-level and disk-level encryption are crucial techniques employed to safeguard sensitive data from unauthorized access and potential security breaches. File-level encryption involves the encryption of individual files or folders, ensuring that only authorized users with the appropriate decryption key or password can access the protected content. This method offers a granular approach, allowing users to selectively encrypt specific files or directories, thus maintaining flexibility in securing sensitive information. One widely used file-level encryption technique is Advanced Encryption Standard (AES), a symmetric encryption algorithm known for its robust security and widespread adoption.

On the other hand, disk-level encryption operates at a broader level, encrypting the entire storage device or disk where data is stored. This comprehensive approach ensures that all data on the disk is protected, irrespective of individual file or folder boundaries. Full Disk Encryption (FDE) is a common disk-level encryption technique that encrypts the entire disk, rendering the data unreadable without the appropriate decryption key. BitLocker and FileVault are examples of FDE implementations on Windows and macOS platforms, respectively. Disk-level encryption provides a seamless and transparent layer of security, as it encrypts data in real-time, reducing the risk of potential vulnerabilities arising during the file transfer process.

The implementation of file-level and disk-level encryption techniques involves a combination of encryption algorithms, key management strategies, and secure protocols to establish a robust security infrastructure. Encryption algorithms play a pivotal role in converting plaintext data into ciphertext, making it incomprehensible to unauthorized entities. AES, a symmetric encryption algorithm, utilizes a specified key size (128, 192, or 256 bits) to encrypt and decrypt data. Asymmetric encryption algorithms, such as RSA, employ a pair of public and private keys, enhancing security by separating the key used for encryption from the one used for decryption.

Effective key management is essential to the success of any encryption system. It involves the generation, distribution, storage, and rotation of encryption keys to ensure their confidentiality and integrity. Key management systems must be designed to prevent unauthorized access to keys while facilitating seamless access for authorized users. Public Key Infrastructure (PKI) is commonly employed for key management in asymmetric encryption, providing a framework for key generation, distribution, and validation through the use of digital certificates.

Secure protocols play a crucial role in facilitating the encrypted communication and exchange of data between systems. Transport Layer Security (TLS) and its predecessor, Secure Sockets Layer (SSL), are widely used protocols for securing data transmission over networks. These protocols establish encrypted channels, ensuring the confidentiality and integrity of data during transit. Implementing secure protocols is particularly vital in scenarios where data is transferred between different devices or over the internet, as it mitigates the risk of interception and unauthorized access during transmission.

File-level encryption provides a targeted approach to securing specific files or folders, making it particularly suitable for scenarios where selective protection is required. It allows organizations to prioritize the encryption of sensitive data while leaving less critical information unencrypted for ease of access. However, the challenge lies in managing encryption keys effectively to avoid potential vulnerabilities. If a user loses their decryption key, accessing encrypted files becomes impossible, emphasizing the need for robust key recovery mechanisms and secure storage practices.

Disk-level encryption, on the other hand, offers a comprehensive solution by encrypting the entire storage medium. This approach ensures that all data, regardless of its nature or location on the disk, is protected uniformly. Full Disk Encryption (FDE) provides a transparent layer of security, as it encrypts data in real-time during read and write operations. While this method simplifies the encryption process for end-users, it requires careful consideration of key management and recovery mechanisms to prevent data loss in case of key-related issues.

The choice between file-level and disk-level encryption often depends on the specific security requirements and use cases of an organization. In scenarios where selective protection of sensitive files is critical, file-level encryption may be preferred. Conversely, disk-level encryption is suitable for situations where a comprehensive and transparent layer of security is necessary, especially in environments where entire disks need to be safeguarded against theft or unauthorized access. Some organizations may even opt for a combination of both techniques to achieve a layered security approach, leveraging the strengths of each method to create a robust defense against potential threats.

The deployment of encryption techniques raises concerns about performance overhead, especially in environments where computational resources are limited. File-level encryption, due to its targeted nature, may incur less performance impact compared to disk-level encryption, which involves encrypting and decrypting all data on the disk. However, advancements in hardware acceleration, such as the use of Trusted Platform Modules (TPM) and dedicated encryption hardware, mitigate these concerns by offloading encryption tasks to specialized components, ensuring optimal system performance even in heavily encrypted environments.

In conclusion, file-level and disk-level encryption techniques are indispensable components of a comprehensive data security strategy. File-level encryption provides a selective and granular approach to securing specific files or folders, while disk-level encryption ensures the protection of entire storage devices. The choice between these techniques depends on the specific security requirements and use cases of an organization. Regardless of the chosen approach, effective key management, encryption algorithms, and secure protocols are essential elements in building a robust and resilient encryption infrastructure. As technology evolves, encryption techniques will continue to play a pivotal role in safeguarding sensitive data against the ever-growing threats in the digital landscape.

The role of audit trails in tracking file access and modifications.

Audit trails play a pivotal role in the realm of cybersecurity, specifically in tracking and monitoring file access and modifications. These digital records serve as a comprehensive and chronological account of activities within a system, providing valuable insights into user interactions with files and directories. The primary purpose of audit trails is to enhance accountability, detect security incidents, and facilitate forensic analysis. By meticulously logging events related to file access and modifications, audit trails contribute to the establishment of a robust security posture, enabling organizations to identify potential security breaches, unauthorized access, or malicious activities.

One of the fundamental aspects of audit trails is the tracking of file access. This involves recording every instance when a user interacts with a file, be it opening, reading, or executing. Audit trails capture crucial details such as the user identity, timestamp, and the specific action performed on the file. This level of granularity allows administrators and security professionals to reconstruct the sequence of events, aiding in the investigation of suspicious activities or compliance audits. Additionally, file access tracking is instrumental in enforcing data privacy policies and ensuring that sensitive information is only accessed by authorized individuals.

In the context of file modifications, audit trails serve as a digital fingerprint of changes made to files over time. Every alteration, whether it involves editing, deleting, or creating a file, is logged in the audit trail with pertinent details. This not only aids in identifying unauthorized modifications but also facilitates version control and rollback in the event of inadvertent changes or data corruption. By maintaining a detailed record of file modifications, organizations can uphold data integrity, ensuring that any alterations to critical files are traceable and accountable.

The implementation of audit trails is closely tied to regulatory compliance requirements in various industries. Many regulatory frameworks, such as the Health Insurance Portability and Accountability Act (HIPAA) and the General Data Protection Regulation (GDPR), mandate the establishment of robust auditing mechanisms to track and monitor access to sensitive information. Compliance with these regulations is essential for organizations to avoid legal repercussions and demonstrate a commitment to safeguarding user privacy and sensitive data. Audit trails, therefore, serve as a crucial tool in meeting these compliance requirements by providing an auditable record of file access and modifications.

Another important dimension of audit trails is user accountability. Each entry in the audit trail includes information about the user responsible for the action, helping organizations attribute specific activities to individuals. This accountability not only discourages malicious behavior but also aids in investigations when security incidents occur. Moreover, audit trails contribute to creating a culture of responsibility within an organization, fostering awareness among users about the significance of adhering to security policies and best practices.

In the event of a security incident or data breach, audit trails become invaluable tools for forensic analysis. Security professionals can leverage these records to trace the origins of an incident, identify the extent of the compromise, and understand the tactics employed by attackers. Forensic analysis of audit trails enables organizations to learn from security incidents, improve their incident response capabilities, and implement proactive measures to prevent similar occurrences in the future. Additionally, audit trails provide crucial evidence that can be used in legal proceedings or investigations, aiding law enforcement in prosecuting cybercriminals.

The effectiveness of audit trails in tracking file access and modifications is contingent upon careful design and implementation. Organizations must define clear audit policies, specifying which events should be logged and the level of detail required. Configuring audit trails to capture relevant information without overwhelming the system with excessive data is a delicate balance that requires thoughtful consideration. Furthermore, secure storage and protection of audit trail data are imperative to prevent tampering or unauthorized access that could compromise the integrity of the records.

Integration with Security Information and Event Management (SIEM) systems enhances the utility of audit trails by providing real-time analysis and correlation of events across an entire IT infrastructure. SIEM systems enable organizations to proactively detect anomalies, potential security threats, or patterns indicative of malicious activities. The synergy between audit trails and SIEM solutions creates a powerful defense mechanism, allowing organizations to respond swiftly to emerging security challenges and fortify their overall cybersecurity posture.

Despite their undeniable benefits, audit trails are not without challenges. The sheer volume of data generated by audit trails can be overwhelming, requiring organizations to implement robust log management and analysis solutions. Additionally, the sensitivity of audit trail data necessitates stringent access controls and encryption to prevent unauthorized tampering or exploitation. Striking a balance between collecting sufficient information for comprehensive auditing and minimizing the impact on system performance remains a continual challenge for organizations striving to implement effective audit trail mechanisms.

In conclusion, audit trails play a critical role in tracking file access and modifications, serving as the digital backbone of cybersecurity efforts. By meticulously recording user interactions with files, audit trails enhance accountability, facilitate forensic analysis, and contribute to regulatory compliance. The granular details captured in audit trails not only aid in detecting and responding to security incidents but also empower organizations to learn from such events and proactively strengthen their security defenses. As technology evolves and cybersecurity threats become more sophisticated, the role of audit trails in securing digital assets continues to be indispensable, offering a reliable and comprehensive approach to monitoring and safeguarding file-related activities within the digital landscape.

Logging mechanisms for detecting unauthorized activities and security breaches.

Logging mechanisms serve as a cornerstone in the proactive detection of unauthorized activities and security breaches within the realm of cybersecurity. These mechanisms involve the systematic recording of events and activities occurring within an information system, generating a chronological record known as logs. The primary purpose of logging is to provide visibility into the inner workings of a system, enabling security professionals to analyze, monitor, and detect anomalous behavior that may indicate a potential security threat. By implementing robust logging practices, organizations can establish a comprehensive audit trail, aiding in the identification of unauthorized access, malicious activities, and security incidents.

One crucial aspect of logging for security detection is the recording of user authentication events. These logs capture information related to user login attempts, successful logins, and failed authentication events. Monitoring authentication logs is essential for detecting unauthorized access attempts, such as brute-force attacks or the use of stolen credentials. Anomalous patterns, such as multiple failed login attempts from a single IP address, can be indicative of malicious activities, prompting security teams to take proactive measures to mitigate potential threats. Additionally, monitoring successful logins is crucial for identifying unauthorized access by legitimate users, as compromised credentials may be exploited by adversaries.

Beyond user authentication events, logging mechanisms extend to the monitoring of privilege changes and authorization activities.

Tracking changes in user privileges or permissions, such as the elevation of user roles or access levels, is vital for detecting unauthorized modifications that may grant adversaries excessive privileges. Authorization logs provide insights into which users are accessing specific resources and the actions they are performing. Analyzing these logs helps identify unusual or suspicious activities that may indicate a security breach, such as unauthorized access to sensitive files or systems.

File and data access logs are integral components of logging mechanisms for security detection. These logs document interactions with files, including reads, writes, and modifications. Monitoring file access logs allows security professionals to identify unusual or unauthorized access patterns, such as a user accessing an unusually high number of files or attempting to access files outside their normal scope of responsibilities. Additionally, tracking changes to sensitive data through modification logs enables the rapid detection of unauthorized alterations or deletions, serving as an early warning system for potential security incidents.

Network activity logs play a crucial role in detecting unauthorized activities that occur at the network level. These logs record communication between devices, including incoming and outgoing traffic, source and destination IP addresses, and protocols used. Unusual network patterns, such as a sudden surge in data transfers or communication with known malicious IP addresses, can be indicative of a security breach or a compromised system. By analyzing network activity logs, security professionals can swiftly identify and respond to unauthorized network access, lateral movement within the network, or suspicious outbound connections.

The integration of logging mechanisms with Intrusion Detection Systems (IDS) and Intrusion Prevention Systems (IPS) enhances the ability to detect and respond to security breaches. IDS monitors network and system activities, comparing them against predefined signatures or behavioral patterns indicative of known threats. When potential security threats are detected, IDS generates alerts that are logged for further analysis. Similarly, IPS actively blocks or mitigates identified threats and logs the details of these preventive actions. The synergy between logging mechanisms and IDS/IPS systems creates a proactive defense mechanism, allowing organizations to swiftly respond to emerging security challenges and fortify their overall cybersecurity posture.

Application-level logging is indispensable for detecting unauthorized activities within software applications or services. These logs capture details about user interactions, application errors, and system events specific to the software. Monitoring application logs helps identify unusual or malicious behavior, such as repeated login failures, abnormal data input, or unauthorized API calls. By analyzing application logs, security teams can gain insights into potential vulnerabilities, identify exploitation attempts, and respond promptly to mitigate the impact of security incidents.

Security Information and Event Management (SIEM) systems play a central role in the aggregation, analysis, and correlation of logs from diverse sources. SIEM solutions provide a centralized platform for managing log data, enabling security professionals to correlate events across an entire IT infrastructure. This correlation enhances the ability to detect complex attack patterns and identify security incidents that may not be apparent when analyzing individual log sources in isolation. SIEM systems also facilitate real-time alerting, allowing security teams to respond promptly to potential threats and conduct in-depth investigations into suspicious activities.

While logging mechanisms are instrumental in detecting unauthorized activities, the effectiveness of these mechanisms hinges on the quality of log data and the implementation of appropriate logging policies. Organizations must define clear logging policies, specifying which events should be logged, the level of detail required, and the retention period for log data. Configuring logging mechanisms to capture relevant information without overwhelming the system with excessive data is crucial for efficient analysis and detection. Furthermore, secure storage and protection of log data are imperative to prevent tampering or unauthorized access that could compromise the integrity of the records.

The continuous monitoring of logs and the timely analysis of log data are vital components of a proactive security strategy. Security professionals must actively review logs to identify patterns, trends, or anomalies that may indicate unauthorized activities or security breaches. Regular log analysis not only aids in the early detection of security incidents but also provides valuable insights into the tactics, techniques, and procedures employed by adversaries. Furthermore, organizations should conduct periodic log reviews and audits to ensure the ongoing effectiveness of logging mechanisms and identify opportunities for refinement.

Despite the evident advantages of logging mechanisms in detecting unauthorized activities, challenges persist in their implementation. The sheer volume of log data generated by diverse sources can be overwhelming, necessitating the use of advanced analytics and machine learning techniques to automate the detection of patterns indicative of security threats. Additionally, organizations face the challenge of retaining log data for an appropriate duration, considering both compliance requirements and the need for historical analysis. Balancing the need for comprehensive logging with the constraints of storage capacity and system performance remains an ongoing consideration for security professionals.

In conclusion, logging mechanisms play a crucial role in the detection of unauthorized activities and security breaches within the dynamic landscape of cybersecurity. By systematically recording events and activities across various dimensions of an information system, logging provides a comprehensive audit trail that enables security professionals to identify anomalies, respond promptly to security incidents, and fortify the overall security posture of an organization. The integration of logging mechanisms with advanced technologies such as SIEM, IDS, and IPS enhances the proactive detection capabilities, allowing organizations to stay ahead of emerging security threats and safeguard their digital assets against the ever-evolving landscape of cyber threats. As technology continues to advance, the role of logging mechanisms in cybersecurity will remain indispensable, offering a foundational layer for building resilient and proactive defense mechanisms.

Techniques for ensuring data integrity through hash functions.

Ensuring data integrity is a critical aspect of information security, and hash functions play a fundamental role in achieving this goal. Hash functions are mathematical algorithms that take an input (or message) and produce a fixed-size string of characters, which is typically a hash value or digest. One of the primary techniques for ensuring data integrity is the use of hash functions to generate checksums or hashes for files or data sets. By calculating the hash value of a piece of data, such as a file, and storing or transmitting this hash alongside the data, users can verify the integrity of the data at a later time by recomputing the hash and comparing it to the original hash value.

The concept of a checksum involves generating a hash value for a specific set of data and then using this hash as a unique identifier for the data. When a user wants to verify the integrity of the data, they recalculate the hash and compare it to the originally generated checksum. If the two hash values match, it indicates that the data has not been altered. This technique is widely used in various scenarios, from file transfers to data storage, as it provides a quick and efficient method to detect accidental or intentional changes to data.

In the context of file verification, hash functions help maintain data integrity during transmission or storage. When a file is transmitted over a network or stored on a server, a hash value is often generated and transmitted along with the file. Recipients can then calculate the hash of the received file and compare it with the transmitted hash to ensure that the file has not been corrupted or tampered with during the transfer process. This technique is particularly useful in preventing data corruption during file downloads, ensuring that the downloaded file matches the original version.

Furthermore, hash functions are integral to the concept of digital signatures, a technique widely employed for data integrity in the context of secure communication. Digital signatures involve the use of asymmetric cryptography, where a private key is used to generate a digital signature, and a corresponding public key is used to verify the signature. Hash functions contribute to digital signatures by generating a hash value of the data to be signed. The digital signature is then created by encrypting this hash value with the private key. Recipients can use the sender's public key to decrypt and verify the signature, ensuring that the data has not been altered since the signature was generated.

In data storage environments, hash functions are applied to ensure the integrity of stored data. This is commonly achieved by calculating and storing hash values for each data block or file. Periodically, or upon retrieval, the hash values can be recalculated and compared to the stored values. Any discrepancies indicate potential data corruption or tampering. This technique is prevalent in systems that prioritize data integrity, such as file systems, databases, and archival storage solutions.

The Merkle tree, named after computer scientist Ralph Merkle, is a hierarchical structure that uses hash functions to ensure data integrity in a scalable and efficient manner. This tree-like structure organizes hash values in a way that allows efficient verification of large datasets. Each leaf node of the tree represents the hash value of a specific data block, and each non-leaf node represents the hash value of its child nodes. The root of the tree, often referred to as the Merkle root, encapsulates the entire hash structure. Verifying the integrity of a specific data block involves only calculating and comparing the relevant hash values along the path from the leaf node to the root. Merkle trees are widely employed in distributed systems, blockchain technology, and file storage systems to efficiently ensure data integrity, especially when dealing with large datasets.

Salting is a technique employed to enhance the security of hash functions, particularly in the context of password storage. While hash functions are valuable for ensuring data integrity, they are not designed to be a one-way function when used for password hashing. Salting involves adding a random value, known as a salt, to the input data before hashing. The salt is unique for each piece of data, ensuring that even identical inputs yield different hash values. This mitigates the risk of attackers using precomputed tables, known as rainbow tables, to reverse engineer hashes and discover original passwords. By incorporating salts, organizations enhance the security of password storage systems, protecting user credentials and maintaining the integrity of authentication processes.

In the realm of blockchain technology, hash functions are fundamental to the creation of blocks and the establishment of an immutable ledger. Each block in a blockchain contains a hash value that is a cryptographic summary of the block's contents. Additionally, the hash of the previous block, often referred to as the "previous hash," is included in each new block. This chaining of blocks through hash functions creates a secure and tamper-evident ledger. Altering the content of any block would necessitate changing the hash value of that block and all subsequent blocks, making the blockchain resistant to tampering and ensuring the integrity of the entire transaction history.

Despite the myriad benefits of hash functions in ensuring data integrity, it's crucial to acknowledge their vulnerability to collision attacks. A collision occurs when two different inputs produce the same hash value. While cryptographic hash functions are designed to minimize the likelihood of collisions, the emergence of more powerful computational capabilities poses a potential threat. In response to this challenge, organizations must stay vigilant and periodically transition to stronger hash functions or algorithms to maintain the resilience of their data integrity mechanisms.

In conclusion, techniques for ensuring data integrity through hash functions are multifaceted and pervasive in the realm of cybersecurity. From checksums and digital signatures to Merkle trees and password hashing with salts, hash functions are versatile tools that safeguard data against corruption, tampering, and unauthorized alterations. The application of hash functions in diverse scenarios, ranging from file transfers to blockchain technology, underscores their universal importance in modern information security. As technology evolves and security threats become more sophisticated, the role of hash functions in ensuring data integrity will continue to be indispensable, providing a robust and efficient foundation for maintaining the trustworthiness of digital information.

Periodic integrity checks to identify and rectify file corruption.

Periodic integrity checks are a vital component of data management strategies, aiming to identify and rectify file corruption in digital systems. The integrity of files, crucial for maintaining the reliability and trustworthiness of data, can be compromised due to various factors, including hardware failures, software bugs, malicious activities, or even environmental conditions. Implementing periodic integrity checks involves systematically examining files and their associated metadata to ensure that they remain unaltered and free from corruption. This proactive approach allows organizations to detect and address file integrity issues before they escalate into significant problems, minimizing the risk of data loss, ensuring the accuracy of information, and maintaining the overall health of digital assets.

One of the common techniques employed in periodic integrity checks is the use of checksums or hash functions. These mathematical algorithms generate unique identifiers, often referred to as checksums or hashes, for files based on their contents. Periodically recalculating these checksums and comparing them with the original values enables the identification of any discrepancies, indicating potential file corruption. This technique is particularly effective for detecting accidental alterations or data corruption that might occur during storage, transmission, or various data manipulation processes. By automating the process of checksum verification, organizations can conduct regular and systematic checks across large datasets without significant manual intervention.

In addition to checksums, cyclic redundancy checks (CRC) are another technique utilized for periodic integrity checks. CRC involves the generation of a checksum based on the binary data within a file. Similar to hash functions, CRC provides a unique value that serves as a fingerprint for the file's content. Periodically recalculating CRC values and comparing them to the original values allows for the detection of changes or corruption within files. CRC is commonly employed in network protocols and storage systems to verify the integrity of transmitted or stored data, contributing to the prevention of data corruption and ensuring the reliability of information.

File verification tools and utilities play a crucial role in automating and streamlining periodic integrity checks. These tools often provide a user-friendly interface for initiating integrity checks on selected files, directories, or entire storage systems. The tools leverage checksums or hash functions to verify the integrity of files, and they may generate reports detailing the status of each file, including information about any detected corruption. By integrating such tools into regular maintenance routines, organizations can systematically examine their digital assets, identify corrupted files, and take appropriate corrective actions.

The ZFS (Zettabyte File System), a file system developed by Sun Microsystems and now commonly used in various operating systems, incorporates built-in integrity checks as a core feature. ZFS uses a technique called data checksumming, where each block of data is assigned a checksum based on its content. During regular scrubbing operations, ZFS automatically compares these checksums with the stored values, identifying and correcting errors as needed. This proactive approach to integrity checks is intrinsic to the design of ZFS, providing a robust solution for ensuring data integrity in storage systems.

Periodic integrity checks are particularly crucial in environments where large volumes of critical data are stored, such as in enterprise storage systems, cloud platforms, or archival repositories. The sheer scale of data in these environments makes manual verification impractical, necessitating automated tools and processes. Implementing periodic integrity checks in these settings helps organizations identify file corruption promptly, preventing the propagation of errors and ensuring that stored data remains reliable and accurate over time.

The practice of periodic integrity checks is also essential in the context of backup and disaster recovery strategies. Organizations routinely create backups of their data to guard against data loss caused by hardware failures, human errors, or malicious activities. However, relying solely on the existence of backups is insufficient without periodic integrity checks to verify the health and accuracy of the backup data. By routinely validating the integrity of backup files and ensuring that they remain uncorrupted, organizations enhance the reliability of their disaster recovery plans and increase the likelihood of successful data restoration in the event of a catastrophe.

Digital forensics, which involves the analysis and investigation of digital evidence, heavily relies on the concept of periodic integrity checks. In legal and investigative scenarios, maintaining the integrity of digital evidence is paramount. Integrity checks are used to verify that forensic images or copies of digital evidence remain unaltered during storage and analysis. Courts and legal proceedings often demand a chain of custody, and periodic integrity checks provide a means to demonstrate the authenticity and reliability of digital evidence, ensuring its admissibility in legal proceedings.

In the domain of content distribution and software delivery, integrity checks are instrumental in guaranteeing the authenticity and security of downloaded files. When users download software, updates, or digital content, integrity checks can be performed using checksums or digital signatures. These checks verify that the downloaded files match the original versions and have not been tampered with during the download process. This practice safeguards users from potential security threats, such as the distribution of compromised or malicious files, providing a layer of trust in the integrity of the downloaded content.

Despite the evident benefits of periodic integrity checks, organizations face challenges in implementing and maintaining effective integrity verification processes. The computational resources required for checksum or hash calculations, especially in large-scale environments, may introduce performance overhead. Balancing the frequency and scope of integrity checks with system performance considerations is an ongoing challenge. Additionally, defining appropriate intervals for periodic checks and ensuring that they align with the organization's operational needs and risk tolerance is crucial for striking a balance between proactive integrity verification and resource efficiency.

Periodic integrity checks are closely tied to the broader concept of continuous monitoring in cybersecurity. While periodic checks are scheduled and routine, continuous monitoring involves real-time or near-real-time monitoring of data and systems to detect and respond to integrity issues promptly. Continuous monitoring complements periodic checks by providing a more immediate response to emerging threats or changes in the integrity of data. Together, these approaches create a comprehensive strategy for safeguarding data integrity throughout its lifecycle.

In conclusion, periodic integrity checks form a fundamental element of robust data management and cybersecurity practices. By systematically verifying the integrity of files through techniques like checksums, CRC, and automated tools, organizations can identify and rectify file corruption proactively. This approach safeguards against data loss, ensures the accuracy of information, and supports the reliability of digital assets. Whether applied in storage systems, backup strategies, digital forensics, or content distribution, periodic integrity checks play a pivotal role in maintaining the trustworthiness of digital data in the face of evolving threats and environmental challenges. As technology continues to advance, the importance of periodic integrity checks will persist, serving as a cornerstone for the ongoing security and reliability of digital information.

Establishing best practices for securing file systems.

Establishing best practices for securing file systems is paramount in safeguarding digital assets, sensitive information, and maintaining the integrity of an organization's data infrastructure. File systems serve as the foundational layer for storing and organizing data on computing devices, making them a critical target for security measures. The multifaceted nature of file system security involves a combination of access controls, encryption, monitoring, auditing, and proactive management to mitigate potential vulnerabilities and protect against various threats.

Access controls are fundamental to file system security, regulating who can access, modify, or delete files and directories. Implementing the principle of least privilege, which grants users the minimum level of access necessary for their roles, is a cornerstone of access control best practices. This approach minimizes the risk of unauthorized access and reduces the potential impact of security breaches. Additionally, organizations often employ role-based access control (RBAC) systems, where users are assigned roles with specific permissions based on their responsibilities. Regularly reviewing and updating access permissions ensures that users only retain access they legitimately require, minimizing the attack surface and enhancing overall file system security.

Encryption plays a pivotal role in protecting sensitive data stored in file systems. Utilizing encryption mechanisms, such as full disk encryption (FDE) or file-level encryption, safeguards data from unauthorized access even if the underlying storage media is compromised. FDE ensures that all data on a disk is encrypted, providing a transparent layer of security against physical theft or unauthorized access. File-level encryption, on the other hand, allows for selective encryption of specific files or directories, enabling organizations to prioritize the protection of sensitive information. Effective key management practices, including secure key storage and rotation, are crucial for maintaining the confidentiality and integrity of encrypted data.

Monitoring file system activities is essential for detecting and responding to security incidents promptly. File integrity monitoring (FIM) systems continuously assess the integrity of files and directories by comparing their current state to a baseline or known good state. Any deviations, whether due to unauthorized modifications or malware, trigger alerts for further investigation. Real-time monitoring solutions provide visibility into user activities, enabling organizations to identify anomalous behavior or potential security threats. Integrating monitoring tools with Security Information and Event Management (SIEM) systems enhances the correlation of events across the entire IT infrastructure, enabling a more comprehensive and proactive approach to file system security.

Auditing file system activities complements monitoring efforts by creating a detailed record of user interactions with files and directories. Audit logs capture information such as file access, modifications, and permission changes, providing a chronological account of events. Regularly reviewing and analyzing these logs not only aids in the detection of unauthorized activities but also contributes to forensic analysis in the event of a security incident. Implementing audit policies aligned with security and compliance requirements ensures that the audit logs capture relevant information without overwhelming the system with excessive data. Additionally, organizations should consider secure storage and protection mechanisms for audit logs to prevent tampering or unauthorized access.

Proactive management of file systems involves maintaining an up-to-date inventory of files, applying patches and updates, and regularly reviewing and updating security configurations. Organizations should conduct routine file system assessments to identify vulnerabilities, outdated software, or misconfigurations that could be exploited by attackers. This includes regularly scanning for malware or malicious files that may have infiltrated the file system. Automating routine tasks, such as software updates and vulnerability assessments, reduces the likelihood of oversights and ensures that file systems remain resilient against emerging threats.

User education and awareness are integral components of file system security best practices. Users, as the end-points of many security protocols, play a crucial role in safeguarding file systems. Training programs should educate users on security policies, safe data handling practices, and the importance of reporting any suspicious activities. Encouraging the use of strong, unique passwords, implementing multi-factor authentication (MFA), and promoting good cyber hygiene habits contribute to a culture of security awareness within the organization.

Regularly backing up data is a foundational practice for file system security. In the event of data loss due to accidental deletion, hardware failure, or a security breach, backups enable organizations to restore critical information and minimize downtime. Best practices for data backups include storing backups in a secure, offsite location, regularly testing the restoration process to ensure its efficacy, and maintaining a backup schedule that aligns with the organization's recovery objectives. This approach not only safeguards against data loss but also enhances the organization's resilience to ransomware attacks or other malicious activities that may compromise data integrity.

Implementing file system security best practices is especially critical in cloud environments, where data is often distributed across various services and storage solutions. Cloud providers typically offer a range of security features, such as access controls, encryption, and monitoring tools, which should be leveraged to augment file system security. Organizations should also conduct regular security assessments of their cloud configurations to identify and rectify misconfigurations or insecure settings that may expose sensitive data to unauthorized access.

In the context of network-attached storage (NAS) or shared file systems, securing access to shared resources is paramount. Properly configuring permissions and access controls on shared folders ensures that users only have access to the files and directories required for their roles. Additionally, monitoring and auditing shared file system activities help detect and respond to potential security incidents involving shared resources. Encryption of data in transit and implementing secure protocols for file transfers further enhances the security posture of shared file systems.

In conclusion, establishing best practices for securing file systems is a multifaceted and dynamic undertaking that requires a holistic approach encompassing access controls, encryption, monitoring, auditing, and proactive management. By adopting the principle of least privilege, implementing encryption mechanisms, and leveraging monitoring and auditing tools, organizations can detect and respond to security threats in a timely manner. Proactive management practices, user education, and regular data backups contribute to the overall resilience of file systems. In an era where data is a critical asset, securing file systems is not only a technical imperative but also a strategic necessity to safeguard against evolving cyber threats and ensure the trustworthiness of digital information.

User education and awareness to mitigate security risks.

User education and awareness play a pivotal role in mitigating security risks within the complex landscape of cybersecurity. In the interconnected and digitized world, where individuals and organizations alike rely on technology for various aspects of their daily lives and operations, the human element remains a significant factor in the overall security posture. Educating users about potential threats, instilling security best practices, and fostering a heightened awareness of cyber risks contribute to a proactive defense against a multitude of security challenges.

One of the foundational aspects of user education is the understanding of common cyber threats. Users need to be aware of the diverse range of threats they may encounter, including phishing attacks, malware, ransomware, social engineering, and other tactics employed by cybercriminals. A comprehensive awareness of these threats enables users to recognize suspicious activities, emails, or links, reducing the likelihood of falling victim to cyberattacks. Regular training sessions, workshops, or awareness campaigns can provide valuable insights into the ever-evolving threat landscape and empower users to make informed decisions to protect themselves and their organizations.

Phishing attacks, in particular, remain a pervasive threat, and user education is a critical defense mechanism. Users should be educated on how to identify phishing emails, which often attempt to deceive individuals into divulging sensitive information or downloading malicious content. Recognizing the characteristics of phishing emails, such as unusual sender addresses, grammatical errors, or urgent requests for personal information, empowers users to exercise caution and report suspicious emails to the appropriate security teams. Simulated phishing exercises, where users are exposed to controlled phishing scenarios, can reinforce these lessons and enhance their ability to discern legitimate communications from phishing attempts.

Social engineering tactics exploit human psychology to manipulate individuals into divulging confidential information or performing actions that may compromise security. User education should emphasize the various forms of social engineering, such as pretexting, baiting, quid pro quo, and tailgating. By understanding these tactics, users can develop a healthy skepticism towards unsolicited requests for information or unexpected interactions, enhancing their ability to resist manipulation. Creating a culture of skepticism and encouraging users to verify the authenticity of requests before taking any action forms a robust defense against social engineering attacks.

Passwords are a fundamental element of security, and user education should emphasize the importance of creating strong, unique passwords for different accounts. Users need to understand the risks associated with weak or reused passwords, which can lead to unauthorized access, identity theft, or compromise of sensitive data. Training programs should guide users on the principles of password hygiene, including the use of complex passwords, regular password updates, and the avoidance of easily guessable information. Implementing multi-factor authentication (MFA) is another crucial aspect of user education, as it adds an additional layer of security beyond passwords, enhancing the overall resilience against unauthorized access.

Mobile devices are ubiquitous in today's digital landscape, and users must be educated about the security risks associated with mobile usage. Awareness programs should cover topics such as secure Wi-Fi connections, the dangers of downloading apps from untrusted sources, and the importance of keeping mobile operating systems and applications up to date. Users should be cautious about accessing sensitive information or conducting financial transactions over public Wi-Fi networks, as these networks may expose them to various security threats. Educating users on the potential risks and best practices for mobile security ensures a more secure digital experience across a wide range of devices.

Remote work has become increasingly prevalent, and the shift to decentralized work environments introduces new security challenges. User education plays a crucial role in ensuring that remote workers are aware of the security risks associated with their home networks and personal devices. Training programs should cover topics such as the use of virtual private networks (VPNs), secure video conferencing practices, and the importance of securing home Wi-Fi networks with strong passwords. Users should be educated on the risks of using personal devices for work-related activities and the necessity of implementing security measures to protect sensitive organizational data.

Data privacy is a growing concern, and user education is instrumental in fostering a culture of privacy awareness. Users should understand the importance of protecting personal and sensitive information, both in professional and personal contexts. Training programs should cover topics such as data encryption, secure communication practices, and the risks associated with oversharing information on social media. Users need to be aware of privacy settings on various platforms and the implications of granting unnecessary permissions to applications. By instilling a sense of responsibility for safeguarding personal and organizational data, user education contributes to a privacy-centric mindset within the digital ecosystem.

Endpoint security is a critical component of overall cybersecurity, and users are often the first line of defense against threats targeting endpoints such as computers, laptops, and mobile devices. User education should emphasize the significance of keeping operating systems, antivirus software, and applications up to date. Users need to understand the risks of downloading files or clicking on links from unknown or untrusted sources. Training programs should also cover the importance of regular system scans and the reporting of any unusual or suspicious activities to IT or security teams. By empowering users to actively participate in endpoint security, organizations enhance their overall resilience against malware, ransomware, and other endpoint-targeted threats.

Data protection regulations, such as the General Data Protection Regulation (GDPR) and the Health Insurance Portability and Accountability Act (HIPAA), impose legal obligations on organizations to safeguard sensitive information. User education should provide an overview of these regulations and their implications for handling and processing personal or sensitive data. Users need to understand their role in compliance efforts, including the proper handling of data, obtaining consent when required, and promptly reporting any data breaches or incidents to the appropriate authorities. Educating users on the legal and ethical considerations surrounding data protection promotes a culture of compliance within the organization.

Incident response is a crucial aspect of cybersecurity, and user education contributes to the effectiveness of incident response efforts. Users should be aware of the importance of promptly reporting any suspicious activities, security incidents, or potential breaches to the designated incident response team. Training programs should provide guidance on the steps users should take in the event of a security incident, including isolating affected systems, preserving evidence, and following established reporting procedures. By fostering a sense of shared responsibility for cybersecurity incidents, organizations can enhance their ability to respond effectively and mitigate the impact of security breaches.

In conclusion, user education and awareness form the cornerstone of a robust cybersecurity strategy, addressing the human factor in the ever-evolving landscape of cyber threats. By educating users on common threats, instilling security best practices, and fostering a culture of security awareness, organizations empower individuals to make informed decisions and actively contribute to the overall security posture. From recognizing phishing attempts to implementing strong password hygiene, user education creates a resilient human firewall against a diverse array of cyber threats. In an era where cyber threats continue to evolve, the investment in user education not only strengthens the organization's defenses but also cultivates a cybersecurity culture that is adaptive, proactive, and collaborative.

Chapter 6: Emerging Trends in File Systems Technology

Exploring the integration of machine learning for predictive file system behavior.

The integration of machine learning (ML) into predictive file system behavior represents a transformative approach to managing and optimizing data storage and retrieval processes. At its core, file systems serve as the backbone for organizing and storing digital information, but the increasing volume and complexity of data pose challenges for traditional approaches to file management. Machine learning, with its ability to discern patterns and make predictions based on data analysis, offers a promising avenue to enhance file system functionality.

One of the key advantages of integrating machine learning into file system behavior lies in its capacity to adapt to dynamic and evolving data landscapes. Traditional file systems often rely on predetermined rules and static structures, which may struggle to efficiently handle the varied and unpredictable nature of modern data usage. Machine learning algorithms, on the other hand, can continuously learn and adjust their behavior based on patterns identified within the data itself. This adaptability enables file systems to better accommodate the diverse needs and characteristics of the data they store.

Furthermore, the predictive capabilities of machine learning contribute to proactive and intelligent file management. By analyzing historical data access patterns, file system behavior can be anticipated, allowing for preemptive optimization of storage and retrieval processes. For instance, ML algorithms can identify files that are likely to be accessed together and strategically position them for faster retrieval, enhancing overall system performance. This predictive approach not only minimizes latency but also optimizes storage space, as less frequently accessed data can be efficiently migrated to secondary storage tiers.

Machine learning's impact on file system security is another crucial aspect of integration. ML algorithms excel in anomaly detection, enabling the identification of unusual or suspicious file access patterns that may indicate unauthorized activities. By continuously learning from normal usage, these algorithms can dynamically adapt to evolving security threats, enhancing the robustness of file system defenses. Moreover, ML-powered file systems can implement access controls based on user behavior analysis, providing a more nuanced and adaptive security framework compared to traditional static permission models.

The scalability of file systems is a fundamental consideration in the era of big data, and machine learning contributes significantly to addressing this challenge. As data volumes continue to grow exponentially, ML algorithms can assist in automating the organization and categorization of massive datasets. By classifying and tagging files based on content, usage patterns, and context, machine learning aids in creating a more structured and navigable file system. This not only facilitates efficient data retrieval but also enhances the overall scalability of file systems to accommodate the ever-expanding data landscape.

Collaboration and interoperability are critical aspects of modern computing environments, and the integration of machine learning into file systems can foster seamless interactions between diverse applications and platforms. ML algorithms can enable intelligent data sharing and synchronization, anticipating the needs of different applications and optimizing file placement accordingly. This collaborative approach enhances overall system efficiency and ensures that file systems align with the varied requirements of interconnected software and services.

While the integration of machine learning into predictive file system behavior offers numerous benefits, challenges and considerations must be addressed. Privacy concerns related to the analysis of user behavior data, the need for robust model interpretability, and the potential biases within training data are among the critical ethical and technical considerations. Striking a balance between optimizing file system performance and safeguarding user privacy is a complex but essential aspect of successful integration.

In conclusion, the integration of machine learning into predictive file system behavior represents a paradigm shift in how we manage and interact with digital data. By leveraging the adaptability, intelligence, and scalability of ML algorithms, file systems can evolve beyond their traditional static nature, offering dynamic, predictive, and secure solutions to the challenges posed by the ever-expanding data landscape. While ethical and technical considerations must be carefully navigated, the potential benefits in terms of performance optimization, security enhancement, and collaborative interoperability make the exploration of machine learning integration a compelling and transformative avenue for the future of file system management.

AI-driven algorithms for automated file system optimization.
The advent of AI-driven algorithms has ushered in a new era of automated file system optimization, revolutionizing the way we manage and interact with digital data. At the core of this transformation is the ability of artificial intelligence (AI) to analyze, learn, and adapt to complex patterns within file systems. Traditional approaches to file system optimization often relied on manual interventions and predefined rules, which struggled to cope with the dynamic nature of modern data usage. AI-driven algorithms, on the other hand,

harness the power of machine learning to continuously analyze data access patterns, predict future needs, and autonomously optimize the file system in real-time.

One of the primary advantages of AI-driven file system optimization lies in its capacity to adapt to evolving data landscapes. In an era where the volume and variety of data are constantly expanding, traditional file management approaches face challenges in efficiently organizing and retrieving information. AI algorithms, through their ability to discern patterns and make predictions based on data analysis, offer a dynamic and adaptive solution. These algorithms can learn from historical data access patterns, adjusting their behavior to accommodate the diverse characteristics of the data they store. This adaptability ensures that file systems remain responsive and efficient in the face of changing data dynamics.

Predictive capabilities represent a cornerstone of AI-driven file system optimization. By leveraging historical data access patterns, AI algorithms can anticipate future file system behavior, enabling preemptive optimization of storage and retrieval processes. For example, the algorithms can identify files that are likely to be accessed together and strategically position them for faster retrieval, thereby minimizing latency and improving overall system performance. This predictive approach not only enhances user experience but also optimizes storage space, as less frequently accessed data can be intelligently migrated to secondary storage tiers.

Security is a paramount concern in file system management, and AI-driven algorithms contribute significantly to enhancing the security posture of file systems. Machine learning algorithms excel in anomaly detection, allowing them to identify unusual or suspicious file access patterns that may indicate unauthorized activities. Through continuous learning from normal usage, these algorithms can dynamically adapt to emerging security threats, providing a robust defense mechanism for file systems. Moreover, AI-powered file systems can implement access controls based on user behavior analysis, offering a more nuanced and adaptive security framework compared to traditional static permission models.

Scalability is another critical consideration in the context of big data, and AI-driven file system optimization plays a pivotal role in addressing this challenge. As data volumes continue to grow exponentially, AI algorithms assist in automating the organization and categorization of massive datasets. By classifying and tagging files based on content, usage patterns, and context, these algorithms contribute to creating a more structured and navigable file system. This not only facilitates efficient data retrieval but also enhances the overall scalability of file systems to accommodate the ever-expanding data landscape.

Collaboration and interoperability are key elements of contemporary computing environments, and AI-driven file system optimization fosters seamless interactions between diverse applications and platforms. Through intelligent data sharing and synchronization, AI algorithms can anticipate the needs of different applications, optimizing file placement accordingly. This collaborative approach enhances overall system efficiency and ensures that file systems align with the varied requirements of interconnected software and services, contributing to a more integrated and cohesive computing environment.

However, the integration of AI-driven algorithms into file system optimization is not without its challenges and considerations. Privacy concerns related to the analysis of user behavior data, the need for robust model interpretability, and the potential biases within training data are among the critical ethical and technical considerations. Striking a balance between optimizing file system performance and safeguarding user privacy is a complex but essential aspect of successful integration. Additionally, ensuring the transparency and explainability of AI algorithms is crucial to building trust among users and administrators.

In conclusion, the integration of AI-driven algorithms into automated file system optimization marks a paradigm shift in how we approach the management of digital data. The adaptability, intelligence, and scalability of AI algorithms offer dynamic solutions to the challenges posed by the ever-expanding data landscape. While ethical and technical considerations must be carefully navigated, the potential benefits in terms of performance optimization, security enhancement, and collaborative interoperability make AI-driven file system optimization a compelling and transformative advancement in the field of data management.

The shift towards object storage as an alternative to traditional file systems.

The paradigm shift towards object storage represents a transformative departure from traditional file systems, ushering in a new era of data management and storage infrastructure. At the heart of this evolution is the recognition that the growing scale and complexity of data require a more scalable, flexible, and efficient storage solution. Traditional file systems, characterized by hierarchical directory structures and limited metadata, face challenges in coping with the massive volumes of unstructured data generated in today's digital landscape. Object storage, on the other hand, introduces a fundamentally different approach by organizing data into discrete, self-contained objects, each accompanied by rich metadata, allowing for a more scalable and versatile storage architecture.

One of the key advantages of object storage is its inherent scalability, which is essential in the face of the explosive growth of data in recent years. Traditional file systems, particularly in network-attached storage (NAS) environments, often encounter limitations when it comes to handling vast amounts of unstructured data. Object storage overcomes these limitations by decoupling the data from a centralized file hierarchy and distributing it across a flat address space. This distributed and scalable architecture enables organizations to seamlessly scale their storage infrastructure to accommodate the ever-expanding volumes of data without the need for complex and manual data sharding or partitioning.

Moreover, object storage systems provide a more flexible and extensible framework for managing diverse types of data. In traditional file systems, the structure imposed by directory hierarchies can be restrictive, making it challenging to efficiently manage and retrieve unstructured or semi-structured data. Object storage allows for the storage of data in its native format, without the constraints of a hierarchical file system. This flexibility is particularly beneficial for organizations dealing with a wide variety of data types, ranging from multimedia files to documents and beyond. Each object within the storage system is accompanied by metadata, enabling efficient indexing and retrieval based on content, usage, or other custom-defined attributes.

The efficiency and cost-effectiveness of storage infrastructure are critical considerations in the era of big data, and object storage systems offer notable advantages in this regard. Traditional file systems often incur higher costs due to the need for complex file hierarchy structures, redundancy mechanisms, and frequent data migrations. Object storage simplifies these processes by adopting a flatter structure, reducing the complexity of data management. Additionally, object storage systems often employ erasure coding or other advanced data protection mechanisms, minimizing the need for costly RAID configurations while ensuring data durability and availability.

Data durability and accessibility are paramount concerns in any storage system, and object storage systems excel in providing robust solutions to these challenges. By distributing data across multiple nodes and geographic locations, object storage inherently enhances data resilience and availability. This distributed architecture, combined with advanced replication and versioning capabilities, ensures that data remains accessible even in the face of hardware failures or other unforeseen events. This increased durability and accessibility make object storage particularly suitable for applications and use cases where high reliability and uninterrupted access to data are critical, such as cloud storage and archival systems.

The adoption of object storage aligns closely with the principles of cloud computing, contributing to the seamless integration of on-premises and cloud-based storage environments. Object storage's distributed nature and the ability to store data in its native format make it well-suited for cloud-native applications and services. Cloud storage providers often leverage object storage as the underlying architecture for their offerings, providing users with scalable and cost-effective solutions for storing and retrieving data in the cloud. This alignment with cloud paradigms facilitates hybrid and multi-cloud deployments, enabling organizations to leverage the benefits of both on-premises and cloud-based storage resources.

Despite the many advantages of object storage, its adoption is not without challenges and considerations. Compatibility with existing applications and workflows, the need for specialized APIs for object storage access, and the learning curve associated with transitioning from traditional file systems are among the factors that organizations must carefully navigate. Moreover, ensuring data security and compliance with regulatory requirements becomes a critical consideration, particularly in industries with stringent data protection standards.

In conclusion, the shift towards object storage marks a significant departure from traditional file systems, offering a scalable, flexible, and efficient solution for the challenges posed by the modern data landscape. The inherent advantages of object storage, including scalability, flexibility, cost-effectiveness, and cloud compatibility, position it as a compelling alternative for organizations seeking to optimize their data storage infrastructure. While challenges exist, the benefits of object storage in enhancing data management, accessibility, and resilience make it a key player in the evolving landscape of storage technologies.

Advantages and challenges of object-based storage.

The adoption of object-based storage has become increasingly prevalent in the realm of data management, bringing forth a host of advantages that address the evolving needs of modern storage architectures. One of the paramount benefits lies in the inherent scalability of object-based storage systems. Traditional storage solutions, based on file systems, often encounter limitations in handling the massive volumes of unstructured and diverse data generated in contemporary digital environments. Object-based storage, by contrast, leverages a flat and distributed architecture, enabling seamless scalability without the complexities associated with traditional hierarchical structures. This scalability is particularly crucial in the era of big data, where organizations grapple with ever-expanding datasets, necessitating storage solutions that can grow dynamically to accommodate these increasing demands.

Flexibility and versatility represent another significant advantage of object-based storage. Unlike traditional file systems that impose rigid hierarchical structures, object storage allows for the storage of data in its native format, unencumbered by the constraints of directory hierarchies. Each piece of data is encapsulated within a self-contained object, accompanied by rich metadata that provides valuable information about the content. This flexibility is particularly beneficial for organizations dealing with a diverse array of data types, ranging from multimedia files to documents and beyond. As a result, object-based storage is well-suited for use cases that involve handling heterogeneous data sets, providing a more adaptable and extensible framework for modern data management needs.

Efficiency and cost-effectiveness are critical considerations in storage infrastructure, and object-based storage systems offer notable advantages in this regard. Traditional file systems may incur higher costs due to complex directory structures, redundancy mechanisms, and frequent data migrations. Object storage simplifies these processes through its flatter structure, reducing the overhead associated with data management. Moreover, object storage systems often implement advanced data protection mechanisms, such as erasure coding, reducing the reliance on costly RAID configurations while ensuring data durability and availability. This increased efficiency and cost-effectiveness make object-based storage an attractive option for organizations seeking to optimize their storage infrastructure without compromising on reliability.

In terms of data durability and accessibility, object-based storage excels by design. The distributed nature of object storage, where data is spread across multiple nodes and potentially across geographic locations, inherently enhances data resilience. Advanced replication and versioning capabilities further contribute to ensuring data availability, even in the face of hardware failures or unforeseen events. This heightened durability makes object-based storage particularly well-suited for critical applications and use cases where data reliability and uninterrupted access are paramount, such as cloud storage and archival systems. The ability to maintain data integrity and accessibility is a key advantage in scenarios where downtime or data loss is not tolerable.

The alignment of object-based storage with cloud computing principles is a noteworthy advantage that facilitates seamless integration between on-premises and cloud-based storage environments. Cloud storage providers often leverage object storage as the underlying architecture for their services, offering users scalable and cost-effective solutions for storing and retrieving data in the cloud. Object storage's distributed nature and compatibility with cloud paradigms make it well-suited for cloud-native applications and services, enabling hybrid and multi-cloud deployments. This alignment supports organizations in leveraging the benefits of both on-premises and cloud-based storage resources, contributing to a more flexible and dynamic storage ecosystem.

However, alongside these advantages, the adoption of object-based storage is not without its challenges. Compatibility with existing applications and workflows is a significant consideration, as transitioning from traditional file systems to object storage may require modifications to applications to integrate with the new storage paradigm. Object storage relies on specialized APIs for access, and ensuring that applications can effectively communicate with and take full advantage of these APIs is a crucial aspect of successful adoption. This challenge often necessitates careful planning and may involve updates or rewrites of existing applications to fully embrace the capabilities of object-based storage.

Furthermore, the learning curve associated with adopting object-based storage can pose challenges for organizations accustomed to traditional file systems. Administrators and IT personnel may need to acquire new skills and understanding to effectively manage and optimize object storage systems. This educational aspect becomes pivotal in ensuring that organizations can unlock the full potential of object-based storage and overcome potential hurdles associated with the shift in storage paradigms.

Security considerations and compliance with regulatory requirements are paramount in any storage solution, and object-based storage is no exception. As organizations migrate to object storage, ensuring that security measures are in place to protect sensitive data becomes crucial. This includes implementing robust access controls, encryption mechanisms, and regular security audits to safeguard data against unauthorized access or breaches. Compliance with industry-specific regulations, such as those governing healthcare or finance, adds an additional layer of complexity that organizations must navigate when adopting object-based storage.

In conclusion, the advantages of object-based storage are substantial, offering scalability, flexibility, efficiency, and compatibility with cloud environments. These attributes make it a compelling option for organizations seeking to address the challenges posed by the ever-expanding volumes and varieties of data. However, the adoption of object-based storage comes with its set of challenges, including compatibility issues, a learning curve, and heightened security considerations. Successful implementation requires a thoughtful and strategic approach, with organizations weighing the benefits against the potential challenges to determine the optimal fit for their specific data management needs.

The concept of immutable file systems for enhanced security.

The concept of immutable file systems represents a groundbreaking approach to enhancing security in the realm of data storage and management. At its core, immutability refers to the quality of being unchanging over time. When applied to file systems, this means that once data is written or stored, it becomes immutable or resistant to modification, deletion, or tampering. Traditional file systems, in contrast, allow for dynamic changes to data, presenting vulnerabilities that malicious actors can exploit. The adoption of immutable file systems is driven by the imperative to fortify data against unauthorized alterations, providing a robust defense mechanism in an era where cybersecurity threats loom large.

One of the primary advantages of immutable file systems lies in their ability to mitigate the risks associated with data tampering and unauthorized access. In traditional file systems, data can be modified, deleted, or replaced, either accidentally or maliciously. Immutable file systems, however, establish a protective barrier by design, preventing any changes to data once it has been written. This immutability is enforced at the file or object level, making it significantly harder for attackers to manipulate critical information. By embracing this proactive approach to security, organizations can ensure data integrity and prevent unauthorized alterations, bolstering their defense against a variety of cyber threats, including ransomware attacks and insider threats.

Data integrity is a cornerstone of information security, and immutable file systems contribute significantly to maintaining the trustworthiness and reliability of stored data. Immutability ensures that once data is written, it remains in its original, unaltered state. This attribute is particularly valuable in sectors such as finance, healthcare, and legal, where the accuracy and unforgeability of data are paramount. By eliminating the risk of unintentional or malicious changes, immutable file systems instill confidence in the authenticity of stored information, fostering a secure environment for critical data assets. This assurance becomes crucial in scenarios where data integrity is not just a preference but a regulatory requirement, aligning with standards such as Sarbanes-Oxley (SOX) or the Health Insurance Portability and Accountability Act (HIPAA).

The prevention of data loss and corruption is another compelling advantage offered by immutable file systems. In traditional setups, accidental deletions or modifications, whether due to human error or system glitches, can result in irretrievable loss of valuable data. Immutable file systems act as a safeguard against such scenarios by prohibiting any changes to existing data. Even in the event of a cybersecurity incident, the original, unaltered data remains intact and recoverable. This aspect enhances the overall resilience of data storage systems, reducing the potential impact of data-related disasters and contributing to the robustness of an organization's data recovery and continuity strategies.

Immutability also plays a pivotal role in addressing the rising threat of ransomware attacks, which have become increasingly sophisticated and targeted. These malicious attacks typically involve encrypting a victim's data and demanding payment for its release. Immutable file systems disrupt the ransomware model by preventing unauthorized alterations to data. Even if a system falls victim to a ransomware attack, the original, unencrypted data remains preserved in its immutable state. This inherent resilience reduces the effectiveness of ransomware tactics, providing organizations with a powerful tool to thwart one of the most pervasive and financially damaging cyber threats.

Moreover, the concept of immutability aligns closely with the principles of auditability and accountability. Immutable file systems create an indelible record of changes, ensuring that every version of data is traceable and attributable to specific actions or users. This audit trail not only aids in forensic analysis in the aftermath of a security incident but also serves as a deterrent, discouraging malicious insiders or external attackers who may be tempted to manipulate or erase their tracks. The transparency and accountability facilitated by immutable file systems contribute to a culture of responsible data stewardship, reinforcing the importance of secure practices throughout an organization.

While the advantages of immutable file systems are compelling, challenges and considerations must be addressed to ensure successful implementation. One notable challenge is the need to strike a balance between immutability and the legitimate need for data modification or deletion. In certain scenarios, such as compliance with data privacy regulations or the right to be forgotten, organizations may need to accommodate requests for the removal or modification of specific data. Achieving this balance requires thoughtful design and implementation of immutable file systems, including the incorporation of flexible access controls and data lifecycle management policies that align with regulatory requirements.

Additionally, the adoption of immutable file systems may entail changes to existing workflows and applications. Traditional approaches to data management often involve regular updates, modifications, or deletions of information. Shifting to an immutable paradigm requires organizations to reassess and potentially redesign their processes to align with the principles of immutability. This adaptation may involve educating users and administrators on the new paradigm, updating existing applications to be compatible with immutable storage, and redefining data governance policies to accommodate the unique characteristics of immutable file systems.

Furthermore, considerations related to performance and storage overhead must be addressed. Immutability often involves creating new versions of data rather than directly modifying existing records. This approach can lead to increased storage requirements over time, particularly in scenarios where data changes frequently. Organizations need to carefully evaluate their storage infrastructure, taking into account factors such as capacity planning, data deduplication, and compression to optimize the balance between immutability and storage efficiency.

In conclusion, the concept of immutable file systems emerges as a powerful and proactive strategy to enhance data security, integrity, and resilience. By rendering data impervious to unauthorized alterations, immutable file systems provide a robust defense against a spectrum of cybersecurity threats, ranging from data tampering to ransomware attacks. The assurance of data integrity, prevention of data loss, and accountability benefits make immutability a compelling approach, especially in industries where trust in data accuracy is paramount. While challenges exist, careful planning, education, and adaptation of workflows can enable organizations to harness the advantages of immutable file systems and elevate the security posture of their data storage environments.

Use cases and implications of immutability in file storage.

The adoption of immutability in file storage introduces a paradigm shift with far-reaching use cases and implications, reshaping how organizations manage, secure, and leverage their data assets. One prominent use case revolves around data integrity assurance, where immutability serves as a safeguard against unintentional or malicious alterations to critical information. In sectors such as finance, healthcare, and legal, where the accuracy and authenticity of data are paramount, the ability to ensure that stored information remains unaltered over time becomes a foundational requirement. Immutability in file storage provides an assurance mechanism, mitigating the risks associated with data tampering and instilling confidence in the reliability of stored records.

Another significant use case arises in the context of cybersecurity, particularly in the battle against ransomware attacks. The increasing sophistication and prevalence of ransomware have heightened the need for robust defense mechanisms. Immutable file storage disrupts the typical ransomware model by preventing unauthorized changes to data. In the event of a ransomware attack, the original, unaltered data remains preserved in its immutable state, rendering the attacker's attempts to encrypt or manipulate data ineffective. This use case underscores the role of immutability as a powerful tool in the cybersecurity arsenal, providing organizations with a means to thwart one of the most pernicious and financially damaging cyber threats.

Data resilience and continuity planning represent another compelling use case for immutability in file storage. Traditional setups, where data can be accidentally deleted or modified, expose organizations to the risk of data loss. Immutability acts as a safeguard against such scenarios by preventing any changes to existing data. This attribute enhances the overall resilience of data storage systems, reducing the potential impact of data-related disasters. In the face of accidental deletions, system glitches, or even cybersecurity incidents, the original, unaltered data remains intact and recoverable, contributing to the robustness of an organization's data recovery and continuity strategies.

In the realm of compliance and auditability, immutability becomes a crucial enabler. Immutable file storage creates an indelible record of changes, establishing a transparent audit trail that is traceable and attributable. This use case aligns with regulatory requirements and industry standards that mandate a comprehensive audit capability for data management practices. Whether it be for financial audits, healthcare compliance, or legal investigations, the immutable nature of file storage ensures that every version of data is verifiable, contributing to forensic analysis in the aftermath of security incidents and fostering a culture of accountability in data stewardship.

The healthcare industry, in particular, stands out as a sector where the implications of immutability in file storage are profound. Electronic Health Records (EHRs) and patient data demand the highest levels of accuracy and security. Immutability ensures that medical records remain tamper-resistant, preserving the integrity of patient information. This use case extends to clinical trials, where maintaining the unalterable nature of research data is critical for regulatory compliance and the credibility of trial outcomes. The implications of immutability in healthcare underscore its role in safeguarding sensitive information and instilling trust in data used for patient care, research, and compliance purposes.

The financial sector also leverages the benefits of immutability, particularly in the context of transactional data. Financial records, transactions, and audit logs require a level of trust and accuracy that is unparalleled. Immutability in file storage provides a safeguard against fraudulent activities, ensuring that once a financial transaction is recorded, it remains unaltered and verifiable. This use case aligns with the stringent regulatory requirements imposed on financial institutions, emphasizing the need for secure and tamper-resistant storage solutions to protect sensitive financial data.

In the context of legal proceedings, where the authenticity and integrity of evidence are paramount, immutability in file storage emerges as a critical tool. Legal documents, contracts, and evidentiary materials stored in an immutable file system become tamper-evident, providing a digital chain of custody that withstands scrutiny in legal proceedings. This use case has implications not only for traditional legal practices but also for the broader legaltech landscape, where technologies supporting legal processes increasingly rely on the assurance of data integrity and the ability to maintain unaltered records.

The media and entertainment industry, characterized by vast amounts of digital assets, benefits from immutability in file storage for content preservation and rights management. Original copies of digital media, creative works, and intellectual property can be safeguarded against accidental modifications or unauthorized alterations. Immutability ensures that the provenance of digital assets remains intact, providing a secure foundation for licensing agreements, royalties, and intellectual property disputes. This use case supports the longevity and integrity of digital content, allowing media and entertainment organizations to protect their creative assets in a tamper-resistant storage environment.

The educational sector also finds value in immutability, particularly for the secure storage of academic records, certificates, and research data. As educational institutions increasingly digitize their records, ensuring the integrity and authenticity of these digital documents becomes paramount. Immutability in file storage guarantees that academic achievements and research findings remain unaltered, providing a trusted repository for credentials and scholarly work. This use case not only contributes to the reliability of academic records but also addresses concerns related to the potential falsification of credentials or research outcomes.

In cloud computing environments, the implications of immutability extend to data governance, compliance, and collaborative workflows. Cloud storage providers often leverage immutable file systems as a foundation for secure and tamper-resistant data storage. Organizations utilizing cloud services can benefit from the assurance that their data remains unaltered, irrespective of the cloud provider's infrastructure or potential security incidents. This use case reinforces the role of immutability as a cornerstone for secure cloud storage solutions, supporting diverse industries and applications that rely on the flexibility and scalability of cloud computing.

However, the adoption of immutability in file storage also introduces implications and considerations that organizations must navigate. One such consideration is the need for balancing immutability with the legitimate need for data modification or deletion. While immutability enhances security, certain scenarios, such as compliance with data privacy regulations or the right to be forgotten, may require organizations to accommodate requests for the removal or modification of specific data. Achieving this balance necessitates thoughtful design and implementation of immutable file systems, incorporating flexible access controls and data lifecycle management policies that align with regulatory requirements.

The performance and storage overhead associated with immutability present another set of considerations. Immutability often involves creating new versions of data rather than directly modifying existing records. This approach can lead to increased storage requirements over time, particularly in scenarios where data changes frequently. Organizations need to carefully evaluate their storage infrastructure, considering factors such as capacity planning, data deduplication, and compression to optimize the balance between immutability and storage efficiency. Performance considerations also extend to the latency introduced by creating new versions of data, especially in environments with stringent requirements for real-time data access.

Moreover, the adoption of immutability may necessitate changes to existing workflows and applications. Traditional approaches to data management often involve regular updates, modifications, or deletions of information. Shifting to an immutable paradigm requires organizations to reassess and potentially redesign their processes to align with the principles of immutability. This adaptation may involve educating users and administrators on the new paradigm, updating existing applications to be compatible with immutable storage, and redefining data governance policies to accommodate the unique characteristics of immutable file systems.

In conclusion, the use cases and implications of immutability in file storage are diverse and impactful, spanning industries and applications where data integrity, security, and resilience are paramount. From ensuring the accuracy of financial transactions to safeguarding patient records in healthcare, immutability emerges as a foundational element in modern data management strategies. While presenting challenges related to data modification needs, performance considerations, and workflow adjustments, the benefits of immutability in enhancing security, compliance, and data reliability position it as a transformative force in the evolving landscape of information management. As organizations continue to grapple with escalating cybersecurity threats and regulatory complexities, the adoption of immutability becomes not just a technological choice but a strategic imperative for safeguarding the trustworthiness and resilience of digital assets.

Evolving trends in distributed file systems for cloud and edge computing.

The landscape of distributed file systems is undergoing transformative evolution, driven by the dynamic requirements of cloud and edge computing environments. Cloud computing, with its emphasis on scalable and on-demand resources, has spurred the development of distributed file systems that can seamlessly scale to meet the demands of modern applications and data storage. One notable trend is the shift towards object storage as a foundational component of distributed file systems in the cloud. Object storage's flat and scalable architecture, coupled with its ability to handle vast amounts of unstructured data, aligns well with the scalability requirements of cloud environments. This evolution reflects a departure from traditional hierarchical file systems, offering greater flexibility and adaptability to the diverse and unpredictable nature of data generated and consumed in the cloud.

The emergence of serverless computing further influences the evolution of distributed file systems in the cloud. Serverless architectures, characterized by the absence of server management and the ability to execute functions on-demand, necessitate file systems that seamlessly integrate with such event-driven paradigms. Distributed file systems tailored for serverless computing prioritize low-latency access and efficient data retrieval, aligning with the ephemeral and stateless nature of serverless functions. These systems enable developers to build applications without the need to manage underlying infrastructure, paving the way for more agile and resource-efficient development in cloud environments.

As the cloud landscape continues to mature, there is a growing emphasis on multi-cloud and hybrid cloud strategies. Distributed file systems are evolving to accommodate these trends, providing seamless interoperability across different cloud providers and on-premises infrastructure. This evolution enables organizations to avoid vendor lock-in, leverage the unique features of multiple cloud providers, and maintain flexibility in choosing the most suitable environment for specific workloads. Inter-cloud file systems are designed to facilitate data mobility, ensuring that data can be seamlessly transferred and accessed across diverse cloud environments without compromising performance or security.

The proliferation of edge computing introduces new dimensions to the evolution of distributed file systems. Edge computing, characterized by the deployment of computing resources closer to the data source, demands file systems that can efficiently manage and store data at the edge. One notable trend is the integration of edge storage solutions with distributed file systems, enabling organizations to process and analyze data locally, reducing latency and enhancing real-time decision-making. Edge-native file systems are optimized for resource-constrained environments, offering a balance between storage efficiency and data accessibility at the edge.

The advent of 5G networks accelerates the convergence of cloud and edge computing, presenting opportunities and challenges for distributed file systems. With the increased bandwidth and low-latency capabilities of 5G, applications can offload more processing to the edge, requiring file systems that can seamlessly span both centralized cloud data centers and edge nodes. This trend emphasizes the need for distributed file systems that are not only agile and scalable but also capable of adapting to the distributed and heterogeneous nature of 5G-enabled environments.

Security and compliance considerations play a central role in the evolution of distributed file systems for cloud and edge computing. As data traverses diverse environments, including public clouds, private clouds, and edge nodes, there is a heightened focus on securing data both in transit and at rest. Distributed file systems are evolving to incorporate robust encryption, access controls, and auditing capabilities to address security concerns. Compliance frameworks, such as those governing data protection and privacy, influence the design of distributed file systems to ensure adherence to regulatory requirements across diverse computing environments.

The rise of containerization and orchestration technologies, exemplified by Docker and Kubernetes, also shapes the evolution of distributed file systems. Containers offer a lightweight and portable means of packaging and deploying applications, and distributed file systems are adapting to seamlessly integrate with containerized workloads. Container-native file systems provide persistent storage for stateful applications running in containerized environments, enabling data to persist across container instances and ensuring consistency in data access and management. Orchestration platforms, such as Kubernetes, orchestrate the deployment and scaling of containerized applications, creating a demand for distributed file systems that seamlessly integrate with these dynamic orchestration frameworks.

The integration of artificial intelligence (AI) and machine learning (ML) into distributed file systems is another noteworthy trend. As organizations harness the power of AI and ML for data-driven insights, there is a growing need for file systems that can efficiently manage and provide access to large datasets used in training and inference workflows. Distributed file systems optimized for AI and ML workloads offer features such as parallelized data access, optimized data locality, and integration with popular ML frameworks. These systems enhance the performance and scalability of AI and ML applications, supporting the growing demand for intelligent data processing in cloud and edge environments.

Furthermore, the evolution of distributed file systems is influenced by the increasing awareness of sustainability and environmental impact. Green computing considerations are prompting organizations to explore energy-efficient storage solutions and distributed file systems that minimize resource consumption. This trend aligns with the broader industry focus on sustainability and reducing the carbon footprint of data centers and computing infrastructure. Distributed file systems designed with energy efficiency in mind contribute to environmentally responsible computing practices, reflecting a holistic approach to technology development in the era of climate consciousness.

Interoperability and standardization efforts also play a critical role in the evolution of distributed file systems for cloud and edge computing. As the diversity of environments increases, organizations seek interoperable solutions that can seamlessly integrate with a variety of platforms, tools, and services. Standardization initiatives, such as the Cloud Native Computing Foundation (CNCF) and the Open Container Initiative (OCI), influence the development of distributed file systems that adhere to industry-wide standards. This drive towards interoperability ensures that organizations can adopt distributed file systems that align with their specific requirements while fostering compatibility with a broad ecosystem of cloud and edge technologies.

In conclusion, the evolving trends in distributed file systems for cloud and edge computing reflect a dynamic landscape shaped by technological advancements, changing computing paradigms, and evolving user expectations. From the shift towards object storage and serverless computing in the cloud to the integration of edge-native solutions and the impact of 5G networks, distributed file systems are adapting to meet the diverse and complex needs of modern computing environments. Security, compliance, containerization, AI integration, sustainability considerations, and interoperability efforts further contribute to the multifaceted evolution of distributed file systems. As organizations navigate the complexities of distributed computing, the evolution of file systems becomes not only a technological journey but a strategic imperative for unlocking the full potential of cloud and edge computing in the digital era.

Challenges and innovations in managing files across distributed nodes.

The management of files across distributed nodes presents a myriad of challenges and necessitates innovative solutions to address the complexities inherent in modern computing environments. One of the central challenges lies in ensuring data consistency and coherence across distributed nodes. In a distributed file system, files may be concurrently accessed and modified by multiple nodes, leading to the potential for conflicts and inconsistencies. Achieving a balance between data consistency and the scalability of distributed systems poses a formidable challenge. Traditional file systems often rely on centralized mechanisms for locking and coordination, which can introduce bottlenecks and hinder scalability. Innovative approaches, such as distributed consensus algorithms and optimistic concurrency control, seek to mitigate these challenges by providing robust mechanisms for coordinating access to files across distributed nodes, ensuring both consistency and performance.

The issue of data durability and fault tolerance adds another layer of complexity to managing files across distributed nodes. In a distributed environment, nodes may experience failures or network partitions, posing a risk of data loss or corruption. Ensuring the durability of files despite node failures requires the implementation of resilient storage mechanisms and distributed replication strategies. Innovations in file systems introduce techniques like erasure coding and distributed replication protocols that enhance fault tolerance. These approaches not only safeguard files against individual node failures but also contribute to the overall reliability and availability of data in distributed environments.

Scalability is a paramount concern when managing files across distributed nodes, particularly as data volumes continue to grow exponentially. Traditional file systems may struggle to scale seamlessly due to centralized metadata management or limitations in the underlying architecture. Innovations in distributed file systems leverage techniques such as sharding, where data is partitioned across multiple nodes, to distribute the storage and processing load efficiently. Additionally, the adoption of object storage, which organizes data into self-contained objects with associated metadata, enhances scalability by eliminating the hierarchical structures of traditional file systems. These innovations facilitate the horizontal scaling of distributed file systems, allowing organizations to accommodate growing datasets and increasing workloads.

Security considerations emerge as a critical challenge in managing files across distributed nodes, as data traverses diverse environments and may be subject to various threats. Traditional security models based on perimeter defenses become less effective in distributed environments where nodes are geographically dispersed and communicate over potentially insecure networks. Innovations in distributed file systems prioritize end-to-end encryption, secure access controls, and robust authentication mechanisms. Additionally, the integration of blockchain technology introduces tamper-resistant ledgers for tracking file access and modifications, enhancing the auditability and accountability of file management in distributed settings. These security innovations aim to protect sensitive data from unauthorized access and ensure the confidentiality and integrity of files across distributed nodes.

The evolving landscape of distributed computing introduces the challenge of managing files in hybrid and multi-cloud environments. Organizations increasingly leverage a combination of on-premises data centers and cloud services, necessitating file systems that seamlessly span diverse infrastructures. Innovations in file management focus on interoperability and data mobility, allowing files to be accessed and migrated across different cloud providers and on-premises nodes. Standardization efforts, such as the Cloud Data Management Interface (CDMI) and advancements in cross-cloud file synchronization tools, contribute to addressing the challenges associated with managing files in hybrid and multi-cloud scenarios. These innovations empower organizations to achieve flexibility and avoid vendor lock-in while efficiently managing files across distributed nodes.

The dynamic nature of distributed environments introduces challenges related to metadata management and access control. In traditional file systems, centralized metadata servers may become performance bottlenecks or points of failure as the number of nodes increases. Innovations in metadata management involve the distribution of metadata across multiple nodes, reducing the burden on individual servers and enhancing overall system performance. Moreover, advances in access control mechanisms, including attribute-based access control (ABAC) and role-based access control (RBAC), provide granular control over file permissions in distributed settings. These innovations ensure that files are securely managed across distributed nodes while accommodating the dynamic and decentralized nature of modern computing architectures.

Data locality and access efficiency present challenges in distributed file systems, particularly as organizations strive to optimize data access times and reduce latency. Traditional file systems may struggle to efficiently retrieve files distributed across geographically dispersed nodes. Innovations in distributed file systems leverage techniques such as content delivery networks (CDNs), which cache frequently accessed files closer to end-users, enhancing data locality and access speed. Additionally, advancements in intelligent caching algorithms and predictive analytics contribute to optimizing file access patterns in distributed environments. These innovations aim to minimize latency and enhance the overall responsiveness of distributed file systems, providing users with efficient access to files regardless of their geographical location.

The rise of edge computing introduces novel challenges and opportunities in managing files across distributed nodes. Edge environments, characterized by the deployment of computing resources closer to data sources, demand file systems that can efficiently handle data at the edge while seamlessly integrating with centralized cloud storage. Innovations in edge-native file systems prioritize low-latency access and data caching at the edge, enabling applications to process and retrieve files locally. Furthermore, advancements in synchronization and data consistency mechanisms between edge nodes and central repositories contribute to maintaining file integrity in distributed edge computing scenarios. These innovations address the unique requirements of edge computing and empower organizations to leverage the benefits of distributed file management in edge environments.

Interoperability and standardization efforts become crucial considerations in managing files across distributed nodes, especially in heterogeneous computing environments. The diversity of storage solutions, operating systems, and communication protocols poses challenges in achieving seamless integration and data mobility. Innovations focus on adopting open standards, such as the Network File System (NFS) and Common Internet File System (CIFS), to facilitate interoperability between different file systems and platforms. Additionally, the development of container-native file systems aligns with containerization trends, allowing applications running in containers to access files efficiently. These innovations contribute to a more cohesive and interoperable ecosystem, enabling organizations to navigate the complexities of managing files across diverse distributed nodes.

In conclusion, the challenges and innovations in managing files across distributed nodes underscore the intricate nature of modern computing environments. From ensuring data consistency and fault tolerance to addressing security concerns and optimizing access efficiency, distributed file systems continue to evolve to meet the demands of contemporary computing paradigms. The innovations discussed, ranging from distributed consensus algorithms to edge-native file systems, collectively contribute to overcoming these challenges and unlocking the full potential of file management in distributed environments. As organizations navigate the complexities of distributed computing, the ongoing pursuit of innovative solutions becomes imperative for achieving efficient, secure, and scalable file management across diverse nodes and environments.

Strategies for integrating and managing file systems across hybrid and multi-cloud environments.

The integration and management of file systems across hybrid and multi-cloud environments present multifaceted challenges and demand strategic approaches to ensure seamless interoperability, data mobility, and efficient file management. One of the foundational strategies involves adopting a hybrid cloud architecture, where organizations leverage a combination of on-premises data centers and cloud services. In this context, implementing a unified file system that spans both on-premises and cloud environments becomes imperative. Technologies like distributed file systems and network-attached storage (NAS) solutions designed for hybrid cloud scenarios enable organizations to manage files consistently across diverse infrastructures. By unifying file management, organizations can achieve a cohesive data strategy that transcends the boundaries between on-premises and cloud-based storage, facilitating a smooth and integrated experience for users and applications.

Embracing cloud-native file systems represents a strategic shift in managing files across hybrid and multi-cloud environments. Cloud-native file systems are purpose-built for cloud architectures, offering scalable and distributed storage solutions that seamlessly integrate with cloud services. These file systems prioritize flexibility and scalability, enabling organizations to leverage the agility and resource efficiency of the cloud. Technologies such as Amazon Elastic File System (EFS), Azure Files, and Google Cloud Filestore provide cloud-native file storage solutions that can be seamlessly integrated into hybrid architectures. By adopting cloud-native file systems, organizations gain the advantages of cloud elasticity while ensuring compatibility with on-premises infrastructure, fostering a unified and streamlined approach to file management.

Interoperability becomes a central focus in managing file systems across hybrid and multi-cloud environments, where diverse storage solutions and platforms coexist. Adopting open standards and protocols, such as the Network File System (NFS) and Common Internet File System (CIFS), facilitates seamless integration between different file systems and environments. These standards ensure that files can be accessed and shared across heterogeneous infrastructure, providing a common language for communication between on-premises data centers and various cloud providers. Additionally, the use of containerized file systems and solutions that align with container orchestration platforms, such as Kubernetes, enhances interoperability in modern application architectures, allowing files to be managed consistently across diverse computing environments.

Data mobility emerges as a critical consideration in managing files across hybrid and multi-cloud environments. Organizations often need the flexibility to move data between on-premises infrastructure and different cloud providers based on changing requirements, cost considerations, or regulatory compliance. Implementing data migration strategies that support seamless movement of files across hybrid and multi-cloud environments is essential. Innovations in cloud services, such as AWS DataSync and Azure Data Box, facilitate efficient and secure data transfer between on-premises environments and cloud storage. These services enable organizations to overcome the challenges associated with data mobility, supporting a dynamic and responsive approach to file management across distributed infrastructure.

The adoption of a multi-cloud strategy introduces complexities in managing files across diverse cloud providers. Organizations may leverage multiple cloud platforms to benefit from specific features, avoid vendor lock-in, or enhance redundancy. However, the heterogeneity of cloud environments poses challenges in achieving consistent file management. Embracing a multi-cloud file management approach involves selecting file systems and storage solutions that offer compatibility with different cloud providers. Additionally, abstraction layers and middleware solutions that provide a unified interface for file access across multiple clouds contribute to simplifying file management complexities. By strategically navigating the nuances of multi-cloud environments, organizations can optimize their file management strategies to align with diverse business objectives and operational needs.

Security considerations play a pivotal role in managing files across hybrid and multi-cloud environments, where data traverses diverse infrastructures and may be subject to various threats. Implementing robust encryption mechanisms, both in transit and at rest, becomes a fundamental strategy to safeguard files against unauthorized access or interception. Role-based access control (RBAC) and identity management solutions ensure that file access privileges are consistently enforced across hybrid and multi-cloud environments, maintaining a secure and compliant posture. Additionally, the adoption of security best practices, such as regular audits, monitoring, and incident response procedures, contributes to a comprehensive security strategy that aligns with the distributed nature of file management in hybrid and multi-cloud architectures.

Cost optimization strategies are crucial for effective file management across hybrid and multi-cloud environments, considering the varying pricing models and cost structures of different cloud providers. Organizations must assess the cost implications of storing, accessing, and transferring files across hybrid environments and strategically allocate resources based on performance requirements and budget constraints. Leveraging cloud services with tiered storage options, such as Amazon S3 storage classes or Azure Blob Storage tiers, allows organizations to align storage costs with the access patterns of their files. Additionally, implementing data lifecycle management policies that automate the movement of files between storage tiers based on usage patterns contributes to cost efficiency. By adopting a proactive and data-centric approach to cost management, organizations can optimize their file management strategies across hybrid and multi-cloud environments.

The orchestration of file management workflows emerges as a strategic imperative in hybrid and multi-cloud environments, where the complexity of distributed infrastructure demands efficient coordination and automation. Container orchestration platforms, such as Kubernetes, provide a framework for orchestrating containerized applications, including those with file management requirements. Organizations can leverage container-native file systems and storage solutions that seamlessly integrate with container orchestration platforms, ensuring consistency in file management across diverse environments. Additionally, workflow automation tools and cloud-native services, such as AWS Step Functions or Azure Logic Apps, enable organizations to design and automate file management workflows that span on-premises infrastructure and multiple cloud providers. Strategic orchestration ensures that file operations are orchestrated in a coordinated and efficient manner, optimizing resource utilization and enhancing overall system agility.

In conclusion, managing file systems across hybrid and multi-cloud environments demands a strategic and holistic approach that addresses interoperability, data mobility, security, cost optimization, and orchestration challenges. By adopting unified file systems that span on premises and cloud environments, embracing cloud-native file systems, prioritizing interoperability through open standards, implementing data mobility strategies, navigating the complexities of multi-cloud environments, ensuring robust security measures, optimizing costs, and orchestrating file management workflows, organizations can navigate the complexities of hybrid and multi-cloud environments effectively. These strategic approaches empower organizations to unlock the benefits of distributed file management, providing a foundation for agility, scalability, and resilience in the dynamic landscape of modern computing architectures.

Ensuring data consistency and accessibility in diverse cloud infrastructures.

Ensuring data consistency and accessibility in diverse cloud infrastructures is a complex and critical challenge that organizations face as they embrace the flexibility and scalability of cloud computing. The distributed nature of cloud environments, encompassing public, private, and hybrid clouds, introduces intricacies in maintaining data consistency across geographically dispersed servers and storage resources. Achieving data consistency becomes paramount, especially when applications and services rely on accurate and up-to-date information. One strategy to address this challenge involves leveraging distributed databases and transactional systems designed for cloud architectures. These systems implement techniques such as distributed transactions and two-phase commit protocols to ensure that changes to data across multiple cloud nodes are atomic and consistent, mitigating the risk of discrepancies and conflicts.

Ensuring data accessibility across diverse cloud infrastructures requires strategic considerations to overcome potential latency and connectivity issues. Organizations often deploy content delivery networks (CDNs) to enhance data accessibility by caching and distributing frequently accessed content closer to end-users. CDNs reduce latency and improve response times by delivering content from edge servers located strategically around the globe. This approach not only enhances user experience but also contributes to data consistency, as users access cached copies of data that are synchronized with the central data repositories. Additionally, organizations may implement global load balancing and traffic management solutions to optimize data access routes, ensuring efficient and reliable connectivity to data stored in diverse cloud locations.

The adoption of cloud-native storage solutions plays a pivotal role in ensuring data consistency and accessibility in diverse cloud infrastructures. Cloud-native storage services, such as Amazon S3, Azure Blob Storage, and Google Cloud Storage, provide scalable and distributed storage that seamlessly integrates with cloud environments. These services often implement strong consistency models and offer features such as versioning and durability to safeguard data integrity. By leveraging cloud-native storage solutions, organizations can ensure that data is consistently accessible across different cloud providers, supporting a unified approach to data management that transcends the boundaries of individual cloud infrastructures.

In heterogeneous cloud environments where multiple cloud providers are utilized, achieving data consistency and accessibility requires interoperability. Embracing open standards and protocols, such as the Network File System (NFS) and Common Internet File System (CIFS), facilitates seamless integration between diverse storage solutions and cloud platforms. These standards provide a common language for communication between on-premises infrastructure and various cloud providers, enabling consistent file access and data sharing. Additionally, the use of containerization technologies, such as Docker and Kubernetes, enhances interoperability by encapsulating applications and their dependencies, allowing them to run consistently across different cloud environments while accessing shared data resources.

Implementing robust data replication strategies is instrumental in ensuring data consistency and accessibility, particularly in scenarios where high availability and fault tolerance are critical. Cloud environments often leverage replication mechanisms to create redundant copies of data across multiple geographic regions or availability zones. Synchronous replication ensures that changes to data are propagated immediately to all replicas, providing strong consistency but potentially introducing latency. Asynchronous replication allows for more flexibility in terms of latency but may result in temporary inconsistencies between replicas. By strategically configuring data replication based on application requirements and performance considerations, organizations can strike a balance between data consistency and accessibility in diverse cloud infrastructures.

The concept of eventual consistency is a notable consideration in achieving data consistency across diverse cloud infrastructures. In distributed systems, eventual consistency acknowledges that, given time, all replicas of data will converge to the same state. This model allows for temporary variations in data between replicas, offering a trade-off between consistency and low-latency access. Implementing eventual consistency in cloud environments involves carefully designing data models, choosing appropriate consistency levels, and leveraging distributed databases and storage systems that support this paradigm. Eventual consistency is particularly relevant in scenarios where low-latency access and high availability are prioritized over immediate consistency.

Ensuring data consistency and accessibility in diverse cloud infrastructures necessitates a proactive approach to monitoring and management. Cloud-native monitoring and observability tools, such as AWS CloudWatch, Azure Monitor, and Google Cloud Operations Suite, enable organizations to track the performance, availability, and consistency of data across different cloud providers. These tools provide insights into latency, error rates, and system behavior, facilitating timely identification and resolution of issues that may impact data consistency and accessibility. Additionally, organizations may implement automated scaling and load balancing mechanisms to dynamically adapt to changing workloads, ensuring optimal performance and responsiveness in diverse cloud environments.

Strategic data governance and metadata management practices contribute significantly to ensuring data consistency and accessibility in diverse cloud infrastructures. Establishing comprehensive data governance policies, including data quality standards, metadata tagging, and access controls, creates a foundation for maintaining consistency and integrity across distributed data sets. Metadata management tools enable organizations to catalog and track the lineage of data, providing transparency into data sources, transformations, and access patterns. By implementing robust data governance practices, organizations can ensure that data is consistently and accurately represented across different cloud infrastructures, supporting a unified and coherent approach to data management.

The integration of edge computing into diverse cloud infrastructures introduces additional considerations for ensuring data consistency and accessibility. Edge computing involves processing data closer to the source of generation, requiring data to be consistently available across both centralized cloud repositories and edge nodes. Edge-native storage solutions and caching mechanisms play a crucial role in enhancing data accessibility at the edge. These solutions enable local storage and retrieval of frequently accessed data, reducing the need for round-trip communication to centralized cloud storage. Implementing edge-native storage architectures ensures that data is consistently accessible, even in scenarios with intermittent connectivity or latency-sensitive edge applications.

Security considerations are paramount in ensuring data consistency and accessibility in diverse cloud infrastructures, where data traverses networks, storage systems, and processing nodes owned and operated by different entities. Implementing robust encryption mechanisms, both in transit and at rest, safeguards data against unauthorized access and interception. Role-based access control (RBAC) and identity management solutions ensure that only authorized users and applications can access and modify data, contributing to a secure and compliant data environment. Additionally, organizations may implement data governance policies that align with regulatory requirements, ensuring that data consistency and accessibility are maintained within the bounds of legal and compliance frameworks.

In conclusion, ensuring data consistency and accessibility in diverse cloud infrastructures is a multifaceted challenge that requires a holistic and strategic approach. Leveraging distributed databases, embracing cloud-native storage solutions, prioritizing interoperability through open standards, implementing robust data replication strategies, considering eventual consistency models, adopting proactive monitoring and management practices, establishing comprehensive data governance, integrating edge-native storage solutions, and prioritizing security considerations collectively contribute to achieving data consistency and accessibility in the dynamic and distributed landscape of modern cloud infrastructures. As organizations navigate the complexities of diverse cloud environments, the strategic considerations outlined become integral to fostering a unified, reliable, and secure approach to data management across geographically dispersed cloud resources.

Chapter 7: Challenges and Solutions in File Systems Management

Addressing challenges related to file fragmentation.

Addressing challenges related to file fragmentation is a critical aspect of maintaining optimal storage performance and efficient data access in modern computing environments. File fragmentation occurs when the data of a file is stored in non-contiguous blocks on a storage device, leading to increased disk I/O operations, longer access times, and reduced overall system performance. One primary strategy to mitigate file fragmentation involves utilizing advanced file systems that implement intelligent allocation algorithms. Traditional file systems, such as FAT32 or NTFS, may suffer from fragmentation over time as files are created, modified, and deleted. However, modern file systems like ZFS, Btrfs, or APFS employ advanced allocation strategies, including copy-on-write mechanisms and dynamic block allocation, to minimize fragmentation and enhance overall storage efficiency.

Defragmentation, a classic technique in addressing file fragmentation, involves reorganizing files and their associated data blocks to ensure contiguous storage. While traditional defragmentation tools have been widely used in the past, modern file systems often incorporate automatic defragmentation routines that operate in the background. These routines intelligently identify and defragment fragmented files during periods of low disk activity, avoiding disruptions to system performance. Additionally, organizations may schedule routine maintenance windows to perform more intensive defragmentation processes on larger storage volumes, ensuring that file fragmentation is proactively addressed without impacting day-to-day operations.

Efficient storage tiering strategies can contribute significantly to mitigating file fragmentation challenges. Storage tiering involves categorizing data based on its access patterns and placing it on storage tiers with varying performance characteristics. Frequently accessed and critical data can reside on high-performance storage tiers like SSDs, while less frequently accessed or archival data can be stored on lower-cost, higher-capacity tiers like traditional hard disk drives (HDDs). By intelligently managing data placement across storage tiers, organizations can minimize the impact of file fragmentation on the performance of critical applications, ensuring that frequently accessed files are stored in a manner that reduces fragmentation and accelerates access times.

The adoption of flash-based storage technologies, such as Solid State Drives (SSDs), presents a transformative solution to file fragmentation challenges. Unlike traditional HDDs, SSDs do not rely on physical read/write heads to access data, allowing for random access to any storage location. This inherent characteristic of SSDs mitigates the performance impact of file fragmentation. Consequently, organizations can leverage SSDs in storage architectures to enhance system responsiveness, reduce access times, and minimize the effects of file fragmentation. The shift towards SSD-based storage infrastructures aligns with the growing demand for improved application performance and responsiveness in various computing environments.

Implementing advanced caching mechanisms is another effective strategy to address challenges related to file fragmentation. Caching involves temporarily storing frequently accessed data in faster, more accessible storage layers, such as RAM or SSDs. By utilizing intelligent caching algorithms, systems can prioritize the caching of frequently accessed files, reducing the need for frequent disk I/O operations and mitigating the impact of file fragmentation on overall performance. Cache management strategies, including read-ahead and write-behind caching, contribute to optimizing data access patterns and minimizing latency associated with fragmented files. Intelligent caching mechanisms are particularly beneficial in scenarios where read and write operations exhibit distinct access patterns.

Dynamic storage provisioning and thin provisioning technologies offer flexibility in addressing file fragmentation challenges by optimizing storage allocation. Traditional storage provisioning methods often allocate fixed-size blocks for files, leading to potential wasted space and increased fragmentation. In contrast, dynamic storage provisioning dynamically adjusts the allocation of storage based on actual data usage, minimizing wasted space and reducing the likelihood of file fragmentation. Thin provisioning takes this concept further by allowing administrators to allocate virtual storage space that is only consumed as data is written. This approach enhances storage utilization efficiency, reduces the occurrence of fragmentation, and provides a more adaptive and scalable solution in modern storage architectures.

Automation and machine learning-driven storage management solutions are becoming increasingly prevalent in addressing file fragmentation challenges. These intelligent systems analyze historical data access patterns, file sizes, and storage utilization to make proactive decisions about data placement and allocation. By leveraging machine learning algorithms, these solutions can predict potential fragmentation issues and take preemptive actions to optimize storage layouts. Automated storage tiering, defragmentation, and caching adjustments are examples of functionalities that benefit from machine learning-driven storage management. These intelligent systems contribute to the proactive and adaptive nature of modern storage architectures, ensuring optimized performance and mitigating the impact of file fragmentation on user experiences.

File system optimization tools, often provided by operating system vendors or third-party software, offer targeted solutions for addressing file fragmentation challenges. These tools typically include features such as defragmentation, disk cleanup, and optimization algorithms designed to enhance file system performance. Organizations can incorporate these tools into their regular maintenance routines to actively manage file fragmentation and maintain the health of their storage infrastructure. Some optimization tools also provide visualizations and reports to help administrators monitor storage health, identify potential fragmentation issues, and make informed decisions about storage configurations and adjustments.

The adoption of containerization technologies, such as Docker, brings a new perspective to addressing file fragmentation challenges in modern application architectures. Containers encapsulate applications and their dependencies, creating portable and isolated environments. Containerized applications often follow a read-only file system model, where the application code and dependencies are immutable, reducing the likelihood of file fragmentation. The stateful data generated by containerized applications can be managed separately, leveraging persistent storage solutions that incorporate optimization techniques. Container orchestration platforms, like Kubernetes, contribute to managing file system challenges by orchestrating the deployment and scaling of containerized applications while providing mechanisms for efficient data access and storage management.

Organizations increasingly explore the benefits of Object Storage as a strategy to address file fragmentation challenges, especially in scenarios where large-scale, unstructured data needs to be efficiently managed. Object Storage systems, such as Amazon S3, Azure Blob Storage, or Google Cloud Storage, store data as objects with associated metadata. The flat and scalable architecture of Object Storage minimizes the impact of file fragmentation, as each object is stored independently. This approach is particularly advantageous for workloads involving large files, multimedia content, and archival data. By adopting Object Storage, organizations can streamline data access, reduce the effects of file fragmentation, and optimize storage efficiency in environments characterized by diverse access patterns and data types.

Strategies for addressing file fragmentation challenges extend beyond technical solutions to include organizational policies and practices. Educating users and administrators about the impact of file fragmentation and promoting best practices for data management contribute to a proactive approach. Encouraging users to regularly perform file maintenance, such as archiving, purging unnecessary files, and organizing data into logical structures, helps prevent fragmentation issues from escalating. Establishing clear data lifecycle management policies ensures that data is appropriately archived or migrated to accommodate changing access patterns and storage requirements, minimizing the risk of file fragmentation over time.

In conclusion, addressing challenges related to file fragmentation requires a multifaceted and adaptive approach that encompasses technological innovations, storage optimization strategies, automation, containerization, and organizational practices. From the adoption of advanced file systems and defragmentation routines to leveraging flash-based storage technologies, dynamic provisioning, and intelligent caching mechanisms, organizations have a rich toolkit to mitigate the impact of file fragmentation on storage performance. Additionally, the growing influence of containerization, object storage, and machine learning-driven solutions contributes to the evolution of strategies aimed at maintaining optimal data access in diverse computing environments. As organizations continue to navigate the complexities of modern storage architectures, the collaborative integration of these strategies becomes imperative for ensuring efficient, reliable, and performant file management.

Strategies for defragmentation and optimizing file allocation.

Strategies for defragmentation and optimizing file allocation are critical components of maintaining efficient storage performance and ensuring streamlined data access in computing environments. File fragmentation occurs when the data associated with a file is scattered across non-contiguous blocks on a storage device, leading to increased disk I/O operations, longer access times, and reduced overall system performance. Defragmentation, a fundamental strategy in addressing fragmentation, involves reorganizing files and their associated data blocks to ensure contiguous storage. Traditional defragmentation tools, both built into operating systems and available as third-party solutions, have been widely used to manually initiate defragmentation processes. These tools analyze file structures, identify fragmented files, and rearrange data blocks to create contiguous storage, minimizing the impact of fragmentation on performance.

Modern file systems often incorporate automatic defragmentation routines, operating seamlessly in the background to address fragmentation without requiring user intervention. These intelligent defragmentation mechanisms leverage algorithms to identify fragmented files during periods of low disk activity, ensuring minimal disruption to ongoing operations. By proactively managing fragmentation, automatic defragmentation contributes to maintaining optimal storage performance, especially in environments with dynamic data changes and frequent file modifications. This approach aligns with the evolving nature of storage management, where automation plays a key role in ensuring consistent performance and responsiveness.

The choice of file system architecture significantly influences defragmentation strategies and the overall optimization of file allocation. Traditional file systems, such as FAT32 or NTFS, may be susceptible to fragmentation over time due to their allocation algorithms. In contrast, modern file systems, including ZFS, Btrfs, and APFS, implement advanced allocation strategies to minimize fragmentation. Copy-on-write mechanisms, dynamic block allocation, and intelligent space management are integral features of these file systems, optimizing file allocation and mitigating the impact of fragmentation. The adoption of modern file systems represents a strategic approach to proactively address fragmentation challenges and enhance storage efficiency in contemporary computing environments.

Storage tiering emerges as a strategic strategy to optimize file allocation by categorizing data based on access patterns and placing it on storage tiers with varying performance characteristics. Frequently accessed and critical data can reside on high-performance storage tiers, such as Solid State Drives (SSDs), while less frequently accessed or archival data is stored on lower-cost, higher-capacity tiers like traditional Hard Disk Drives (HDDs). This tiered storage approach not only optimizes data access but also minimizes the impact of file fragmentation on critical applications. Storage tiering aligns with the principles of efficient resource utilization, providing a balanced solution that caters to the diverse performance requirements of different data sets.

The adoption of flash-based storage technologies, particularly Solid State Drives (SSDs), revolutionizes file allocation and defragmentation strategies. Unlike traditional Hard Disk Drives (HDDs) with physical read/write heads, SSDs allow for random access to any storage location. This inherent characteristic significantly reduces the impact of file fragmentation on access times and overall performance. As organizations increasingly transition to SSD-based storage infrastructures, they benefit from improved application responsiveness, faster data access, and a reduction in the traditional challenges associated with file fragmentation. The strategic incorporation of SSDs aligns with the ongoing pursuit of enhanced storage performance in various computing environments.

Dynamic storage provisioning and thin provisioning technologies offer adaptive solutions for optimizing file allocation. Traditional storage provisioning methods allocate fixed-size blocks for files, potentially leading to wasted space and increased fragmentation. Dynamic storage provisioning adjusts the allocation of storage based on actual data usage, minimizing wasted space and reducing the likelihood of fragmentation. Thin provisioning takes this concept further by allowing administrators to allocate virtual storage space that is only consumed as data is written. These approaches contribute to optimized storage allocation, ensuring efficient space utilization and mitigating the challenges associated with file fragmentation in modern storage architectures.

Automation and machine learning-driven storage management solutions play a pivotal role in optimizing file allocation and addressing fragmentation challenges. These intelligent systems analyze historical data access patterns, file sizes, and storage utilization to make proactive decisions about data placement and allocation. By leveraging machine learning algorithms, these solutions can predict potential fragmentation issues and take preemptive actions to optimize storage layouts. Automated storage tiering, defragmentation, and caching adjustments are examples of functionalities that benefit from machine learning-driven storage management. These intelligent systems contribute to the proactive and adaptive nature of modern storage architectures, ensuring optimized performance and mitigating the impact of file fragmentation on user experiences.

Advanced caching mechanisms contribute significantly to optimizing file allocation and mitigating the challenges associated with fragmentation. Caching involves temporarily storing frequently accessed data in faster, more accessible storage layers, such as RAM or SSDs. By utilizing intelligent caching algorithms, systems can prioritize the caching of frequently accessed files, reducing the need for frequent disk I/O operations and minimizing the impact of file fragmentation on overall performance. Read-ahead and write-behind caching strategies further enhance data access patterns and reduce latency associated with fragmented files. Intelligent caching mechanisms are particularly beneficial in scenarios where read and write operations exhibit distinct access patterns, contributing to an overall improvement in storage efficiency.

Containerization technologies, such as Docker, introduce a novel perspective to optimizing file allocation, especially in modern application architectures. Containers encapsulate applications and their dependencies, creating portable and isolated environments. Containerized applications often follow a read-only file system model, where the application code and dependencies are immutable, reducing the likelihood of file fragmentation. The stateful data generated by containerized applications can be managed separately, leveraging persistent storage solutions that incorporate optimization techniques. Container orchestration platforms, like Kubernetes, contribute to managing file allocation challenges by orchestrating the deployment and scaling of containerized applications while providing mechanisms for efficient data access and storage management.

Organizational policies and practices play a vital role in optimizing file allocation and addressing fragmentation challenges. Educating users and administrators about the impact of file fragmentation and promoting best practices for data management contribute to a proactive approach. Encouraging users to perform regular file maintenance, such as archiving, purging unnecessary files, and organizing data into logical structures, helps prevent fragmentation issues from escalating. Establishing clear data lifecycle management policies ensures that data is appropriately archived or migrated to accommodate changing access patterns and storage requirements, minimizing the risk of file fragmentation over time. Aligning organizational practices with storage optimization strategies creates a collaborative and proactive environment for addressing file allocation challenges.

In conclusion, strategies for defragmentation and optimizing file allocation are integral components of maintaining efficient storage performance in modern computing environments. From the adoption of advanced file systems, storage tiering, and flash-based storage technologies to dynamic provisioning, automation-driven solutions, and caching mechanisms, organizations have a diverse toolkit to optimize file allocation and mitigate the impact of fragmentation. Containerization technologies and organizational practices further contribute to a holistic approach to storage optimization. As organizations continue to navigate the complexities of modern storage architectures, the collaborative integration of these strategies becomes imperative for ensuring efficient, reliable, and performant file management in diverse computing environments.

Identifying challenges associated with managing large-scale file systems.

Identifying challenges associated with managing large-scale file systems is essential in navigating the complexities that arise when dealing with vast amounts of data in diverse computing environments. One prominent challenge is the sheer volume of data generated and stored within large-scale file systems. As data continues to proliferate exponentially, managing the growth becomes a substantial task. This challenge extends to capacity planning, where organizations must anticipate future storage needs, allocate resources effectively, and ensure scalability to accommodate expanding datasets. Large-scale file systems often encounter issues related to data sprawl, where unstructured data is distributed across various locations, making it challenging to maintain a centralized and coherent data management strategy.

The diversity of data types within large-scale file systems introduces another layer of complexity. Unstructured data, including documents, images, videos, and logs, can vary significantly in size, format, and access patterns. Managing this heterogeneity requires adaptable storage solutions capable of efficiently handling diverse data types while providing optimized access mechanisms. Furthermore, addressing the challenges associated with diverse data often involves implementing metadata management strategies to categorize, tag, and organize files effectively, facilitating efficient search, retrieval, and data lifecycle management.

Ensuring data consistency and integrity becomes a critical challenge in large-scale file systems, especially in distributed environments. With data distributed across multiple nodes or storage clusters, maintaining consistency becomes complex. Synchronization issues, conflicting updates, and potential data corruption are inherent risks in large-scale distributed file systems. Implementing robust replication mechanisms, distributed transactions, and versioning controls becomes imperative to ensure that all instances of data across the file system remain coherent and accurate. The challenge is heightened in scenarios where data is concurrently accessed and modified by multiple users or applications, requiring sophisticated coordination and conflict resolution mechanisms.

Access control and security present significant challenges in large-scale file systems, particularly when dealing with diverse user groups, varying data sensitivity levels, and compliance requirements. Establishing and enforcing granular access policies, authentication mechanisms, and encryption protocols are essential components of a robust security strategy. Balancing the need for accessibility with stringent security measures is a delicate task, and organizations must navigate the complexities of implementing role-based access controls (RBAC), encryption at rest and in transit, and audit trails to meet both regulatory requirements and organizational security standards.

Performance optimization poses a considerable challenge in large-scale file systems, where the sheer volume and diversity of data can lead to latency issues and decreased system responsiveness. Efficient data retrieval, storage, and processing become critical factors in maintaining optimal performance. Implementing techniques such as caching, indexing, and parallel processing can contribute to performance optimization. Additionally, organizations may leverage technologies like distributed file systems, object storage, and tiered storage architectures to balance performance and cost-effectiveness based on data access patterns and usage requirements.

Data mobility and interoperability challenges arise when managing large-scale file systems across heterogeneous environments, encompassing on-premises infrastructure, cloud platforms, and edge computing nodes. Organizations often face the need to move data seamlessly between different storage solutions, implement hybrid cloud strategies, or accommodate evolving technology landscapes. Ensuring compatibility and smooth data transfer between diverse systems and platforms necessitates the adoption of open standards, protocols, and data migration strategies. Overcoming these challenges enables organizations to leverage the advantages of diverse computing environments without compromising data accessibility, integrity, or security.

Metadata management becomes increasingly crucial in large-scale file systems to enhance searchability, categorization, and overall data organization. As the volume of data grows, maintaining an efficient and scalable metadata infrastructure is essential for quick and accurate file retrieval. Metadata solutions must accommodate diverse data types, provide flexibility for tagging and categorization, and integrate seamlessly with search and indexing mechanisms. The challenge lies in designing and implementing a metadata framework that aligns with the specific requirements and access patterns of the large-scale file system while ensuring minimal impact on overall performance.

Data lifecycle management presents a multifaceted challenge in large-scale file systems, where organizations must navigate the entire lifespan of data from creation to deletion or archival. Balancing the need for data accessibility with storage efficiency and cost-effectiveness requires the implementation of policies for data retention, archiving, and deletion. Developing automated workflows for data migration between storage tiers based on access patterns, and defining clear criteria for data archival or deletion, becomes essential. Striking the right balance between data availability and storage optimization while adhering to regulatory compliance requirements poses a constant challenge in large-scale file system management.

Disaster recovery and data resilience are critical considerations in large-scale file systems, given the potential impact of system failures, hardware malfunctions, or unforeseen events. Implementing robust backup and recovery strategies, ensuring data durability, and incorporating redundancy mechanisms are essential components of a comprehensive data resilience plan. The challenge lies in designing and maintaining a resilient architecture that can withstand failures, minimize downtime, and facilitate rapid recovery. Large-scale file systems often require geographically distributed backup locations, efficient snapshot mechanisms, and continuous monitoring to ensure data integrity and availability in the face of unexpected disruptions.

Scalability challenges emerge as a fundamental consideration in large-scale file systems, especially as organizations experience growth in data volumes, user bases, and computing infrastructure. Scalability encompasses both vertical scalability, where individual components can handle increasing workloads, and horizontal scalability, involving the ability to add new nodes or storage clusters seamlessly. Ensuring that the file system architecture can scale effectively to meet growing demands without sacrificing performance, accessibility, or security becomes a persistent challenge. Implementing scalable storage solutions, distributed file systems, and load balancing mechanisms are integral strategies to address scalability challenges in large-scale file systems.

Regulatory compliance introduces an additional layer of complexity in managing large-scale file systems, as organizations must adhere to industry-specific and regional data protection and privacy regulations. Compliance requirements may dictate data storage practices, access controls, encryption standards, and auditability measures. Navigating the intricacies of compliance frameworks and ensuring that large-scale file systems align with these regulations requires ongoing monitoring, policy enforcement, and collaboration with legal and compliance teams. Organizations must be agile in adapting their file system management practices to evolving regulatory landscapes to avoid potential legal repercussions.

The evolution of technology and the continuous introduction of new storage solutions and computing paradigms present a challenge in large-scale file system management. Staying abreast of technological advancements, assessing their relevance to specific use cases, and strategically incorporating innovations without disrupting existing operations become essential. The challenge lies in adopting a future-proof approach that allows organizations to harness the benefits of emerging technologies while maintaining compatibility with legacy systems and data. Continuous training and development of IT teams, along with strategic partnerships with technology vendors, contribute to navigating the dynamic landscape of large-scale file system management.

In conclusion, identifying challenges associated with managing large-scale file systems is paramount in developing effective strategies to overcome the complexities inherent in handling vast amounts of data. From addressing the sheer volume and diversity of data, ensuring data consistency and security, to optimizing performance, scalability, and compliance with regulatory frameworks, organizations must adopt a holistic and adaptive approach. The challenges discussed underscore the need for a comprehensive understanding of the intricate interplay between technology, data management practices, and organizational policies to successfully navigate the landscape of large-scale file system management in modern computing environments.

Scalability solutions, including sharding and distributed file storage.

Scalability solutions, encompassing concepts such as sharding and distributed file storage, play a pivotal role in addressing the ever-growing demands for processing power, storage capacity, and data access in modern computing environments. Scalability, defined as the ability of a system to handle increasing workloads and adapt to growing demands, is a fundamental consideration as organizations strive to accommodate expanding user bases, larger datasets, and dynamic computing infrastructures. Sharding, a prominent scalability technique, involves partitioning a database or dataset into smaller, more manageable fragments called shards. Each shard is a self-contained subset of the overall data, and the distribution of data across shards allows for parallel processing and improved performance. Sharding is particularly valuable in distributed databases, where the separation of data enables parallel queries and transactions, alleviating the load on individual database nodes and contributing to horizontal scalability.

Distributed file storage systems represent a key component of scalability solutions, offering a paradigm shift from traditional centralized storage models. In a distributed file storage system, data is distributed across multiple nodes or servers, forming a decentralized architecture that enables efficient data access and storage. This approach addresses the limitations of centralized storage systems, which may encounter bottlenecks as data volumes increase. Distributed file storage systems, exemplified by technologies like Hadoop

Distributed File System (HDFS), Google File System (GFS), and Amazon S3, distribute data across a cluster of nodes, providing scalability by allowing organizations to add nodes to accommodate growing storage needs seamlessly.

Sharding, as a strategy for achieving scalability, involves breaking down large datasets or databases into smaller, more manageable units called shards. Each shard functions as an independent subset of the complete dataset, containing a specific portion of the data. The distribution of shards across different nodes or servers enables parallel processing of queries and transactions, distributing the computational load and improving overall system performance. Sharding is particularly effective in scenarios where a centralized database becomes a bottleneck due to increased data volumes and query complexity. By distributing data across multiple shards, organizations can achieve horizontal scalability, allowing the system to scale out by adding more nodes or servers to the infrastructure.

There are several approaches to implementing sharding, each with its advantages and considerations. Range-based sharding involves dividing the dataset based on a specific range of values, such as partitioning data based on a range of user IDs or timestamps. Hash-based sharding, on the other hand, leverages a hashing function to determine which shard a particular piece of data belongs to, ensuring a more even distribution of data across shards. Directory-based sharding maintains a central directory that maps data to specific shards, providing a level of abstraction and flexibility in managing the sharding configuration. Dynamic sharding allows for the automatic redistribution of data as the system scales, adapting to changing workloads and data distribution patterns.

Distributed file storage systems represent a paradigm shift from traditional monolithic storage architectures, providing a scalable and fault-tolerant solution for managing large volumes of data. In a distributed file storage system, data is distributed across multiple nodes or servers, each equipped with its storage capacity. This decentralized approach eliminates the limitations associated with a single, centralized storage location, allowing organizations to scale their storage infrastructure horizontally by adding more nodes as needed. Distributed file storage systems excel in handling massive datasets and are designed to provide high availability, fault tolerance, and efficient data access.

The Hadoop Distributed File System (HDFS) is an exemplary distributed file storage system widely used in big data processing. HDFS divides large files into smaller blocks, typically 128 megabytes or 256 megabytes in size, and distributes these blocks across multiple nodes in a cluster. This distribution enables parallel processing of data, as each node can independently process its allocated data blocks. Moreover, HDFS incorporates replication for fault tolerance, ensuring that multiple copies of each data block are stored across different nodes to mitigate the risk of data loss in the event of node failures.

Google File System (GFS) is another notable distributed file storage system designed to handle large-scale data across multiple servers. GFS employs a master-server architecture, where a central master server manages metadata and coordinates data access across distributed chunkservers. The system is optimized for scalability, fault tolerance, and high throughput, making it suitable for applications with vast data storage and retrieval requirements.

Amazon Simple Storage Service (S3) is a widely used cloud-based distributed file storage solution that provides scalable and durable object storage. S3 allows organizations to store and retrieve any amount of data, offering high availability and reliability through data replication across multiple data centers. Its simple and scalable architecture makes it a preferred choice for a wide range of applications, from small-scale projects to large-scale enterprise solutions.

The benefits of distributed file storage systems extend beyond scalability to include fault tolerance, high availability, and improved data access performance. These systems distribute data across multiple nodes, reducing the risk of data loss due to hardware failures or node outages. Additionally, the parallel processing capabilities inherent in distributed file storage systems enhance data access performance, enabling organizations to achieve efficient and responsive data retrieval for diverse workloads.

Scalability solutions, including sharding and distributed file storage, are not mutually exclusive but can be complementary in addressing the complexities of modern computing environments. Sharding focuses on partitioning large datasets or databases to enable parallel processing and improve query performance. It is particularly effective in scenarios where data distribution patterns align with sharding strategies, such as when data can be logically divided based on ranges or hash functions. Distributed file storage systems, on the other hand, provide a holistic approach to scalable data storage, distributing data across multiple nodes and enabling horizontal scaling as storage needs grow.

The integration of sharding and distributed file storage systems becomes particularly powerful in large-scale applications and systems dealing with massive datasets. For example, a system handling vast amounts of user-generated content, such as images, videos, or documents, could leverage sharding to partition user data based on user IDs or content types. Simultaneously, a distributed file storage system could be employed to store and manage these large files efficiently, distributing the load across a cluster of nodes. This combined approach leverages the strengths of both sharding and distributed file storage to achieve a scalable, high-performance solution.

Challenges associated with scalability solutions, including sharding and distributed file storage, involve careful consideration of factors such as data consistency, system complexity, and potential trade-offs. In sharding, ensuring data consistency across distributed shards can be challenging, requiring robust synchronization mechanisms and coordination. Additionally, the design and maintenance of a sharded architecture introduce complexities in managing metadata, transactional consistency, and potential challenges related to uneven data distribution. Organizations must carefully assess their data access patterns, workload characteristics, and scalability requirements to determine the most suitable sharding strategy for their specific use case.

Distributed file storage systems face challenges related to data access latency, synchronization, and ensuring fault tolerance in dynamic environments. The distribution of data across multiple nodes necessitates efficient coordination and communication mechanisms to maintain data consistency and integrity. Additionally, organizations must consider trade-offs between consistency and availability, especially in distributed systems where achieving both simultaneously can be challenging. Effective load balancing, fault detection, and recovery mechanisms are essential components of a robust distributed file storage system.

In conclusion, scalability solutions, including sharding and distributed file storage, represent crucial approaches to addressing the challenges posed by the ever-increasing demands for data processing and storage in modern computing environments. Sharding provides a means to partition large datasets for parallel processing, improving query performance and scalability. Distributed file storage systems offer a decentralized, scalable architecture for efficient data storage, retrieval, and high availability. The integration of these solutions requires a thoughtful consideration of data distribution patterns, workload characteristics, and the specific requirements of the organization's use case. By leveraging the strengths of sharding and distributed file storage, organizations can achieve scalable, responsive, and fault-tolerant solutions to meet the dynamic demands of contemporary computing.

Common challenges in implementing reliable backup and recovery strategies.

Implementing reliable backup and recovery strategies is a critical aspect of ensuring data integrity, availability, and resilience in modern computing environments. Despite the importance of these strategies, organizations face a myriad of common challenges that must be navigated to establish robust and effective backup and recovery processes. One of the primary challenges is the sheer volume and diversity of data generated by organizations today. As data continues to grow exponentially, backup and recovery solutions must contend with large datasets, various data types, and complex structures. Ensuring the efficient and timely backup of diverse data sets becomes a considerable undertaking, requiring careful planning, resource allocation, and the selection of appropriate backup technologies.

The complexity of modern IT infrastructures introduces another challenge in implementing reliable backup and recovery strategies. Organizations often operate in hybrid environments that span on-premises data centers, cloud platforms, and edge computing nodes. Managing backup processes across these heterogeneous environments requires a cohesive and adaptable strategy. Compatibility issues, differing technologies, and diverse storage architectures necessitate a comprehensive approach that ensures seamless data protection and recovery regardless of the underlying infrastructure. Achieving a unified backup and recovery solution across hybrid environments is crucial to mitigating the risk of data loss and ensuring consistent business continuity.

Data growth and complexity are further compounded by the increasing frequency of data changes and updates within organizations. Continuous changes to files, databases, and applications demand backup solutions that can perform frequent and incremental backups to capture only the modified or newly added data. Traditional full backups can be resource-intensive and time-consuming, posing challenges in meeting stringent backup windows. Incremental and differential backup strategies become essential components of reliable backup solutions, enabling organizations to balance data protection with operational efficiency. However, implementing these strategies requires careful consideration of data dependencies, recovery point objectives (RPO), and the coordination of backup schedules to ensure data consistency.

Ensuring data consistency and integrity across distributed environments presents a significant challenge in backup and recovery efforts. In distributed systems, where data may reside on various nodes, servers, or cloud instances, maintaining a coherent and synchronized backup becomes complex. Coordinating backup processes to capture consistent snapshots of interdependent data while avoiding issues such as data skew or partial backups is crucial. Organizations must implement mechanisms, such as distributed transactional consistency and synchronization protocols, to address challenges associated with data consistency in distributed environments. Additionally, ensuring that backup copies accurately reflect the state of the data at the time of backup is essential for reliable recovery.

The ever-evolving threat landscape introduces security challenges in backup and recovery strategies. Cybersecurity threats, including ransomware attacks, malware, and unauthorized access, pose a significant risk to data integrity and availability. Attackers increasingly target backup systems to compromise or delete backup copies, rendering organizations unable to recover their data without paying a ransom. Implementing secure and isolated backup repositories, leveraging encryption for data in transit and at rest, and employing access controls and authentication mechanisms are essential elements of a resilient backup strategy. Organizations must also regularly test their backup and recovery processes to ensure their effectiveness in the face of emerging security threats.

Scalability challenges emerge as organizations experience data growth and expanding IT infrastructures. Backup solutions must scale seamlessly to accommodate the increasing volume of data, the addition of new applications, and the deployment of additional infrastructure components. Ensuring that backup processes can scale horizontally by adding resources or vertically by leveraging advanced backup technologies becomes critical. Organizations may also encounter challenges related to the scalability of backup infrastructure components, such as backup servers, storage repositories, and network bandwidth. Addressing scalability challenges requires strategic planning, the adoption of scalable backup architectures, and regular assessments of infrastructure requirements.

Meeting recovery time objectives (RTO) and recovery point objectives (RPO) is a common challenge that organizations face in designing and implementing reliable backup and recovery strategies. RTO defines the acceptable downtime for systems and applications, while RPO specifies the maximum allowable data loss in the event of a recovery. Striking the right balance between achieving low RTO and RPO and minimizing the associated costs is a complex task. High-frequency backups and advanced technologies, such as continuous data protection (CDP) and near-instant recovery solutions, contribute to meeting stringent RTO and RPO requirements. However, organizations must carefully assess their specific recovery needs, data criticality, and budget constraints to tailor their backup and recovery strategies accordingly.

The human factor introduces challenges related to the management and oversight of backup and recovery processes. Organizations often struggle with the human elements of backup strategy implementation, such as defining and enforcing backup policies, ensuring regular testing of recovery processes, and providing adequate training for backup administrators. Human errors, such as misconfigurations, accidental deletions, or oversight in backup scheduling, can compromise the effectiveness of backup solutions. Establishing clear backup policies, conducting training programs, and implementing role-based access controls contribute to minimizing the impact of human-related challenges on the reliability of backup and recovery processes.

Cost considerations play a crucial role in the implementation of backup and recovery strategies. Organizations must balance the need for comprehensive data protection with budget constraints and operational efficiency. Traditional backup solutions may incur high upfront costs for hardware, software licenses, and ongoing maintenance. Cloud-based backup services offer an alternative, allowing organizations to leverage scalable and pay-as-you-go models. However, cloud costs can vary based on data volume, storage requirements, and data transfer. Organizations must conduct thorough cost-benefit analyses to determine the most cost-effective backup and recovery approach while meeting their data protection and compliance requirements.

Compliance requirements, often dictated by industry regulations and data protection laws, introduce additional challenges in backup and recovery efforts. Organizations must align their backup strategies with specific compliance frameworks, ensuring that data is securely stored, retained for the required periods, and can be audited for regulatory purposes. Implementing features such as data encryption, audit trails, and access controls becomes essential to meet compliance standards. Additionally, organizations must stay informed about changes in regulatory landscapes and adapt their backup and recovery processes accordingly to avoid legal repercussions and financial penalties.

In conclusion, implementing reliable backup and recovery strategies is a multifaceted challenge that organizations must navigate to ensure the integrity, availability, and resilience of their data. From addressing the complexities of modern IT infrastructures, data growth, and security threats to achieving data consistency in distributed environments, organizations must adopt holistic and adaptive approaches. Balancing factors such as scalability, cost-effectiveness, and compliance requirements requires strategic planning, careful technology selection, and ongoing evaluation of backup and recovery processes. By addressing these common challenges, organizations can establish robust backup and recovery strategies that safeguard their data assets and enable swift and effective recovery in the face of unforeseen events.

Techniques for ensuring data resilience and rapid recovery.

Ensuring data resilience and rapid recovery is a paramount concern for organizations seeking to safeguard their critical information assets in the face of various challenges, including hardware failures, cyber threats, and natural disasters. One fundamental technique for enhancing data resilience is the implementation of robust backup strategies. Organizations often employ regular and automated backups of their data to create redundant copies that can be restored in the event of data loss. The choice between full, incremental, or differential backups depends on factors such as data change frequency, recovery time objectives (RTO), and available resources. By maintaining multiple copies distributed across different locations or storage tiers, organizations fortify their resilience against various data loss scenarios and lay the foundation for efficient recovery processes.

In conjunction with traditional backup methods, continuous data protection (CDP) emerges as a valuable technique to enhance data resilience. CDP involves capturing and replicating every change made to data in real-time or near-real-time. This granular approach minimizes data loss, as organizations can recover from any point in time, often down to the level of individual file changes. CDP is particularly effective in scenarios where minimizing RPO (Recovery Point Objective) is critical, as it allows for the recovery of data with minimal loss, sometimes seconds before an incident occurs. The implementation of CDP involves capturing changes at the source, transmitting them to a secondary location, and storing them in a manner that enables rapid recovery. This technique is instrumental in bolstering data resilience by significantly reducing the potential for data loss and downtime.

Utilizing snapshot technologies represents another technique for ensuring data resilience and facilitating rapid recovery. Snapshots capture the state of a file system or storage volume at a specific point in time, creating a read-only copy of the data. These point-in-time copies provide a consistent view of the data for backup and recovery purposes. Snapshots are particularly valuable for quickly recovering from data corruption, accidental deletions, or other issues, as they offer a point of reference from which to restore the system or individual files. The efficient use of snapshots requires a balance between storage capacity and the frequency of snapshot creation, ensuring that organizations can meet their recovery objectives without incurring excessive storage costs.

Redundant Array of Independent Disks (RAID) configurations contribute to data resilience by distributing data across multiple disk drives, providing fault tolerance and improved performance. RAID employs various levels, such as RAID 1 (mirroring), RAID 5 (striping with parity), and RAID 6 (striping with dual parity), each offering a different balance of performance and resilience. In the event of a disk failure, RAID systems can continue to operate, and data can be reconstructed from the remaining drives. While RAID enhances data resilience against hardware failures, it is not a substitute for comprehensive backup strategies, as it does not protect against logical errors, data corruption, or catastrophic events affecting the entire RAID array.

Cloud-based backup and disaster recovery services play a pivotal role in ensuring data resilience and rapid recovery, particularly for organizations leveraging cloud infrastructures. Cloud services offer scalable and secure storage solutions that facilitate offsite backups and data redundancy. By leveraging cloud-based backup services, organizations can benefit from automatic data replication, geographic redundancy, and the ability to restore data from anywhere with an internet connection. Cloud-based disaster recovery solutions provide organizations with the flexibility to quickly spin up virtualized environments in the cloud in the event of a local infrastructure failure. This approach minimizes downtime and enables organizations to resume operations swiftly, even in the face of catastrophic events.

The implementation of high-availability (HA) architectures is a key technique for ensuring data resilience and rapid recovery in mission-critical systems. HA architectures are designed to minimize downtime by providing redundant components and failover mechanisms. Redundant servers, storage, and network components are configured to operate in tandem, and in the event of a failure, the workload seamlessly transitions to the redundant components. HA architectures are often employed in conjunction with load balancing mechanisms to ensure optimal resource utilization and prevent service disruptions. While HA architectures contribute significantly to minimizing downtime, they are not a one-size-fits-all solution and should be complemented by comprehensive backup and recovery strategies to address a broader range of data loss scenarios.

Implementing a tiered storage strategy is instrumental in optimizing data resilience and recovery. This technique involves categorizing data based on its criticality and access frequency and assigning it to different storage tiers accordingly. Frequently accessed and critical data can be stored on high-performance storage tiers, such as Solid State Drives (SSDs), while less frequently accessed or archival data is stored on lower-cost, higher-capacity tiers like traditional Hard Disk Drives (HDDs). By adopting a tiered storage approach, organizations can enhance performance for critical applications while optimizing costs. Additionally, tiered storage facilitates the implementation of backup and recovery strategies that prioritize the backup of critical data, allowing for faster recovery in the event of data loss or system failures.

Automation plays a crucial role in ensuring data resilience and expediting recovery processes. Automated backup and recovery solutions enable organizations to schedule and execute routine backups without manual intervention. Automation ensures consistency, reduces the risk of human errors, and allows organizations to meet stringent backup schedules. Additionally, automated recovery processes can streamline the restoration of data and systems, minimizing downtime and accelerating the recovery timeline. Intelligent automation technologies, such as machine learning-driven analytics, contribute to proactive monitoring, identification of potential issues, and predictive decision-making in data protection and recovery efforts.

Embracing a culture of proactive testing and validation is a foundational technique for ensuring data resilience and rapid recovery. Regularly testing backup and recovery processes, including the restoration of data and systems, helps organizations identify potential issues, assess the effectiveness of their strategies, and validate the reliability of their backups. By conducting simulated recovery scenarios, organizations can uncover weaknesses in their processes, address any shortcomings, and refine their strategies to ensure optimal performance in real-world scenarios. Proactive testing is instrumental in building confidence in the efficacy of backup and recovery solutions and contributes to a swift response in the event of actual data loss or system failures.

Encryption technologies play a dual role in enhancing data resilience and securing the recovery process. By encrypting data both in transit and at rest, organizations safeguard sensitive information from unauthorized access, mitigating the risk of data breaches and ensuring compliance with data protection regulations. Encryption also contributes to the integrity of backup and recovery processes by preventing tampering or unauthorized alterations of backup data. Implementing robust encryption mechanisms, including key management practices, enhances the overall security posture of backup and recovery strategies, reinforcing data resilience against both external threats and internal vulnerabilities.

In conclusion, ensuring data resilience and rapid recovery requires a multifaceted approach that integrates various techniques and technologies. Robust backup strategies, continuous data protection, snapshot technologies, RAID configurations, and cloud-based services contribute to creating redundant copies of data and minimizing the impact of hardware failures or data corruption. High-availability architectures enhance system reliability, and tiered storage strategies optimize data access and recovery performance. Automation and proactive testing ensure the consistency and reliability of backup and recovery processes, while encryption technologies bolster data security and integrity. By adopting a comprehensive and adaptive approach that leverages these techniques, organizations can establish resilient data protection mechanisms and expedite recovery in the face of diverse challenges.

The importance of routine maintenance for file systems.

Routine maintenance for file systems is of paramount importance in ensuring the health, performance, and longevity of the underlying data infrastructure within computing environments. A file system serves as the critical layer responsible for organizing, storing, and retrieving data on storage devices. The significance of routine maintenance lies in its ability to proactively address potential issues, optimize performance, and mitigate risks associated with data loss or corruption. One fundamental aspect of routine maintenance involves regular file system checks and integrity validations. These checks help identify and rectify inconsistencies, errors, or corruption within the file system structure, preventing the escalation of minor issues into critical problems that could compromise data integrity.

Moreover, routine maintenance encompasses the application of updates and patches to the file system software. As technology evolves, file system developers release updates to address security vulnerabilities, improve performance, and introduce new features. Regularly applying these updates ensures that the file system remains resilient against emerging threats, adheres to the latest security standards, and leverages optimizations for enhanced efficiency. Failure to keep the file system software up-to-date may expose vulnerabilities that could be exploited by malicious actors, compromising the confidentiality and integrity of stored data. Therefore, routine maintenance acts as a proactive measure to fortify the file system against evolving security challenges.

File system optimization is a crucial aspect of routine maintenance that focuses on enhancing performance and responsiveness. Over time, file systems can become fragmented, leading to scattered data blocks across storage devices. This fragmentation can result in slower data access times and reduced overall system performance. Routine maintenance tasks, such as defragmentation and optimization processes, help rearrange data blocks, minimizing fragmentation and improving data retrieval efficiency. Additionally, optimization efforts may involve the removal of unnecessary or obsolete files, freeing up storage space and contributing to a more streamlined and responsive file system.

Capacity planning is an integral component of routine maintenance, ensuring that the file system can accommodate the growing volume of data generated by organizations. Regular assessments of storage capacity, usage patterns, and data growth projections enable administrators to anticipate and address potential capacity constraints before they impact system performance or lead to data loss. By proactively expanding storage resources, redistributing data across storage tiers, or implementing efficient data archiving strategies, organizations can maintain an optimal balance between storage capacity and performance, ensuring uninterrupted access to data.

Backup and recovery procedures are essential elements of routine maintenance for file systems. Establishing regular backup schedules, testing recovery processes, and verifying the integrity of backup copies are critical tasks to safeguard against data loss due to accidental deletions, hardware failures, or other unforeseen events. Routine maintenance ensures that backup mechanisms are consistently operational, and backup copies are up-to-date, providing a reliable safety net for data recovery. Furthermore, periodic disaster recovery drills and simulations contribute to the preparedness of organizations, allowing them to validate the effectiveness of their backup and recovery strategies in a controlled environment.

Routine maintenance extends to the monitoring and analysis of file system performance metrics. Continuous monitoring allows administrators to proactively identify bottlenecks, anomalies, or signs of potential issues affecting the file system's performance. By leveraging monitoring tools and analytics, administrators can gain insights into data access patterns, resource utilization, and overall system health. This information enables informed decision-making, facilitates the early detection of performance degradation, and supports the implementation of preemptive measures to optimize file system performance.

Security is a paramount consideration in routine maintenance for file systems, given the increasing sophistication of cyber threats and the critical role file systems play in data storage. Regular security audits, vulnerability assessments, and access control reviews are essential components of maintaining a secure file system environment. Ensuring that users have appropriate permissions, employing encryption mechanisms for sensitive data, and implementing multi-factor authentication contribute to a robust security posture. Routine security maintenance addresses potential weaknesses, mitigates the risk of unauthorized access or data breaches, and aligns the file system with evolving cybersecurity best practices.

Compliance with regulatory requirements and industry standards is a critical aspect of routine maintenance for file systems, especially in sectors handling sensitive or confidential data. Organizations must regularly review and update their file system configurations to align with evolving compliance frameworks. This includes implementing encryption, access controls, and audit trails to meet specific regulatory mandates. Routine compliance audits and assessments help organizations demonstrate adherence to data protection and privacy regulations, minimizing the risk of legal consequences and ensuring the responsible handling of sensitive information stored within the file system.

Another key consideration in routine maintenance is the implementation of disaster recovery planning and testing. While backups provide a crucial mechanism for data recovery, disaster recovery planning goes beyond simple backup strategies. Organizations need to formulate comprehensive plans that outline procedures for system restoration, alternative infrastructure arrangements, and communication protocols in the event of a catastrophic incident. Routine maintenance involves regular reviews and updates of these disaster recovery plans, ensuring they remain aligned with organizational changes, technological advancements, and evolving risk landscapes. Conducting periodic disaster recovery drills allows organizations to validate the efficacy of their plans and refine them based on lessons learned.

File system housekeeping is a routine maintenance task that involves the management of obsolete or temporary files, log files, and outdated configurations. Accumulation of unnecessary files can impact storage efficiency, hinder data access times, and contribute to clutter within the file system. Regular housekeeping activities, such as the removal of redundant files, archiving of outdated data, and periodic log file rotation, help maintain a clean and organized file system environment. This not only contributes to optimal performance but also simplifies troubleshooting and system administration tasks.

Training and skill development for administrators and IT personnel are integral aspects of routine maintenance. The technology landscape evolves, and new features, tools, or best practices may emerge. Regular training ensures that personnel responsible for file system maintenance stay informed about the latest advancements, security considerations, and efficient operational practices. This ongoing skill development contributes to the effectiveness of routine maintenance tasks, empowers administrators to make informed decisions, and enhances their ability to address evolving challenges in file system management.

In conclusion, the importance of routine maintenance for file systems cannot be overstated in the context of modern computing environments. From addressing potential data integrity issues to optimizing performance, ensuring security, and meeting regulatory compliance requirements, routine maintenance serves as a proactive and holistic approach to file system management. By incorporating regular checks, updates, optimization efforts, capacity planning, and security measures, organizations can foster a resilient and reliable file system infrastructure. Routine maintenance not only prevents potential issues from escalating but also contributes to the longevity and efficiency of file systems, providing a solid foundation for the storage, retrieval, and protection of valuable data assets.

Automating maintenance tasks to minimize downtime and disruptions.

Automating maintenance tasks has emerged as a pivotal strategy to minimize downtime and disruptions in modern computing environments. The proactive automation of routine and repetitive maintenance activities not only enhances operational efficiency but also significantly reduces the risk of human errors and accelerates the overall maintenance process. One of the key advantages of automation lies in its ability to streamline the execution of routine tasks, such as software updates, system patches, and security configurations. Automated maintenance workflows ensure that critical updates are applied promptly, minimizing vulnerabilities and enhancing the overall security posture of the IT infrastructure. By removing the manual intervention traditionally associated with these tasks, automation reduces the window of exposure to potential security threats, contributing to a more robust and resilient system.

Efficient and timely patch management is a critical aspect of system maintenance, and automation plays a pivotal role in ensuring that patches are applied promptly and consistently across the IT landscape. Automated patching solutions can systematically assess the system's current state, identify missing patches, and apply updates seamlessly. This not only minimizes the risk of security breaches resulting from unpatched vulnerabilities but also alleviates the burden on IT teams, allowing them to focus on strategic initiatives rather than the time-consuming task of manually managing patches. Moreover, automated patching helps organizations maintain compliance with industry regulations and security standards by ensuring that systems are consistently updated with the latest security patches.

Automated maintenance extends to the realm of configuration management, where it becomes instrumental in enforcing standardized configurations across diverse IT environments. Configuration drift, caused by manual changes or inconsistencies in configurations, can lead to system instability and vulnerabilities. Automation tools facilitate the creation and enforcement of desired configurations, ensuring uniformity across servers, workstations, and network devices. This not only reduces the risk of misconfigurations but also streamlines troubleshooting and enhances the overall reliability of the IT infrastructure. Automated configuration management contributes to a more predictable and stable environment, minimizing the likelihood of disruptions caused by configuration-related issues.

The automation of routine backup and recovery tasks is paramount for minimizing data loss and downtime. Automated backup schedules, snapshot creation, and replication processes ensure that critical data is consistently and securely backed up without reliance on manual intervention. Automation also extends to the verification of backup integrity, enabling organizations to regularly test and validate the recoverability of their data. In the event of data loss or system failures, automated recovery processes can expedite the restoration of systems and services, reducing downtime and enhancing overall business continuity. The reliability and consistency achieved through automated backup and recovery procedures contribute to a robust data protection strategy, safeguarding organizations against the impact of unforeseen events.

Automated monitoring and alerting systems play a crucial role in proactive maintenance by continuously assessing the health and performance of IT infrastructure components. These systems can automatically detect anomalies, irregularities, or potential issues in real-time, allowing administrators to address emerging problems before they escalate into critical disruptions. Automated alerts enable a swift response to incidents, facilitating rapid diagnosis and resolution. By leveraging artificial intelligence and machine learning, automated monitoring systems can even predict potential issues based on historical data patterns, allowing organizations to take preventive actions and minimize the impact on system availability. This proactive approach to maintenance contributes to a more resilient and reliable IT environment.

In the realm of cybersecurity, automated threat detection and response mechanisms are indispensable for minimizing downtime and disruptions caused by security incidents. Automated security solutions can continuously monitor network traffic, analyze system logs, and identify patterns indicative of malicious activities. In the event of a security threat, automated response mechanisms can trigger predefined actions, such as isolating compromised systems, blocking malicious traffic, or initiating incident response procedures. The speed and efficiency of automated threat detection and response are critical in minimizing the dwell time of attackers within the network, reducing the potential impact of security incidents, and maintaining the integrity of sensitive data.

Automated maintenance extends its benefits to the realm of performance optimization, where it can proactively address issues affecting system responsiveness and efficiency. Automated performance monitoring tools can analyze resource utilization, identify bottlenecks, and recommend or implement adjustments to optimize system performance. Tasks such as load balancing, resource allocation, and capacity planning can be automated to ensure that systems operate within optimal parameters. This proactive approach to performance maintenance contributes to a more responsive and scalable IT infrastructure, minimizing the risk of performance-related disruptions and enhancing the overall user experience.

The automation of routine hardware maintenance tasks, such as firmware updates and diagnostic checks, is crucial for ensuring the reliability and longevity of physical infrastructure components. Automated firmware updates can be scheduled during low-impact periods to minimize disruptions while ensuring that hardware components are running the latest and most secure firmware versions. Automated diagnostic checks can continuously monitor hardware health, detect potential failures or degradation, and trigger alerts or preemptive actions. By automating these tasks, organizations can prolong the lifespan of hardware components, reduce the risk of unexpected failures, and optimize the overall performance of the physical infrastructure.

In the context of cloud computing and virtualized environments, automation is integral to achieving the agility and scalability that these platforms promise. Automated provisioning and de-provisioning of virtual machines, containers, and cloud resources enable organizations to dynamically adjust their computing infrastructure based on demand. Scaling resources up or down in response to workload fluctuations becomes seamless, minimizing the risk of performance bottlenecks or overprovisioning. Automated deployment pipelines and configuration management tools further enhance the efficiency of managing cloud-based and virtualized environments, contributing to the rapid and consistent delivery of applications and services.

Automation also plays a pivotal role in ensuring compliance with regulatory requirements and industry standards. Automated compliance management tools can assess system configurations, monitor access controls, and generate reports to demonstrate adherence to specific compliance frameworks. This not only reduces the manual effort required for compliance audits but also ensures that organizations consistently meet regulatory obligations. By automating compliance checks, organizations can proactively address any deviations from compliance standards, minimizing the risk of non-compliance-related disruptions and legal consequences.

Collaborative and communication tools, when integrated into automated maintenance workflows, enhance the coordination and transparency of maintenance activities across teams. Automated notifications, status updates, and reporting mechanisms enable stakeholders to stay informed about ongoing maintenance tasks, scheduled downtimes, or potential issues. Collaboration platforms facilitate the sharing of information, documentation, and best practices among team members involved in maintenance activities. This collaborative approach ensures that all relevant parties are well-informed, aligned, and can contribute effectively to the success of automated maintenance initiatives.

While automation offers numerous benefits in minimizing downtime and disruptions, organizations must approach it with a strategic mindset. The design and implementation of automated maintenance processes should align with the specific needs, objectives, and characteristics of the organization's IT environment. Careful consideration of factors such as scalability, integration with existing systems, security implications, and the human element in overseeing automated processes is essential. Furthermore, organizations should continuously evaluate and refine their automated maintenance strategies in response to evolving technologies, operational requirements, and emerging threats. By adopting a thoughtful and adaptive approach to automation, organizations can harness its transformative potential to achieve resilient, efficient, and highly available IT infrastructures while minimizing downtime and disruptions.

Challenges arising from file system compatibility issues.

File system compatibility issues pose significant challenges in the realm of information technology, impacting data interoperability, accessibility, and overall system functionality. The diversity of file systems used across different operating systems and storage devices contributes to this complexity, requiring a nuanced understanding of the issues that can arise. One of the primary challenges stems from the inherent differences in the structures and conventions employed by various file systems. Each operating system tends to have its preferred file system, such as NTFS for Windows, HFS+ for macOS, and ext4 for Linux. When data needs to be shared or transferred across systems with disparate file systems, compatibility challenges arise, leading to potential data corruption, loss of metadata, or even incompatibility issues that hinder access to the shared information.

Moreover, variations in file system features and capabilities contribute to compatibility challenges. Different file systems support distinct sets of features, such as file permissions, encryption, compression, and symbolic links, to name a few. When data is moved or accessed across systems with varying capabilities, certain features may not be supported or may be interpreted differently. For instance, a file with complex permissions on a Windows NTFS file system may encounter issues when transferred to a Linux ext4 file system that employs a different permission model. These compatibility gaps can lead to a loss of functionality, security vulnerabilities, or unintended changes to the file attributes.

File system compatibility challenges become particularly pronounced in heterogeneous IT environments where multiple operating systems coexist. In enterprise settings, organizations often deploy a mix of Windows, macOS, and Linux systems to meet diverse user and application requirements. In such scenarios, ensuring seamless data sharing and collaboration across different file systems becomes a formidable task. Users may encounter difficulties when attempting to open files created on one platform with applications running on another, leading to disruptions in workflow, reduced productivity, and potential data integrity issues. Bridging the gap between disparate file systems in a heterogeneous environment requires careful planning, standardized practices, and sometimes the implementation of intermediary solutions.

Cross-platform data exchange, especially in the context of external storage devices like USB drives or external hard disks, introduces additional compatibility challenges. These devices may be formatted with a specific file system that is not natively supported by all operating systems. For instance, a USB drive formatted with the macOS-specific HFS+ file system may encounter difficulties when connected to a Windows system that does not have native HFS+ support. While some operating systems have introduced support for multiple file systems to enhance compatibility, discrepancies in implementation or versioning can still lead to issues. Users relying on external storage for data transfer must navigate these compatibility challenges, potentially resorting to third-party tools or workarounds to ensure seamless cross-platform access.

Networked storage solutions, such as Network Attached Storage (NAS) or Storage Area Networks (SAN), introduce their own set of compatibility challenges. These storage systems often run specialized file systems optimized for performance, scalability, or specific features. When users attempt to access data stored on networked drives from different operating systems, compatibility issues may arise due to differences in file system support or network protocols. Organizations relying on networked storage for collaborative work may face difficulties in maintaining consistent access and functionality across diverse platforms, necessitating careful consideration of file system compatibility when designing and implementing storage solutions.

Virtualization technologies, which enable the deployment of multiple operating systems on a single physical server, introduce compatibility challenges at the intersection of host and guest file systems. Virtual machines may use file systems that differ from the host environment, requiring effective mechanisms for data exchange and communication. File sharing between the host and guest systems, as well as among different virtual machines, demands compatibility considerations to ensure seamless data transfer and consistent behavior. Virtualization administrators must navigate the complexities of file system compatibility to optimize performance, prevent data corruption, and facilitate efficient resource utilization.

The evolution of file systems over time introduces versioning and compatibility challenges, especially when transitioning between different generations of a file system. Newer versions may introduce enhancements, optimizations, or additional features that may not be fully backward-compatible with older implementations. Upgrading a file system on a storage device or migrating data to a newer file system version can result in compatibility issues with legacy systems that do not support the updated features. Compatibility challenges may also manifest during data migrations between storage devices or platforms, requiring careful planning and validation to ensure a smooth transition without loss of functionality or data.

File system compatibility issues also manifest in the context of cloud computing, where data may be stored, accessed, and processed across various cloud platforms with different file system architectures. Each cloud provider typically employs its own file system or storage solution, and organizations leveraging multi-cloud or hybrid cloud strategies may encounter challenges when attempting to seamlessly move or synchronize data across these environments. The lack of standardized file system interfaces across cloud platforms can lead to integration complexities, necessitating the development of robust data management strategies, middleware solutions, or cloud-agnostic file system approaches to address compatibility challenges effectively.

Security considerations add another layer of complexity to file system compatibility challenges. Encryption, access control mechanisms, and security features embedded within file systems vary across different platforms. When encrypted files are transferred between systems with incompatible encryption methods or key management practices, decryption becomes problematic, leading to potential data loss or compromise. Ensuring secure and compliant data handling across disparate file systems requires a comprehensive understanding of the security features supported by each system and the implementation of protocols that maintain data confidentiality and integrity.

As technology continues to advance, new file system formats and architectures are introduced, further exacerbating compatibility challenges. Emerging storage technologies, such as Non-Volatile Memory Express (NVMe) drives, may utilize file systems optimized for high-speed storage access. Compatibility issues may arise when attempting to integrate these advanced storage solutions with older systems or legacy applications that lack support for the latest file system formats. Organizations must carefully evaluate the compatibility of storage technologies with existing infrastructure, considering factors such as hardware support, operating system compatibility, and application integration.

Mitigating file system compatibility challenges requires a multifaceted approach that considers both technical and organizational aspects. Standardization efforts to establish common file system interfaces or formats across operating systems could alleviate many compatibility issues. Initiatives such as cross-platform file system support or the adoption of open standards for data interchange could contribute to a more interoperable computing landscape. Additionally, the development and utilization of middleware solutions, virtualization technologies, and file system abstraction layers can help bridge the gaps between disparate file systems, enabling smoother data exchange and access in heterogeneous environments.

Organizations must also prioritize education and awareness among users and IT professionals regarding file system compatibility considerations. Training programs and guidelines on best practices for cross-platform data exchange, storage management, and collaborative work in heterogeneous environments can empower users to navigate compatibility challenges effectively. Furthermore, collaboration between hardware manufacturers, operating system developers, and storage solution providers is essential to drive industry-wide efforts aimed at enhancing file system compatibility, promoting standardized interfaces, and addressing interoperability concerns.

In conclusion, file system compatibility issues represent a pervasive and intricate challenge in the landscape of information technology. The diversity of file systems across operating systems, storage devices, and cloud platforms necessitates careful consideration and strategic planning to ensure seamless data interoperability. Organizations must navigate the complexities of cross-platform data exchange, storage management, and collaborative work, employing a combination of standardized practices, middleware solutions, and user education to mitigate compatibility challenges effectively. As technology continues to evolve, fostering collaboration, standardization, and innovation remains essential to address the ever-growing complexity of file system compatibility in the dynamic and interconnected world of computing.

Strategies for achieving interoperability between different file system types.

Achieving interoperability between different file system types is a multifaceted challenge that requires a strategic and comprehensive approach. Interoperability, in this context, refers to the seamless exchange and access of data across diverse file systems, each with its own structures, conventions, and features. Strategies for addressing this challenge encompass various aspects, including the development of standardized interfaces, the implementation of middleware solutions, the adoption of open standards, and the establishment of collaborative industry practices.

One fundamental strategy for achieving interoperability involves the development and adoption of standardized interfaces that facilitate communication between different file systems. Standardization efforts aim to define common protocols, file formats, and data structures that can be universally recognized and implemented across various platforms. Initiatives such as the Common Internet File System (CIFS) and Network File System (NFS) exemplify standardized interfaces designed to enable file sharing and access across heterogeneous environments. By adhering to agreed-upon standards, operating systems and storage solutions can ensure compatibility and seamless communication, fostering interoperability in mixed IT ecosystems.

Middleware solutions play a crucial role in bridging the gap between disparate file systems by providing a layer of abstraction and translation. Middleware acts as an intermediary software layer that sits between applications and underlying file systems, translating requests and data formats as needed. This abstraction layer shields applications from the intricacies of individual file system implementations, allowing them to interact with a standardized interface provided by the middleware. Solutions like File System in Userspace (FUSE) enable the development of user-space file systems, decoupling them from the kernel and providing a flexible framework for implementing interoperability across different platforms. Middleware solutions not only enhance interoperability but also contribute to the adaptability and extensibility of file system interactions.

Open standards play a pivotal role in promoting interoperability by providing a shared framework for the design and implementation of file systems. The adoption of open standards ensures transparency, encourages collaboration, and facilitates the development of interoperable solutions. For example, the use of open standards for file formats, such as the Extensible Markup Language (XML) or JavaScript Object Notation (JSON), allows data to be represented in a universally understandable and exchangeable manner. Similarly, protocols like the Internet Protocol (IP) and Transmission Control Protocol (TCP) provide a standardized foundation for networked file system communications, fostering compatibility between diverse systems. Embracing open standards promotes a vendor-agnostic approach, reducing dependencies on proprietary technologies and enhancing the potential for seamless interoperability.

Collaborative industry practices and initiatives play a crucial role in addressing interoperability challenges by fostering a shared commitment to compatibility. Industry consortia, standards organizations, and collaborative development efforts bring together stakeholders from diverse backgrounds to define common practices and guidelines. For example, organizations like the Storage Networking Industry Association (SNIA) work towards developing standards and best practices for storage systems, including file systems. Collaborative efforts can lead to the establishment of reference architectures, interoperability testing frameworks, and shared knowledge repositories that empower organizations to navigate interoperability challenges effectively. By fostering a collective approach, industry collaboration contributes to the development of interoperable solutions that benefit the entire ecosystem.

Cross-platform file system support is a strategic approach aimed at enhancing interoperability by enabling operating systems to read and write data across multiple file system types. Some file systems, such as exFAT, are designed to be compatible with various operating systems, allowing users to transfer data between Windows, macOS, and Linux systems seamlessly. The implementation of cross-platform support mitigates the need for complex translation layers or middleware solutions, simplifying the process of sharing data across different environments. While cross-platform file systems represent a practical solution, challenges may arise due to variations in feature sets or limitations imposed by certain operating systems.

Virtualization technologies provide an innovative strategy for achieving file system interoperability by abstracting underlying hardware and enabling the deployment of multiple operating systems on a single physical server. Virtual machines (VMs) or containers encapsulate entire operating system environments, each with its own file system, within a virtualized container. Virtualization platforms, such as VMware or Hyper-V, facilitate the coexistence of different file systems on the same infrastructure. This approach not only promotes interoperability but also enhances resource utilization by consolidating multiple virtualized environments on a single physical machine. However, challenges related to performance overhead and resource contention must be carefully addressed when employing virtualization for achieving file system interoperability.

The use of intermediary translation layers, known as file system bridges or converters, represents a targeted strategy for achieving interoperability between specific file systems. These solutions aim to translate file system operations and data formats on the fly, allowing applications or operating systems to interact with file systems that would otherwise be incompatible. Tools like UFS Explorer or Paragon Software's UFSD technology provide file system drivers and converters that enable cross-platform access to various file systems. While effective in specific scenarios, file system bridges may introduce performance overhead and compatibility limitations, and their success depends on the extent of feature translation required.

Cloud-based storage and file-sharing solutions offer a contemporary strategy for achieving interoperability by providing a centralized and platform-agnostic environment. Cloud platforms, such as Amazon S3, Microsoft Azure Blob Storage, or Google Cloud Storage, often support standardized interfaces and protocols for data access. Organizations can leverage cloud storage as a common repository, enabling users and applications across different platforms to access and share data seamlessly. Cloud-based file-sharing services, such as Dropbox or Google Drive, extend this approach to end-users, providing a user-friendly interface for storing and collaborating on files across diverse operating systems.

The implementation of hybrid file systems, which combine elements from different file system types, represents an innovative strategy for achieving interoperability while preserving specific functionalities. Hybrid file systems may incorporate features from multiple file systems, allowing them to adapt to diverse use cases or environments. For example, the ZFS file system combines the strengths of traditional file systems with advanced storage management capabilities. Hybrid approaches aim to provide a balance between compatibility and specialized functionalities, catering to the evolving needs of modern computing environments.

Embracing containerization and container orchestration frameworks, such as Docker and Kubernetes, introduces a strategy for achieving file system interoperability in distributed and microservices architectures. Containers encapsulate applications and their dependencies, including file system components, in a portable and reproducible manner. Container orchestration frameworks facilitate the deployment and management of containers across diverse environments. This approach not only enhances portability but also simplifies the management of file system dependencies, promoting interoperability in dynamically changing and distributed computing landscapes.

Education and training initiatives that promote awareness and understanding of file system interoperability issues play a vital role in equipping IT professionals and users with the knowledge to navigate challenges effectively. Training programs focused on best practices, standardized approaches, and interoperability considerations empower individuals to make informed decisions when dealing with diverse file systems. A well-informed user base contributes to a culture that values interoperability, prompting organizations to prioritize solutions and practices that facilitate seamless data exchange across different file system types.

In conclusion, achieving interoperability between different file system types demands a holistic and strategic approach that encompasses standardization, middleware solutions, collaborative practices, and innovative technologies. By adopting standardized interfaces, leveraging middleware solutions, embracing open standards, and fostering industry collaboration, organizations can create a foundation for seamless data exchange across diverse file systems. Additionally, the strategic use of cross-platform support, virtualization, cloud-based solutions, and containerization introduces practical approaches to address interoperability challenges in modern computing environments. Education and training initiatives further empower individuals to navigate interoperability issues effectively, fostering a culture that values compatibility and facilitates the development of interoperable solutions across the IT landscape.

Chapter 8: Future Horizons: Innovations in Operating System File Systems

Exploring the integration of non-volatile memory technologies in file systems.

The integration of non-volatile memory (NVM) technologies in file systems represents a transformative paradigm shift in storage architectures, offering unprecedented opportunities for enhanced performance, durability, and efficiency. NVM, such as NAND Flash and emerging technologies like 3D XPoint, provides persistent storage capabilities with significantly lower latency than traditional storage media like hard disk drives (HDDs) or even solid-state drives (SSDs). The unique characteristics of NVM, such as byte-addressability and non-volatility, present both challenges and opportunities for file system design and implementation.

One of the primary advantages of integrating NVM technologies into file systems is the potential for substantially improved storage performance. Unlike traditional storage media, NVM allows for direct access to individual bytes, eliminating the need for block-based access. This byte-addressability enables more efficient data retrieval and storage, reducing access times and latency. File systems designed to harness this capability can capitalize on the inherent speed of NVM, providing applications with faster read and write operations. The integration of NVM technologies introduces the prospect of achieving near-memory speeds for storage operations, thereby revolutionizing the overall responsiveness of computing systems.

Durability and resilience are critical considerations in file system design, and NVM technologies contribute significantly to addressing these concerns. NVM exhibits superior endurance compared to traditional storage media, as it does not have mechanical components susceptible to wear and tear. The elimination of moving parts, such as spinning disks or magnetic heads, reduces the likelihood of mechanical failures, enhancing the overall reliability and lifespan of storage systems. This increased durability is particularly advantageous in scenarios where file systems experience frequent write operations, as is often the case in databases, log files, or other write-intensive workloads.

The non-volatile nature of NVM technologies ensures data persistence even in the absence of power, aligning well with the expectations of modern file systems. In the event of power loss or system shutdowns, NVM retains stored data without the need for energy-consuming mechanisms like uninterruptible power supplies (UPS) or complex journaling systems. File systems designed for NVM can leverage these characteristics to implement more streamlined and energy-efficient mechanisms for ensuring data consistency and durability. The elimination of power-dependent volatile storage elements enhances the resilience of file systems, making them well-suited for deployment in scenarios where power fluctuations or outages are a concern.

Integrating NVM technologies into file systems also opens avenues for novel approaches to data management and storage optimization. The fast and direct access to data afforded by NVM enables the implementation of efficient storage tiering strategies, where frequently accessed or critical data is dynamically placed in the NVM layer for accelerated performance. This tiered storage architecture optimizes resource utilization, ensuring that the most relevant data resides in the high-speed NVM tier while less frequently accessed data may be stored in lower-speed, higher-capacity tiers. File systems can leverage these capabilities to adapt to changing access patterns, delivering optimal performance while maintaining cost-effective storage solutions.

Furthermore, the byte-addressability of NVM allows file systems to explore innovative mechanisms for managing metadata, such as file system structures, directory information, and access control data. Traditional block-based storage imposes limitations on the granularity of metadata updates, potentially leading to inefficiencies in managing small-sized files or directories. NVM's byte-addressable nature enables more fine-grained control over metadata updates, reducing overhead and optimizing metadata operations. File systems designed to capitalize on NVM can therefore achieve more efficient metadata handling, resulting in improved overall system responsiveness.

While the integration of NVM technologies brings forth numerous benefits, it also introduces unique challenges that necessitate careful consideration in file system design. One such challenge is the endurance limitations inherent in NVM. While NVM technologies exhibit significantly higher endurance than traditional storage media, they are not immune to wear and degradation over time. File systems must implement effective wear-leveling algorithms and error correction mechanisms to mitigate the impact of endurance issues, ensuring uniform utilization of NVM cells and prolonging the lifespan of storage devices.

The increased density of NVM technologies also introduces considerations related to storage efficiency and data integrity. As NVM storage capacities continue to grow, file systems must address the efficient organization and management of large volumes of data. Advanced compression algorithms and deduplication techniques become crucial for optimizing storage space and reducing redundancy. Additionally, file systems must implement robust error detection and correction mechanisms to safeguard data integrity, particularly in scenarios where silent data corruption or bit flips may occur.

Concurrency and parallelism considerations become paramount in file systems leveraging NVM technologies to harness their full potential. NVM's low-latency characteristics enable multiple parallel access streams, making it imperative for file systems to support concurrent read and write operations efficiently. Traditional file system designs optimized for HDDs or SSDs may face challenges in fully exploiting the parallelism offered by NVM. New concurrency-aware file system architectures need to be developed to ensure that the benefits of NVM's speed are not hampered by bottlenecks in the file system layer.

Another consideration in the integration of NVM technologies is the development of optimized file system interfaces and access patterns that fully leverage the capabilities of NVM. Existing file system protocols and interfaces may not be fully aligned with the strengths of NVM, potentially limiting performance gains. File systems need to be designed with NVM-aware interfaces that exploit byte-addressability, reduce unnecessary overhead, and enable applications to capitalize on the speed and efficiency of NVM storage. This requires collaboration between file system designers, application developers, and industry standards organizations to establish interfaces that unlock the full potential of NVM technologies.

Security considerations also come to the forefront in NVM-enabled file systems. The non-volatile nature of NVM introduces challenges related to secure data erasure. Traditional methods of secure deletion, such as overwriting data blocks, may not be as effective in NVM environments. File systems must implement secure erasure mechanisms that align with the characteristics of NVM, ensuring that sensitive data is reliably and irreversibly removed. Additionally, encryption becomes a critical component in securing data stored in

NVM, with file systems needing to support robust encryption algorithms and key management practices to protect data at rest.

In conclusion, the integration of non-volatile memory technologies in file systems represents a paradigm shift with far-reaching implications for storage performance, durability, and efficiency. NVM's byte-addressable and non-volatile characteristics offer the potential for transformative changes in data management and access patterns. While the benefits are substantial, challenges related to endurance, storage efficiency, concurrency, and security necessitate careful consideration in file system design. As the technology landscape continues to evolve, collaborative efforts between storage industry stakeholders, standards organizations, and researchers are essential to unlocking the full potential of NVM technologies in file systems and realizing the promise of a new era in storage innovation.

The impact on data access speed and system responsiveness.

The impact of data access speed on system responsiveness is a critical aspect that underpins the overall user experience and performance of computing systems. The speed at which data can be accessed directly influences how quickly applications respond to user input, how rapidly files are opened and saved, and, by extension, the efficiency of the entire computing environment. In contemporary computing, where users expect instantaneous responses and seamless interactions with their devices, the speed of data access plays a pivotal role in shaping the perceived performance and usability of systems.

Data access speed refers to the rate at which a system can retrieve or store information from or to its storage media, encompassing both read and write operations. Traditional storage media, such as hard disk drives (HDDs), have long been a bottleneck in terms of data access speed due to their mechanical nature, relying on spinning disks and moving read/write heads. As a result, accessing data from HDDs involves latency introduced by the physical movement of these components, leading to relatively slower response times.

The advent of solid-state drives (SSDs) has heralded a significant improvement in data access speed compared to HDDs. SSDs, based on NAND Flash memory, offer much faster read and write speeds, lower latency, and improved random access performance. This transition from HDDs to SSDs has had a profound impact on system responsiveness, reducing the time it takes to boot the operating system, launch applications, and load large files. The elimination of mechanical components in SSDs allows for near-instantaneous access to data, contributing to a perceptible boost in overall system speed and responsiveness.

Nonetheless, the pursuit of even faster data access speeds has led to the exploration and integration of non-volatile memory (NVM) technologies, such as NAND Flash, 3D XPoint, and other emerging solutions. NVM offers advantages like byte-addressability, which allows for direct access to individual bytes of data, and lower latency compared to traditional storage media. The impact on data access speed when transitioning to NVM is transformative, enabling systems to achieve read and write speeds that approach those of system memory (RAM). This proximity to memory speeds results in unparalleled responsiveness, with applications loading almost instantly and file operations completing in the blink of an eye.

The impact of enhanced data access speed extends beyond individual applications to influence the overall multitasking capabilities of computing systems. Faster access to data means that the system can rapidly switch between different tasks and applications, allowing users to seamlessly navigate between workflows without experiencing noticeable delays. This fluidity in multitasking contributes to a more immersive and efficient user experience, where the system adapts swiftly to user input and accommodates diverse computing needs.

In the context of system boot times, the impact of faster data access is particularly pronounced. Traditional HDDs often entail extended boot times as the operating system and essential files are loaded. With the adoption of SSDs and NVM technologies, boot times are drastically reduced, and users can access their systems within seconds of powering on. This immediacy in system availability enhances user satisfaction and productivity, eliminating the frustration associated with waiting for the system to become operational.

Application launch times represent another facet of system responsiveness influenced by data access speed. Slow application launches can hinder productivity and disrupt the user experience. Faster data access, facilitated by SSDs and NVM, ensures that applications load swiftly, allowing users to initiate tasks without enduring prolonged waiting times. This acceleration in application responsiveness is particularly advantageous in scenarios where quick access to tools and software is crucial, such as in professional environments or creative workflows.

The impact of data access speed is not confined to the realm of user-facing applications; it also extends to system-level operations, such as file transfers, data backups, and software installations. Faster data access speeds contribute to more efficient handling of large datasets, reducing the time required for tasks like copying files, creating backups, or installing software updates. The efficiency gained in these background operations translates into an overall smoother computing experience, as system resources are utilized more judiciously and with minimal disruptions to user activities.

Real-time responsiveness is a crucial consideration in scenarios where systems are deployed for mission-critical tasks or time-sensitive applications. Industries such as finance, healthcare, and autonomous vehicles rely on systems that can rapidly process and retrieve data in real-time. The impact of faster data access speed in these contexts is not merely a matter of user convenience but a fundamental requirement for ensuring the reliability and effectiveness of critical applications. Systems equipped with high-speed data access capabilities can deliver near-instantaneous responses to real-time inputs, meeting the stringent demands of applications where split-second decisions are paramount.

The impact of data access speed is particularly pronounced in gaming environments, where rapid data retrieval is essential for delivering immersive and responsive gaming experiences. Slow loading times, texture pop-ins, and delays in rendering graphical elements can detract from the gaming experience. SSDs and NVM technologies significantly mitigate these issues, allowing games to load quickly, reducing in-game loading screens, and providing a more fluid and seamless gaming experience. The impact of enhanced data access speed in gaming environments is not only appreciated by gamers but is also a critical factor in maintaining the competitive edge in online multiplayer scenarios.

The efficiency of data access speed is contingent not only on the underlying storage technologies but also on the optimization of file systems and storage architectures. File systems designed to leverage the capabilities of high-speed storage media can further enhance the impact on system responsiveness. Techniques such as wear leveling, garbage collection, and efficient data organization become critical in ensuring sustained performance and longevity, especially in the case of NAND Flash-based storage solutions.

The impact of faster data access speed also reverberates in the realm of virtualization and cloud computing. In virtualized environments, where multiple virtual machines may contend for storage resources, faster data access ensures that each virtual instance can swiftly access its storage space, leading to improved overall system performance. Cloud-based services, which rely on efficient data retrieval and storage to deliver applications and content to users, benefit from the accelerated data access speeds provided by NVM technologies. These advancements in data access speed contribute to the scalability and responsiveness of cloud-based infrastructures, enabling them to handle increasing workloads and user demands.

However, it's crucial to acknowledge that the impact of data access speed is part of a broader system performance landscape influenced by various components, including processors, memory, and interconnectivity. While faster data access speeds contribute significantly to improved system responsiveness, the overall performance is a synergistic outcome of the harmonious interplay of these components. Achieving optimal system responsiveness requires a holistic approach that considers the entire computing stack, from storage media to processing units and system architecture.

In conclusion, the impact of data access speed on system responsiveness is profound and far-reaching, shaping the user experience, application performance, and overall efficiency of computing systems. The transition from traditional HDDs to SSDs and the integration of NVM technologies represent pivotal advancements that have elevated data access speeds to unprecedented levels. The resulting immediacy in system responses, faster application launches, and enhanced multitasking capabilities contribute to a computing environment that aligns with the expectations of modern users. As computing technologies continue to evolve, the pursuit of even faster data access speeds remains a focal point, promising continued improvements in system responsiveness and a more dynamic and efficient user experience.

Leveraging machine-generated metadata for enhanced file categorization.

Leveraging machine-generated metadata for enhanced file categorization represents a pivotal advancement in information management, offering the potential to revolutionize the efficiency, accuracy, and scalability of organizing vast amounts of digital data. In the contemporary landscape, where the proliferation of data is exponential, traditional manual methods of file categorization and organization fall short in coping with the sheer volume and complexity of information. Machine-generated metadata, powered by artificial intelligence (AI) and machine learning algorithms, introduces a paradigm shift by automating the extraction of meaningful descriptors from files, augmenting human-defined metadata, and providing a more nuanced understanding of content.

One of the key pillars of this transformative approach is the integration of machine learning models capable of comprehending the semantic content of files. Natural Language Processing (NLP) algorithms, for instance, enable machines to understand textual content within documents, extracting keywords, topics, and contextual information. Image recognition models, on the other hand, decipher visual elements within files, allowing for the extraction of features such as objects, scenes, or even sentiments. These machine learning models serve as engines for generating metadata that encapsulates the essence of the file's content, surpassing the limitations of traditional categorization methods that rely solely on manual annotations or predefined tags.

The integration of machine-generated metadata not only augments human-defined metadata but also addresses the scalability challenge associated with the ever-expanding volume of digital content. As the number of files grows exponentially, automating the categorization process becomes imperative to maintain efficiency. Machine learning models, fueled by extensive training datasets, learn to recognize patterns, relationships, and context within files, enabling them to categorize documents, images, or other types of data autonomously. This scalability empowers organizations to handle large datasets with ease, ensuring that the categorization process remains efficient and adaptable to the dynamic nature of digital content.

Furthermore, leveraging machine-generated metadata enhances the accuracy of file categorization by reducing reliance on manual input and overcoming human biases or inconsistencies. Traditional methods of file tagging or categorization often involve human operators, introducing the potential for errors, oversights, or variations in the application of metadata. Machine learning models, when properly trained, exhibit a remarkable ability to consistently and objectively analyze content, discerning relevant features and attributes that might elude manual categorization. This automated precision not only minimizes errors but also ensures a more standardized and reliable categorization process across diverse datasets.

The utilization of machine-generated metadata is particularly impactful in scenarios where files exhibit multi-modal characteristics, combining text, images, and potentially other data types. Traditional manual categorization struggles to capture the intricate relationships between different modalities, often leading to oversimplified or fragmented metadata structures. Machine learning models excel in recognizing patterns across modalities, enabling a holistic understanding of file content. For instance, a document containing both textual information and embedded images can be accurately categorized based on the combined insights derived from NLP and image recognition algorithms. This multi-modal approach enhances the granularity and richness of metadata, facilitating more nuanced categorization in complex data scenarios.

Context-aware file categorization represents another dimension of the transformative potential of machine-generated metadata. By understanding the context in which files are created, modified, or utilized, machine learning models can infer relationships, dependencies, and relevance that may elude manual categorization efforts. For instance, a document created during a specific project, associated with particular collaborators, or aligned with a certain phase of a workflow can be contextually categorized based on the dynamic interplay of metadata generated from the content itself and external contextual factors. This context-aware categorization adds a layer of sophistication to information management, enabling systems to adapt and evolve in tandem with the evolving context of data usage.

The integration of machine-generated metadata also paves the way for personalized and adaptive file categorization, catering to the diverse needs and preferences of individual users. Machine learning models, when trained on user-specific data patterns, can discern unique categorization preferences, predicting the relevance of files to specific users or user groups. This personalization extends beyond simple categorization and can influence the presentation, recommendation, and prioritization of files based on individual usage patterns, ultimately enhancing the user experience and efficiency in accessing relevant information.

However, the deployment of machine-generated metadata for file categorization is not without its challenges and considerations. Ensuring the interpretability and explainability of machine learning models is crucial, especially in scenarios where decisions impact critical processes or involve sensitive data. Transparent models that provide insights into how and why certain metadata was assigned contribute to user trust and facilitate human oversight, addressing concerns related to algorithmic bias or unexpected outcomes.

The dynamic nature of content evolution and the emergence of new data types pose challenges in maintaining the relevance and adaptability of machine-generated metadata models. Continuous training and refinement of machine learning algorithms are essential to ensure that the categorization models stay abreast of evolving content structures and patterns. Incorporating mechanisms for user feedback and corrections also contributes to the iterative improvement of models, aligning them more closely with user expectations and evolving information contexts.

Security and privacy considerations are paramount in the realm of machine-generated metadata, especially when dealing with sensitive or confidential information. Ensuring that categorization models comply with data protection regulations, implement robust encryption protocols, and minimize the risk of unauthorized access is critical. Striking a balance between the utility of machine-generated metadata and the protection of sensitive data requires thoughtful design and implementation, safeguarding against potential vulnerabilities or misuse.

In conclusion, leveraging machine-generated metadata for enhanced file categorization represents a transformative leap in information management, offering unprecedented efficiency, scalability, and adaptability. Machine learning models, driven by advancements in NLP, image recognition, and context-aware algorithms, empower organizations to categorize vast datasets autonomously, overcoming the limitations of traditional manual methods. The integration of machine-generated metadata augments human-defined metadata, providing a more nuanced understanding of content and enabling sophisticated categorization in multi-modal and context-rich scenarios. While challenges related to interpretability, model adaptability, and security persist, the potential for improved accuracy, scalability, and personalized categorization positions machine-generated metadata as a cornerstone in the evolution of information management systems. As technology continues to advance, the integration of machine-generated metadata is poised to play a central role in reshaping how organizations organize, access, and derive value from their ever-expanding digital repositories.

Automating metadata management for improved efficiency.

Automating metadata management represents a pivotal advancement in information governance, offering transformative benefits in terms of efficiency, accuracy, and scalability. Metadata, encompassing descriptive information about data, plays a crucial role in organizing, retrieving, and understanding the content of digital assets. Traditionally, managing metadata has been a labor-intensive and error-prone process, relying heavily on manual input and human oversight.

However, the advent of automation technologies, powered by artificial intelligence (AI) and machine learning algorithms, has ushered in a new era where the extraction, enrichment, and maintenance of metadata can be accomplished with unprecedented speed and precision.

One of the key facets of automating metadata management lies in the deployment of machine learning models designed to comprehend and interpret the intrinsic characteristics of data. Natural Language Processing (NLP) algorithms, for instance, enable systems to analyze textual content, extracting relevant keywords, topics, and context. Image recognition models, on the other hand, allow for the identification of visual elements within files, contributing to a more comprehensive understanding of content. These machine learning models serve as intelligent engines that can automatically generate descriptive metadata, transcending the limitations of manual efforts and offering a scalable solution for handling the ever-growing volumes of digital data.

Automation in metadata management is particularly impactful in scenarios where datasets are vast and diverse, spanning various file types, formats, and modalities. Manual metadata entry struggles to keep pace with the sheer volume and heterogeneity of digital assets, often resulting in incomplete or inconsistent metadata. Automated solutions, leveraging machine learning models trained on diverse datasets, excel in recognizing patterns and attributes within different types of data. Whether dealing with text documents, images, audio files, or other data modalities, automation ensures a uniform and accurate application of metadata, fostering a standardized approach to information organization.

Efficiency gains in metadata management are evident in the automation of repetitive tasks that consume significant human resources. For example, the bulk tagging or categorization of files based on content, context, or usage patterns can be automated, allowing human operators to focus on more complex and value-added aspects of information management. Routine tasks such as updating time-stamps, versioning, or ensuring data consistency across multiple repositories can be seamlessly handled by automated systems, contributing to a streamlined and error-free metadata management process.

The integration of automation in metadata management also addresses the challenge of maintaining metadata accuracy and consistency over time. Human-centric approaches may introduce errors, oversights, or inconsistencies in metadata application, especially as datasets evolve or undergo modifications. Automated solutions, backed by machine learning models that continuously learn from data patterns, ensure a higher degree of accuracy and consistency in metadata assignment. This adaptability is crucial in dynamic data environments where information undergoes frequent updates, ensuring that metadata remains reflective of the evolving nature of digital assets.

Machine learning models that underpin automated metadata management systems have the ability to discern complex relationships and interdependencies within data, contributing to enhanced metadata enrichment. Beyond basic descriptors, automation can uncover hidden patterns, semantic connections, and contextual nuances within content. For instance, understanding the relationships between entities mentioned in text documents or identifying recurring visual themes in images adds layers of intelligence to metadata, facilitating more sophisticated categorization and retrieval of information.

In addition to extraction and enrichment, automation in metadata management extends to the maintenance and updates of metadata over the entire lifecycle of digital assets. Traditional manual approaches may struggle to keep metadata relevant and up-to-date as datasets undergo changes. Automated systems, equipped with machine learning models capable of recognizing modifications, additions, or deletions within data, can dynamically adjust metadata to reflect the current state of digital assets. This real-time adaptability ensures that metadata remains accurate and aligned with the evolving context of data usage.

The role of automation in metadata management becomes even more pronounced in scenarios involving big data, where the scale and complexity of datasets surpass the capabilities of traditional manual methods. Big data environments, characterized by massive volumes of diverse and unstructured data, demand agile and scalable solutions for metadata management. Automated systems, driven by machine learning algorithms, thrive in such environments by swiftly analyzing and categorizing vast datasets, providing a foundation for efficient data discovery, analytics, and decision-making.

Context-aware metadata management represents an advanced dimension of automation, where systems go beyond simple descriptive tags to understand the broader context in which data operates. By considering factors such as temporal relevance, user context, or data dependencies, automated systems can assign metadata that aligns with the dynamic nature of information usage. For instance, a document created during a specific project phase or associated with a particular user group can be contextually tagged based on the dynamic interplay of metadata generated from the content and external contextual factors. This context-aware automation adds a layer of sophistication to metadata management, ensuring that metadata remains relevant and meaningful in diverse usage scenarios.

The adoption of automation in metadata management is not without challenges, and careful considerations must be given to factors such as interpretability, explainability, and bias. Transparency in how machine learning models interpret data and assign metadata is crucial for user trust and oversight. Explainable AI techniques, which provide insights into the decision-making process of models, contribute to a clearer understanding of how automated systems arrive at metadata assignments. Additionally, efforts must be made to address biases that may be present in training data, ensuring that automated metadata management systems do not inadvertently introduce or perpetuate biases in metadata assignment.

The integration of automation in metadata management also necessitates robust security and privacy measures. Automated systems dealing with sensitive or confidential information must comply with data protection regulations, implement encryption protocols, and safeguard against unauthorized access. Striking a balance between the efficiency gains offered by automation and the protection of sensitive data requires a comprehensive approach that encompasses secure design, rigorous testing, and ongoing monitoring.

In conclusion, automating metadata management through the integration of machine learning models represents a paradigm shift in information governance, offering unprecedented efficiency, accuracy, and adaptability. Machine-generated metadata, driven by NLP, image recognition, and context-aware algorithms, transcends the limitations of manual methods, providing a scalable solution for handling diverse and vast datasets. The efficiency gains in automating repetitive tasks, ensuring accuracy over time, and enriching metadata with contextual intelligence contribute to a streamlined and sophisticated approach to information organization. As technology continues to advance, the integration of automation in metadata management is poised to play a central role in reshaping how organizations derive value from their digital repositories, unlocking new possibilities for data discovery, analytics, and knowledge extraction.

The potential for blockchain technology in creating secure and transparent file systems.

The potential for blockchain technology in creating secure and transparent file systems represents a groundbreaking intersection of distributed ledger technology and data management, offering a paradigm shift in how we conceive, store, and secure digital information. At its core, blockchain is a decentralized and tamper-resistant ledger that operates across a network of nodes, ensuring transparency, immutability, and consensus in recording transactions. When applied to file systems, these characteristics address longstanding challenges in data security, integrity, and accountability. Blockchain's decentralized architecture eliminates the need for a central authority, reducing the risk of single points of failure and enhancing the overall resilience of file systems against unauthorized access, data corruption, or malicious tampering.

Security is a paramount concern in file systems, especially in an era where cyber threats and data breaches are pervasive. Blockchain introduces a new dimension of security by leveraging cryptographic techniques to secure data and transactions. Each block in the blockchain is cryptographically linked to the previous one, forming an unbroken chain of blocks. This inherent linkage ensures that any attempt to alter a block would require recalculating the cryptographic hashes for all subsequent blocks, an computationally infeasible task that provides a robust defense against tampering. By anchoring file system transactions in the blockchain, data integrity is assured, and the risk of unauthorized modifications or data manipulation is significantly mitigated.

The transparency afforded by blockchain technology is instrumental in fostering trust and accountability within file systems. Every participant in the network has access to a transparent and immutable record of file-related transactions. This transparency not only enhances visibility into data activities but also serves as a powerful deterrent against malicious actions. In traditional file systems, audit trails may be susceptible to manipulation or deletion, compromising the verifiability of file-related activities. Blockchain addresses this by providing an auditable and decentralized ledger where every change, access, or transfer of files is recorded in a tamper-evident manner.

This transparency cultivates a culture of accountability, as participants are held accountable for their actions, and the entire history of file-related events is traceable.

Decentralization, a foundational principle of blockchain, contributes to the creation of secure and resilient file systems. Unlike centralized file storage systems vulnerable to single points of failure, a decentralized blockchain-based file system distributes data across a network of nodes, ensuring redundancy and fault tolerance. This not only enhances data availability but also safeguards against data loss due to hardware failures, cyber attacks, or natural disasters. Decentralization also reduces the risk of unauthorized access, as compromising a single node does not compromise the entire file system. The distributed nature of blockchain-based file systems aligns with the principles of data sovereignty, giving users greater control over their data and reducing dependence on centralized entities for storage and access.

Smart contracts, programmable self-executing contracts running on the blockchain, introduce a layer of automation and enforceability to file systems. Smart contracts can be employed to define and automate access control rules, file permissions, and data sharing agreements. For instance, a smart contract could specify that only authorized individuals or entities have access to certain files, automating the enforcement of access policies without requiring manual intervention. The self-executing nature of smart contracts ensures that predefined rules are automatically enforced, reducing the risk of human error and enhancing the overall security posture of the file system. Smart contracts also facilitate secure and transparent collaboration, enabling parties to interact with files based on predefined and tamper-resistant contractual agreements.

The immutability of data recorded on the blockchain contributes to the creation of reliable and tamper-proof audit trails within file systems. In traditional file systems, audit logs may be susceptible to manipulation, deletion, or unauthorized access. Blockchain, with its append-only structure, ensures that once data is recorded, it cannot be altered or deleted. This immutability enhances the reliability of audit trails, providing a secure and verifiable record of all file-related activities. The integrity of audit logs is crucial in forensic investigations, compliance adherence, and maintaining a clear chain of custody for sensitive data. Blockchain's immutability guarantees that audit trails remain intact and trustworthy, even in the face of sophisticated cyber attacks or attempts to conceal unauthorized activities.

Blockchain-based file systems also hold promise in addressing the challenges of data provenance and authenticity. In scenarios where the origin and authenticity of files are critical, blockchain provides a transparent and unforgeable record of a file's journey from creation to its current state. Each transaction recorded on the blockchain includes information about the file, its hash, and the parties involved, creating an immutable trail of provenance. This provenance information can be crucial in verifying the authenticity of documents, artworks, or any digital asset, fostering trust in the integrity of the data. Blockchain's role in ensuring data provenance has applications in various domains, including intellectual property, supply chain management, and the verification of digital content.

The integration of blockchain technology in file systems aligns with the principles of user-centric data ownership and privacy. Traditional file storage systems often require users to entrust their data to centralized entities, raising concerns about data privacy, ownership, and potential misuse. Blockchain's decentralized architecture allows users to maintain control over their data, with cryptographic keys serving as the mechanism for access control. Users can grant or revoke access to their files securely, without relying on intermediaries. This shift towards user-centric data ownership empowers individuals and organizations to have greater control over who can access their files, enhancing privacy and aligning with evolving regulatory frameworks focused on data protection.

The use of blockchain in file systems also introduces the potential for tokenization, where digital tokens or assets on the blockchain represent ownership or access rights to specific files. This tokenization mechanism enables new models for monetizing digital content, creating decentralized marketplaces for file sharing, or even enabling micropayments for access to premium content. Blockchain-based tokenization adds a layer of programmability to digital assets, allowing for the creation of decentralized applications (dApps) that leverage tokens to facilitate secure and transparent transactions within the file system. This token-based economy has the potential to revolutionize how digital content is shared, accessed, and monetized.

While the potential benefits of blockchain in creating secure and transparent file systems are substantial, it's essential to acknowledge certain challenges and considerations. Scalability, a recurring concern in blockchain applications, is critical in the context of file systems that handle large volumes of data. Ensuring that blockchain networks can scale to accommodate the storage and retrieval demands of extensive file systems is imperative for widespread adoption. Solutions such as off-chain storage mechanisms or layer-2 scaling solutions are being explored to address scalability challenges without compromising the security and transparency of blockchain-based file systems.

Interoperability with existing file systems and standards is another consideration. Integrating blockchain technology into established data management infrastructures requires thoughtful design to ensure compatibility and smooth transitions. Standards for interoperability and data exchange between traditional file systems and blockchain-based file systems need to be established to facilitate seamless integration and data portability.

The energy consumption associated with certain blockchain consensus mechanisms, such as Proof of Work (PoW), has been a subject of environmental concern. Exploring more energy-efficient consensus algorithms, such as Proof of Stake (PoS) or hybrid approaches, is crucial to address sustainability concerns while maintaining the security and transparency of blockchain-based file systems.

In conclusion, the potential for blockchain technology in creating secure and transparent file systems heralds a new era in data management, ushering in unparalleled security, transparency, and user-centric control. The decentralized and tamper-resistant nature of blockchain addresses long-standing challenges in data security, integrity, and accountability. From ensuring the immutability of data to fostering transparent collaboration through smart contracts, blockchain's impact on file systems extends across various domains. As the technology continues to mature and address scalability and interoperability challenges, the adoption of blockchain-based file systems has the potential to reshape how we conceive, interact with, and derive value from our digital assets, ushering in a future where security, transparency, and user empowerment are at the forefront of data management.

The concept of self-healing file systems capable of automatic error correction.

The concept of self-healing file systems, capable of automatic error correction, represents a transformative paradigm in data storage and management, where the traditional notion of static, error-prone file systems is replaced by dynamic, resilient architectures that autonomously detect and rectify errors. At its core, self-healing file systems embody the principle of proactively addressing data inconsistencies, corruption, or hardware failures without requiring explicit user intervention. This innovation holds profound implications for data integrity, system reliability, and overall user experience, promising a future where digital assets are safeguarded against disruptions, and data remains dependable in the face of unforeseen challenges.

Central to the concept of self-healing file systems is the integration of advanced algorithms and mechanisms that continuously monitor the health and integrity of stored data. These algorithms operate in the background, scrutinizing file structures, checksums, or other integrity verification methods to detect anomalies or discrepancies. The ability to automatically identify errors, whether caused by hardware malfunctions, data corruption, or environmental factors, is a cornerstone of self-healing file systems. This capability transcends traditional file management approaches, where errors often require manual detection and correction, introducing delays, potential data loss, and disruptions to system availability.

Automatic error correction, a hallmark of self-healing file systems, relies on sophisticated mechanisms designed to rectify identified errors without user intervention. When an error is detected, these systems employ redundant data, error-correcting codes, or other resilience mechanisms to restore the affected files or data structures to their correct state. By automating the error correction process, self-healing file systems not only mitigate the impact of errors but also ensure that data inconsistencies are swiftly and seamlessly resolved, minimizing the risk of cascading issues that could compromise the overall system integrity.

A fundamental aspect of self-healing file systems is their ability to adapt and evolve in response to changing environmental conditions, hardware variations, or emerging threats. Machine learning algorithms, for instance, can be integrated to enable self-healing file systems to learn from past errors, predict potential issues, and preemptively implement corrective measures. This adaptive intelligence ensures that the file system becomes increasingly proficient in identifying and correcting errors over time, contributing to a continuously improving and resilient data storage infrastructure.

Redundancy, a key strategy in self-healing file systems, involves the creation and maintenance of duplicate or parity data to withstand potential failures. Redundancy mechanisms such as RAID (Redundant Array of Independent Disks) or erasure coding ensure that even if certain components or portions of data become corrupted or inaccessible, the system can rebuild the original data from the redundant information. The redundancy approach not only bolsters data resilience but also facilitates automatic error correction by leveraging the available redundant information to restore compromised data integrity.

Checksums and hash functions play a vital role in the self-healing capabilities of these file systems. These cryptographic methods generate unique identifiers for files or data blocks, and any corruption or alteration in the file content results in a change in the checksum or hash value. By regularly verifying these checksums or hashes, self-healing file systems can detect errors and trigger automatic correction processes, replacing corrupted data with intact copies or redundant information. This checksum-based approach adds an additional layer of validation and correction, enhancing the overall reliability of the file system.

Continuous monitoring and real-time error detection are fundamental attributes of self-healing file systems. These systems employ a combination of periodic scans, real-time monitoring tools, and background processes to assess the health of stored data. In the event of discrepancies or errors, immediate alerts are generated, prompting the system to initiate corrective actions. This proactive approach ensures that errors are identified swiftly, reducing the window of vulnerability and enhancing the system's ability to maintain data integrity even in dynamic and unpredictable operational environments.

Self-healing file systems are particularly beneficial in large-scale, distributed, or cloud-based storage infrastructures, where the sheer volume of data and diverse operational conditions pose significant challenges. In such environments, the automatic detection and correction of errors become essential for maintaining uninterrupted service, preventing data loss, and upholding the reliability of critical applications. The resilience offered by self-healing file systems is crucial in scenarios where manual intervention may not be feasible or may incur significant downtime, such as in cloud storage solutions where data is distributed across geographically dispersed servers.

The concept of self-healing file systems extends beyond error correction to encompass the restoration of data consistency and coherency. In distributed or multi-node environments, where files may be simultaneously accessed or modified by multiple entities, ensuring data consistency becomes a complex challenge. Self-healing file systems address this challenge by automatically resolving conflicts, reconciling changes, and synchronizing data across distributed nodes to maintain a coherent and consistent view of information. This holistic approach to data management contributes to the overall robustness of the file system, ensuring that users are presented with a unified and accurate representation of their data.

Another key facet of self-healing file systems is their ability to recover from catastrophic events or disasters. In traditional file systems, the impact of hardware failures, natural disasters, or cyber-attacks can be severe, leading to data loss and extended periods of system unavailability. Self-healing file systems, however, integrate features such as data replication, backup mechanisms, and distributed architectures that enable them to withstand and recover from catastrophic events. These systems can automatically rebuild data from redundant copies, switch to alternative storage locations, or initiate failover processes, minimizing downtime and preserving data accessibility in the face of adversity.

The integration of self-healing capabilities aligns with broader trends in autonomous systems and edge computing, where the emphasis is on reducing reliance on manual interventions and empowering systems to independently manage and optimize their operations. In edge computing environments, where decentralized processing occurs closer to data sources, the ability of self-healing file systems to autonomously correct errors becomes particularly valuable. This decentralized autonomy enhances the efficiency of edge devices, reduces dependency on centralized data centers, and contributes to the overall reliability of distributed computing infrastructures.

However, the implementation of self-healing file systems is not without challenges and considerations. Balancing the trade-off between computational overhead and the timeliness of error correction is crucial, especially in resource-constrained environments. The continuous monitoring, verification, and correction processes inherent in self-healing file systems may consume computational resources, and careful optimization is required to ensure that the benefits of error correction do not come at the expense of system performance.

Security considerations are paramount in the context of self-healing file systems, as automated correction processes must be protected against unauthorized manipulation or exploitation. Ensuring that only authorized entities can trigger error correction mechanisms, validating the integrity of correction actions, and safeguarding against malicious attempts to subvert the self-healing process are critical aspects of security design. The integration of encryption and secure communication protocols further enhances the overall security posture of self-healing file systems.

In conclusion, the concept of self-healing file systems capable of automatic error correction heralds a new era in data storage and management, promising resilience, reliability, and autonomy. By integrating advanced algorithms, redundancy mechanisms, and real-time monitoring, these systems proactively detect and rectify errors without user intervention, ensuring data integrity in dynamic and challenging operational environments. The ability to automatically correct errors, recover from catastrophic events, and maintain data consistency positions self-healing file systems as a transformative solution in the evolving landscape of data storage and management. As technology continues to advance, the integration of self-healing capabilities is poised to redefine expectations for data reliability and system robustness, offering a glimpse into a future where digital assets remain secure, dependable, and resilient against the complexities of modern computing environments.

Exploring the integration of augmented reality in file system interactions.

The exploration of augmented reality (AR) in file system interactions represents a revolutionary convergence of digital and physical worlds, introducing transformative possibilities for how users perceive, interact with, and manage their digital files. At its core, augmented reality seamlessly overlays virtual information onto the user's real-world environment, creating an immersive and interactive experience. When applied to file systems, this integration promises to redefine traditional approaches to data organization, retrieval, and collaboration, ushering in a new era where digital content becomes spatially aware and intricately woven into the fabric of everyday physical surroundings.

One of the fundamental aspects of integrating augmented reality into file system interactions is the creation of a spatial computing paradigm. In traditional file management interfaces, users navigate through hierarchical folder structures or search for files based on metadata. Augmented reality, however, introduces spatial awareness, allowing users to place and organize files in a three-dimensional space. This spatial organization aligns with the human cognitive understanding of physical space, enabling users to associate files with specific locations, contexts, or real-world objects. Files can be visually represented as virtual objects in the user's environment, creating a tangible and intuitive link between digital content and physical space.

In the context of augmented reality file systems, physical locations or objects can serve as anchors for organizing and retrieving digital files. For example, a user might choose to associate work-related documents with a virtual shelf in their office, images with a specific room, or music files with a virtual audio station. This spatial organization provides a natural and contextually rich way of managing files, leveraging the user's spatial memory and environmental cues. The ability to visually place and organize files in the physical world enhances the user experience, making file management more intuitive and closely aligned with real-world contexts.

The interaction with files in augmented reality extends beyond conventional input methods, introducing immersive gestures, voice commands, and spatial interactions. Users can physically reach out, grab, or move virtual files in their augmented environment. Gestures such as swiping, pinching, or rotating become natural ways to interact with and manipulate digital content. Voice commands enable users to perform actions like opening files, creating folders, or initiating searches, adding a layer of convenience to file system interactions. This multimodal interaction paradigm in augmented reality enhances the user's sense of agency and control, providing a more engaging and intuitive means of managing digital files.

Visualization plays a pivotal role in the augmented reality file system, where digital content is dynamically overlaid onto the physical environment. Files can be represented as 3D objects, holograms, or interactive widgets, each with its own visual attributes based on file type, content, or metadata. For instance, a document might be represented as a virtual paper stack with visible titles, an image could manifest as a floating holographic preview, and a music file might appear as a virtual audio player. This visual richness not only makes file interactions more engaging but also provides cues and context about the nature of the files, aiding in quick identification and retrieval.

Augmented reality file systems also offer innovative approaches to file discovery and exploration. Users can employ spatial exploration techniques to navigate through their digital content, physically moving around and interacting with virtual representations of files. For instance, files associated with a particular project may be scattered across a virtual workspace, and users can explore these files by navigating through the augmented space. This spatial exploration adds a novel dimension to file discovery, allowing users to visually traverse their digital content as if it were a physical landscape, fostering a more immersive and memorable experience.

Collaborative file interactions take on a new dimension in augmented reality, where multiple users can share a common virtual space to collaborate on files in real-time. Remote collaboration becomes more immersive as users can see and interact with shared files in a shared augmented environment. Whether co-editing a document, reviewing designs, or collaboratively organizing files, augmented reality facilitates a sense of presence and shared spatial understanding among remote collaborators. This collaborative aspect extends beyond traditional file-sharing platforms, offering a more interactive and spatially aware approach to joint digital workspaces.

The integration of augmented reality in file systems opens avenues for innovative data visualization techniques. Data-driven visualizations, such as charts, graphs, or interactive infographics, can be seamlessly overlaid onto the physical world, providing users with a spatial understanding of complex datasets. For example, a user exploring a set of financial reports may visualize revenue trends as virtual graphs hovering above a table, or geographic data could be represented as a 3D map superimposed onto the floor. Augmented reality transforms data analysis into a more immersive and contextual experience, enabling users to gain insights through spatially situated visualizations.

In educational contexts, augmented reality file systems have the potential to revolutionize how students interact with and learn from digital content. Textbooks, documents, or educational materials can be enriched with interactive 3D models, animations, or supplementary information seamlessly integrated into the physical learning environment. For instance, students studying biology might interact with virtual 3D models of cells or organisms, bringing textbook illustrations to life. Augmented reality file systems thus become powerful tools for enhancing educational content delivery, making learning more engaging, interactive, and spatially contextualized.

The integration of augmented reality also facilitates the creation of context-aware file systems, where the system adapts and presents relevant files based on the user's location, activities, or preferences. For instance, as a user enters their home office, the augmented reality file system may automatically display work-related files associated with that environment. Similarly, during a meeting, relevant documents, notes, or collaborative materials could be dynamically presented in the augmented space. This context-awareness leverages spatial cues to anticipate user needs and streamline file interactions based on the user's immediate context.

Security and privacy considerations are integral to the implementation of augmented reality file systems. As digital content becomes spatially situated in the physical world, ensuring that sensitive files are appropriately protected from unauthorized access or unintended visibility is paramount. Robust authentication mechanisms, encryption protocols, and access controls are crucial to safeguarding digital content within augmented reality environments. Striking a balance between the immersive user experience and stringent security measures becomes a key challenge, requiring careful design to address potential vulnerabilities and privacy concerns.

The hardware landscape plays a significant role in the realization of augmented reality file systems. The availability of advanced AR devices, such as smart glasses or headsets, with sufficient processing power, sensors, and display capabilities, influences the overall user experience. As technology advances and AR hardware becomes more accessible, the potential for widespread adoption of augmented reality file systems increases, making these immersive interactions more seamlessly integrated into daily workflows.

In conclusion, the exploration of augmented reality in file system interactions unveils a transformative approach to digital content management, where files become spatially aware, interactive, and seamlessly integrated into the physical environment. The spatial computing paradigm, multimodal interactions, and immersive visualization techniques redefine how users organize, discover, and collaborate on digital files. Whether enhancing educational experiences, facilitating collaborative workspaces, or providing context-aware file interactions, augmented reality file systems open new frontiers in human-computer interaction. As technology continues to evolve and AR capabilities become more pervasive, the integration of augmented reality in file systems holds the promise of redefining how we engage with and derive value from our digital content in the spatially enriched landscapes of the future.

User interfaces and file management through augmented reality applications.

User interfaces and file management through augmented reality (AR) applications represent a paradigm shift in the way users interact with digital content, blending the physical and virtual realms to create a seamless and immersive experience. At the core of this transformation is the concept of spatial computing, where digital information is overlaid onto the user's real-world environment, fundamentally altering the traditional approaches to file organization, navigation, and manipulation. AR user interfaces introduce a new dimension of interaction, leveraging the spatial awareness of the environment to redefine how users visualize, access, and manage their files.

The essence of AR file management lies in the spatial organization of digital content, transcending the conventional hierarchical folder structures into a three-dimensional space. In AR interfaces, users have the ability to place files and folders in specific locations within their physical environment, creating a spatial map that aligns with their cognitive understanding of space. For instance, a user may choose to place work-related documents on a virtual desk, images on a virtual wall, and music files around a designated audio station. This spatial arrangement adds a layer of tangibility to file organization, allowing users to navigate their digital content as if it were a physical space, fostering a more intuitive and context-aware approach to file management.

The interaction paradigm in AR file management extends beyond traditional input methods, introducing a multimodal experience that combines gestures, voice commands, and spatial interactions. Users can use hand gestures to reach out, grab, or move virtual files within their augmented environment, mimicking physical interactions with tangible objects. Voice commands enhance the hands-free nature of interaction, enabling users to perform actions like opening files, creating folders, or initiating searches through natural language. Spatial interactions, such as physically walking around virtual file clusters or using hand gestures to manipulate files in 3D space, contribute to a more immersive and engaging user experience, breaking away from the constraints of traditional two-dimensional interfaces.

The visualization of files in AR applications is a key aspect of the user interface, where digital content is dynamically overlaid onto the physical world. Files can be represented as 3D objects, holograms, or interactive widgets, each with visual attributes based on file type, content, or metadata. For example, a document might appear as a virtual stack of papers with visible titles, an image could manifest as a floating holographic preview, and a music file might be represented as a virtual audio player. This visual richness not only makes file interactions more engaging but also provides cues and context about the nature of the files, aiding in quick identification and retrieval.

Spatial computing in AR file management transforms the act of file discovery into an exploratory and visually rich experience. Users can physically move around and interact with their digital content as if navigating a physical space. For example, files associated with a specific project might be scattered across a virtual workspace, and users can explore and discover these files by moving through the augmented space. This spatial exploration adds a novel dimension to file discovery, encouraging users to visually traverse their digital content in a way that aligns with their physical movements, fostering a deeper connection between the user and their files.

Collaborative file interactions take on a new dimension in AR applications, where multiple users can share a common virtual space to collaborate on files in real-time. Remote collaboration becomes more immersive as users can see and interact with shared files in a shared augmented environment. Whether co-editing a document, reviewing designs, or collaboratively organizing files, AR applications facilitate a sense of presence and shared spatial understanding among remote collaborators. This collaborative aspect extends beyond traditional file-sharing platforms, offering a more interactive and spatially aware approach to joint digital workspaces.

The integration of AR in file management introduces innovative data visualization techniques. Augmented reality provides an opportunity to overlay data-driven visualizations onto the physical world, offering users a spatial understanding of complex datasets. For instance, financial reports may be visualized as virtual graphs hovering above a table, or geographic data could be represented as a 3D map superimposed onto the floor. This spatial visualization transforms data analysis into an immersive and contextual experience, allowing users to gain insights through interactive and visually situated representations of their data.

In educational contexts, AR applications for file management have the potential to revolutionize how students interact with and learn from digital content. Textbooks, documents, or educational materials can be enhanced with interactive 3D models, animations, or supplementary information seamlessly integrated into the physical learning environment. For example, students studying biology might interact with virtual 3D models of cells or organisms, bringing textbook illustrations to life. AR applications in education provide a more engaging, interactive, and spatially contextualized approach to learning, making educational content more accessible and captivating.

Context-aware file management is another dimension facilitated by AR interfaces. These interfaces adapt to the user's location, activities, or preferences, presenting relevant files based on the immediate context. For instance, as a user enters their home office, the AR application may automatically display work-related files associated with that environment. Similarly, during a meeting, relevant documents, notes, or collaborative materials could be dynamically presented in the augmented space. This context-awareness leverages spatial cues to anticipate user needs and streamline file interactions based on the user's immediate context.

Security and privacy considerations are integral to AR file management applications. As digital content becomes spatially situated in the physical world, ensuring that sensitive files are appropriately protected from unauthorized access or unintended visibility is paramount. Robust authentication mechanisms, encryption protocols, and access controls are crucial to safeguarding digital content within AR environments. Striking a balance between the immersive user experience and stringent security measures becomes a key challenge, requiring careful design to address potential vulnerabilities and privacy concerns.

The hardware landscape plays a significant role in the realization of AR file management applications. The availability of advanced AR devices, such as smart glasses or headsets, with sufficient processing power, sensors, and display capabilities, influences the overall user experience. As technology advances and AR hardware becomes more accessible, the potential for widespread adoption of AR file management applications increases, making these immersive interactions more seamlessly integrated into daily workflows.

In conclusion, user interfaces and file management through augmented reality applications redefine the way users interact with and manage their digital content. The spatial computing paradigm, multimodal interactions, and immersive visualization techniques usher in a new era of file management, where files become spatially aware, interactive, and seamlessly integrated into the physical environment. Whether enhancing collaborative workspaces, facilitating educational experiences, or providing context-aware file interactions, AR applications transform digital content management into an immersive and engaging spatial experience. As technology continues to evolve, the integration of augmented reality in file management applications holds the promise of redefining how we interact with and derive value from our digital content in the spatially enriched landscapes of the future.

Implementing dynamic policies for file system management based on real-time conditions.

Implementing dynamic policies for file system management based on real-time conditions represents a paradigm shift in the approach to optimizing and governing data storage. Traditional file system management often relies on static, predetermined policies that may not adequately adapt to the dynamic and evolving nature of data usage, access patterns, and system conditions. Dynamic policies leverage real-time information, contextual awareness, and adaptive algorithms to continuously adjust file system behavior, ensuring efficient resource utilization, enhanced performance, and responsiveness to changing operational environments.

At the core of dynamic policy implementation is the recognition that file systems are dynamic entities influenced by various factors such as user activities, system load, storage capacity, and security considerations. Unlike static policies, which are predefined and may not account for these fluctuating conditions, dynamic policies are designed to evolve in response to the real-time state of the file system. This adaptability is particularly crucial in modern computing environments where data volumes are vast, access patterns are diverse, and the demand for responsive and efficient file system management is paramount.

Real-time conditions encompass a spectrum of factors that influence file system behavior. Monitoring and analyzing these conditions involve the continuous collection of data on storage usage, access patterns, system performance metrics, and environmental variables. For instance, file access frequency, file sizes, and user interactions contribute to the evolving state of the file system. Concurrently, system-level metrics such as CPU utilization, memory availability, and network bandwidth provide insights into the broader operational context. Dynamic policies harness this real-time data to inform decision-making processes and adjust file system configurations accordingly.

One of the key aspects of dynamic policies is the ability to adapt storage allocation based on the changing demands of the file system. Adaptive storage allocation involves dynamically adjusting the distribution of available storage space among different file types, directories, or users in response to real-time usage patterns. For instance, frequently accessed files or directories may be allocated more storage resources to optimize performance, while less accessed or archival data may have their allocation adjusted to free up space. This adaptability ensures that storage resources are efficiently utilized, minimizing the risk of capacity constraints and optimizing the overall performance of the file system.

Dynamic policies also play a crucial role in optimizing file placement and retrieval strategies. By continuously analyzing real-time access patterns, these policies can intelligently determine the most suitable locations for frequently accessed files, thereby reducing access latency and enhancing overall system responsiveness. Additionally, as data access patterns evolve, dynamic policies can influence caching mechanisms to ensure that frequently accessed data is readily available in memory, further improving access times. This adaptability in file placement strategies aligns file system behavior with the changing requirements of applications and users.

In the context of security, dynamic policies offer the ability to adjust access controls and permissions based on real-time conditions. Continuous monitoring of user behavior, authentication events, and potential security threats enables dynamic policies to dynamically modify access privileges and permissions. For example, in the event of a security incident or unauthorized access attempt, the file system can dynamically enforce stricter access controls or initiate automated responses to mitigate potential risks. This real-time adaptability enhances the security posture of the file system, responding promptly to emerging threats and vulnerabilities.

The concept of Quality of Service (QoS) in file system management is another area where dynamic policies prove invaluable. QoS aims to prioritize certain types of file access or system operations based on defined criteria. Dynamic QoS policies adjust these prioritization criteria in real-time, ensuring that critical applications or users receive the necessary resources and responsiveness. For example, during peak usage periods, dynamic policies may prioritize read and write operations for mission-critical applications over less time-sensitive tasks, contributing to a more responsive and efficient file system.

In distributed file systems, where data is distributed across multiple nodes or storage locations, dynamic policies become instrumental in load balancing and data distribution. Real-time monitoring of node utilization, network conditions, and data access patterns allows dynamic policies to redistribute data dynamically, ensuring an equitable distribution of workload across nodes. This adaptability contributes to improved performance, fault tolerance, and scalability in distributed file systems, addressing the challenges posed by varying workloads and environmental conditions.

Automation is a key enabler of dynamic policies, allowing for the seamless execution of policy adjustments without manual intervention. Automated processes, driven by real-time data and adaptive algorithms, can implement changes in storage allocations, access controls, caching strategies, and other aspects of file system management. This automation not only ensures responsiveness to real-time conditions but also reduces the administrative burden associated with manual policy adjustments. By leveraging automation, dynamic policies enable file systems to operate with agility and efficiency in dynamic computing environments.

Machine learning algorithms play a significant role in the implementation of dynamic policies, particularly in scenarios where patterns and correlations in real-time data may not be immediately apparent. These algorithms can analyze historical data, learn from past file system behaviors, and predict future trends. For example, machine learning models can identify patterns of peak usage times, allowing dynamic policies to proactively adjust resource allocations and prioritize critical operations during anticipated high-demand periods. The adaptive learning capabilities of machine learning contribute to the proactive nature of dynamic policies, enhancing their ability to anticipate and respond to changing file system conditions.

Real-time analytics and monitoring are foundational components of dynamic policy implementation, providing the continuous stream of data necessary for informed decision-making. Advanced analytics tools enable file system administrators to gain insights into usage patterns, performance metrics, and potential anomalies in real-time. These insights empower dynamic policies to make data-driven decisions, adjusting configurations and parameters to align with the observed conditions. The integration of real-time analytics ensures that the file system management remains responsive, adaptive, and aligned with the evolving needs of users and applications.

The concept of dynamic policies extends to backup and data protection strategies, where real-time conditions influence the frequency, granularity, and methodologies employed in data backup and recovery. Dynamic backup policies can adjust the backup frequency based on changes in data volatility, ensuring that critical data is backed up more frequently during periods of heightened activity or modification. Additionally, real-time monitoring of data integrity and potential threats can trigger dynamic policies to initiate proactive measures such as snapshot creation or backup replication to safeguard against data loss or corruption.

In the context of cloud environments, where file systems often span diverse infrastructures and services, dynamic policies become essential for optimizing cost-efficiency. Real-time monitoring of cloud resource utilization, pricing models, and data access patterns enables dynamic policies to make informed decisions regarding data placement, resource scaling, and cost optimization. For instance, during periods of reduced demand, dynamic policies may trigger the scaling down of cloud resources to minimize costs, while scaling up during periods of increased demand to ensure performance requirements are met.

Challenges in implementing dynamic policies revolve around striking a balance between adaptability and stability. Excessive and frequent policy adjustments may introduce operational overhead, resource contention, or unintended consequences. Careful tuning and validation of dynamic policies are crucial to ensuring that the system responds effectively to real-time conditions without introducing instability or compromising overall reliability. Additionally, considerations related to user privacy, security, and regulatory compliance must be carefully addressed to mitigate potential risks associated with dynamic adjustments in file system management.

In conclusion, implementing dynamic policies for file system management based on real-time conditions heralds a transformative approach to data storage and optimization. These policies, driven by real-time data, adapt to changing usage patterns, system conditions, and security threats, ensuring that file systems operate with agility, efficiency, and responsiveness. The dynamic allocation of storage resources, adaptive file placement strategies, real-time security adjustments, and automated processes contribute to a file system that aligns seamlessly with the evolving needs of modern computing environments. As technology continues to advance, the integration of dynamic policies is poised to redefine expectations for file system management, ushering in an era where data storage is not only efficient and reliable but also inherently adaptive to the dynamic nature of contemporary computing landscapes.

Speculating on the potential impact of quantum computing on file systems.

Speculating on the potential impact of quantum computing on file systems opens a realm of transformative possibilities that could reshape the very foundations of data storage, processing, and security. Quantum computing, harnessing the principles of quantum mechanics, introduces a paradigm shift by leveraging quantum bits or qubits, which can exist in multiple states simultaneously. This unprecedented computational power has the potential to revolutionize how file systems operate, impacting aspects ranging from storage efficiency and data processing to encryption and security.

One of the most significant potential impacts of quantum computing on file systems lies in its ability to redefine data processing capabilities. Traditional computing systems, based on classical bits that exist in either a 0 or 1 state, face limitations in handling complex algorithms and computations, especially in scenarios involving vast datasets. Quantum computers, with their inherent ability to exist in superpositions of states, can process a multitude of possibilities simultaneously. This quantum parallelism could lead to exponential speedups in tasks such as indexing, searching, and analyzing large volumes of data within file systems, transforming the landscape of data processing efficiency.

Quantum computing's impact on encryption algorithms holds profound implications for the security of file systems. Current cryptographic methods, including widely used ones like RSA and ECC, rely on the difficulty of certain mathematical problems for their security. However, quantum algorithms, such as Shor's algorithm, have demonstrated the potential to efficiently solve these mathematical challenges. As a result, the advent of practical quantum computers poses a threat to the traditional security infrastructure of file systems. The widespread adoption of quantum-resistant encryption techniques, known as post-quantum cryptography, becomes imperative to safeguard sensitive data stored within file systems from the vulnerabilities introduced by quantum computing.

Quantum computing's impact on data storage efficiency is another area of exploration. Quantum algorithms could potentially optimize storage and retrieval processes within file systems, leveraging quantum principles to represent and manipulate data in more compact forms. Quantum data compression techniques, for instance, may offer novel ways to store information with reduced redundancy, enhancing storage efficiency and minimizing the physical footprint of file systems. This could be particularly beneficial in managing the exponentially growing volumes of data generated in today's digital age.

The potential for quantum-enhanced machine learning algorithms holds promise for file systems in terms of data classification, pattern recognition, and predictive analytics. Quantum machine learning models, leveraging quantum parallelism and entanglement, may outperform classical models in tasks such as content-based indexing, contextual search, and personalized recommendations within file systems. This could lead to more intelligent and responsive file management systems, enhancing user experiences and optimizing the organization of digital content.

Quantum entanglement, a unique quantum phenomenon where particles become correlated in such a way that the state of one instantly influences the state of another, could introduce novel approaches to distributed file systems. The entanglement-based quantum communication may facilitate secure and instantaneous transmission of information between distributed nodes. This could redefine how data is shared, replicated, and synchronized across geographically dispersed locations within a file system, potentially leading to unprecedented advancements in the field of distributed and decentralized storage architectures.

The impact of quantum computing on error correction mechanisms is also a critical consideration for file systems. Quantum computers are susceptible to errors due to the fragile nature of quantum states. Quantum error correction techniques, such as those based on qubits' entanglement, may play a pivotal role in ensuring the reliability and integrity of data stored within quantum-enhanced file systems. The development of robust quantum error correction mechanisms becomes paramount to maintaining the accuracy of stored information and preventing the degradation of file system performance.

Quantum sensing technologies could further augment file system capabilities, especially in scenarios requiring precise data retrieval or monitoring. Quantum sensors, leveraging quantum properties for enhanced sensitivity, could be employed in file systems for tasks such as monitoring data access patterns, detecting anomalies, or optimizing storage allocation based on real-time conditions. This integration of quantum sensing within file systems could contribute to a more adaptive, context-aware, and efficient data management infrastructure.

Despite the promises and potentials, the realization of practical quantum computing and its impact on file systems faces several challenges. Quantum computers are notoriously sensitive to environmental factors, requiring extremely low temperatures and isolated conditions to maintain quantum coherence. The development of scalable and stable quantum hardware remains a significant hurdle. Additionally, the creation of error-resistant quantum bits and the mitigation of decoherence, where quantum states lose coherence over time, are active areas of research. The practical integration of quantum technologies into existing file system architectures demands careful consideration of these technical challenges and necessitates advancements in quantum hardware and error correction methodologies.

Ethical considerations and potential societal impacts also accompany the integration of quantum computing into file systems. Quantum computing's unprecedented computing power raises concerns about the security and privacy implications of breaking current encryption methods. The development and deployment of post-quantum cryptographic solutions become crucial to mitigate these risks. Additionally, the accessibility and equitable distribution of quantum computing resources pose questions about potential disparities in technological capabilities and data access. Ensuring that the benefits of quantum-enhanced file systems are accessible to a broad spectrum of users without exacerbating digital divides is an ethical consideration that must be addressed.

In conclusion, speculating on the potential impact of quantum computing on file systems reveals a landscape of transformative possibilities and challenges. From redefining data processing efficiency and storage optimization to posing challenges for traditional encryption methods, quantum computing holds the promise of reshaping the fundamental aspects of how file systems operate. As ongoing research progresses, the realization of practical quantum computers and their integration into file systems will likely be a gradual evolution, with ethical, technical, and societal considerations shaping the trajectory of this quantum future for data storage and management.